Three
Beams
of
Light

Chronicles of a lighthouse keeper's family

by Norma Engel

Tecolote Publications

Tecolote Publications
Box 70205
San Diego, CA 92107

Cover design by Jodi Baca

Library of Congress Catalog Card Number: 86-50408

ISBN 0-938711-00-8

Printed in the United States of America

For Mom and Dad

Contents

List of Illustrations vii

Preface ix

Acknowledgments xi

Part One: Oakland Harbor Light Station

    1. The First Beam 5

    2. The Shake-Up 15

Part Two: Point Bonita Light Station

    3. Back on Dry Land 23

    4. Settling In Again 31

    5. The City Falls 41

    6. Three Bags Full 51

    7. You Can Get There From Here But It Isn't Easy 59

    8. Nellie Was a Lady 65

Part Three: Ballast Point Light Station

    9. Headed For Ballast Point 75

    10. Our Journey Ends 85

    11. Home Again 97

    12. School Daze 105

    13. The First and the Last 111

    14. Feathers and Fur 117

    15. Just for the Looking 123

    16. The Canine Brigade 129

    17. The Initiation 135

    18. We Welcome a Stranger 141

    19. And Say Goodbye to a Friend 151

20. That Wasn't Funny 157

21. Water, Water, Go Away 165

22. Bounty Hunters 171

23. The Young Entrepreneurs 179

24. Fish and Chips 187

25. Pelicans and Picnickers 195

26. A Distant Conflict Draws Near 201

27. And Then Some More Pets 207

28. Fortune Hunters 215

29. Unscheduled Dunkings 223

30. The Big Splash 229

31. Battle Stations 233

32. Olaf and the Chinaman 237

33. Thar They Blow 243

34. High and Dry 251

35. Time to Leave 257

Bibliography 257

Appendix 259

Illustrations

Oakland Harbor Light Station 1
Hermann and Freda Engel 4
Floor Plan, Oakland Harbor Light Station 8
Oakland Harbor Beacon 11
Steamer *Newark* 14
Point Bonita Light Station 19
The Engel Family, Point Bonita 22
Original Dwelling, Point Bonita 27
Point Bonita, Aerial View of Dwellings 30
Old Fog Signal, Point Bonita 36
Telegraph Hill Burning 40
New Dwellings, Point Bonita 49
Point Bonita Lens 50
Promotion Letter, Point Bonita 55
Walkway to Light Station, Point Bonita 58
Point Bonita Station and Trail 61
Mr. and Mrs. Engel Walking Home from Sausalito 64
Freda Engel and Children at Beach 70
Letter of Appointment to Ballast Point 74
Birdseye View of Ballast Point 84
Ballast Point from Fort Rosecrans 93
The Engel Family in "Useless" 96
San Diego Harbor 104
Map of Fort Rosecrans and Ballast Point 110
Light Tower, Ballast Point 122
Rover 128
Pilot Boat, San Diego Harbor 134
Brother El 134
Fur Seal 140
Ballast Point Dwellings 154
Mr. and Mrs. Engel Relaxing on Lawn 160
Freda Engel Tending Her Garden 164
Charles Hatfield 168
Stray Torpedo 170
Steamer *Harvard* 194
Gunnery Targets, 1918 200
Journal Entry, "Horse Out to Sea" 206
Map, San Diego Harbor 214
Keeping Downed Plane Afloat 222

Channel Swim   228
Crowds at Channel Swim   230
Parking at Channel Swim   230
Cove at Ballast Point   236
Hermann Engel in Uniform   242
Lumber Freighter   250

Preface

There have been many sources of information, official and personal, for material in this book, but the one I relied on greatly was my mother's remarkable memory.

After Dad's death, Mom and I lived together from 1935 until her passing in 1979 at the age of ninety-eight. Her mind was always clear and her memory faultless and during those forty-four years of companionship, I jotted down my notes.

If events in this book are at variance with the *Annual Record,* during the years at Point Bonita, I trust my mother's memory. She *lived* at that light station. The short paragraph entries in the *Annual Record* were made by visiting inspectors, really conscientious men who spent most of their time checking the operation and working parts of the light and fog signal, giving only a cursory glance at the family living quarters. What they observed in the dwelling areas in a short space of time did not always agree with my mother's assessment of the situation. It's too bad the keepers' wives were not asked to write their comments about the miserable dwellings.

The government was very shortsighted in providing such poor housing for the men and their families who really dedicated their lives to the U.S. Lighthouse Service. The responsibilities were great, the pay was poor, the hours long, and the stations almost always situated far from stores or schools, and many were subject to the battering storms that hit the coastal regions.

In those early days, the Service found it extremely difficult to find enough qualified men to fill its needs, and so accepted even those truly not fit for the arduous duty, those in poor physical condition, ones who could not cope with the hardships, others whose families found the life too hazardous, or adventurers who found the Service too much hard work and responsibility and not enough adventure.

But out of the few who applied there also came individuals hardy of spirit and body, firm in purpose to make this their way of life, understanding of the meaning of dedication to duty, blessed with a supportive family, and unflagging in their efforts to keep the seas safe.

They toiled side by side with others who formed the backbone of this demanding life, and kept the lights burning. These good men and women found a satisfaction and happiness in a job well done that outweighed the many hardships of the early days. Dad and Mom worked day by day with outstanding individuals such as the Cobbs, the Martins, the Ingersolls, and the Frankes, happy in the knowledge of the important job they were doing.

Acknowledgments

I have obtained research material from the following sources:
    San Diego Historical Society
    National Maritime Museum, San Francisco
    Bancroft Library, University of California
    U.S. National Archives
        Copies of: 1005 pages of the Lighthouse Keepers' log
            entries. 1900-1915
            Annual Records—1900-1931
    My father's official correspondence
    And most of all, my mother's remarkable memory

Part One

National Archives.

Oakland Harbor Light Station
1900-1901

Annual Record, 1890:

The Oakland Harbor, California—The bids for the construction of this station were opened July 31, 1889 and contract made. Work was commenced in September and finished November 30, on which date it was accepted by the Government. On January 27, 1890, the light, which is a fixed light of the fifth order, illuminating the whole horizon, was exhibited and the fog signal was ready for service. This signal is a bell struck by clock work once every five seconds. The station is a frame dwelling surmounted by an iron lantern, and stands upon eleven piles.

Mom and Dad

1

The First Beam

U.S. Lighthouse log entry:
    Nov. 4, 1900. Mod. N (wind) Fog. Assigned Mr. Hermann Engel as assistant keeper to duty at this station.

U.S. Lighthouse log entry:
    Nov. 6, 1900. Hermann Engel left station at 1:00 p.m. on liberty. Returned 4:00 p.m., NW Foggy.

The woman sat quietly in the stern of the little rowboat, her right hand clutching the handle of a bulging suitcase. She shivered in the dampness of the late afternoon, and drew her coat closer around her slight figure. A bell toned mournfully in the distance.

My father stopped rowing, rested his muscular arms on the oars, and let the boat drift idly while he turned to stare ahead. When he swung back he reached out to touch my mother's hand. "There it is, Freda, dead ahead."

Dimly outlined in the afternoon haze stood a small white structure perched precariously on old wooden pilings braced by a crisscross of planks. This was the Oakland Harbor Light Station, Dad's first assignment in the U.S. Lighthouse Service. And it was Mom's first view of her new home somewhere on the bay between Oakland and San Francisco.

Dad spied the wide-eyed astonishment in her blue eyes and hastened to reassure her. "Don't worry, Freda, I've been placed at the top of the list for shore duty. We won't be here long, but we'll have to keep quiet about your staying here. Family members have orders to live ashore. We can't have you breaking regulations." There was a hint of a twinkle in his warm brown eyes, and a little smile just visible under a handsome black mustache.

A few more easy strokes brought the skiff close to the station ladder where it could be tied. When all was secure, my father leaned over to help Mom. She stepped gingerly from the boat, and with his arm around her, went easily up the ladder. Halfway up she hesitated. "Well it certainly looks better than the dark hotel room in Oakland." Her casual remark somehow implied a complete acceptance of this new life.

At the top awaiting their arrival stood the keeper, Charles McCarthy. His weatherbeaten Irish face beamed with delight at the sight of his new helper and the lovely bride. He hastened to steady Mom as she neared the top. "Welcome to Oakland Harbor Light," and he beamed again. By the time the introductions were over, the old keeper was completely charmed by my mother, and she quickly warmed to his gallantry. What a strange trio, the young married couple and the ancient mariner. They moved inside.

A quick survey of the room disclosed only bare necessities for a kitchen: a small coal stove, some limited shelf space holding battered enamel dishes, and a scattering of staple foods. A freshly scrubbed sink gleamed in one corner. Against the south wall stood a shining golden oak table and two matching chairs, part of an impulsive furniture purchase that had plunged my father even further into debt.

The short silence was broken when my mother asked quietly, "Are you sure there's room enough for all of us?"

"Oh, yes," Mr. McCarthy spoke quickly as he swung his arm in a small arc. "You can have all of this. Just leave me a little corner where I can smoke my pipe."

Mom laughed and edged closer to the warm stove. Its heat penetrated her damp clothing. It had not been a long trip from the Oakland Ferry Landing, but she was not used to being out in an open boat. The glow from the fire brightened her spirits. Dad was glad to hear that laugh.

"Well, I'd better bring up the suitcases and the other things before they get wet."

"Yep, and I'm going to take a look at that fog bank. It's going to roll in pretty soon." And the keeper followed Dad out the door.

Left to her inspection, Mom opened one door and found herself in the little appendage that had been built next to the outside wall which housed a toilet and wooden tub. The draft that blew through was cold enough to discourage anyone from lingering in that space. The old wooden tub would have to be dragged into the kitchen when it came bath time. She retreated and went back through the kitchen to the bedroom door Dad had pointed out to her. There, in a little eight-by-eight foot space, an oak bed, dresser and washstand crowded each other for space. The lighthouse tender had brought over all their furniture a few days before during a spell of good weather and with a high tide. Incredulous seamen hoisted over the massive pieces. With much lifting, hauling, groaning and shoving, the crew at last maneuvered it all into the little station. It definitely gave an air of simple elegance to this strange little abode on the bay.

In the midst of Mom's perusal a horrendous "BONG" resounded throughout the room. The 3500-pound fog bell had begun its task of alerting mariners. It was disconcerting to find, however, that the bell hung just ten feet from the head of their bed. Its lusty tone gave hints of sleepless nights to come. This bronze monster was not going to render any Brahms "Lullaby."

Dad came in with his load and found a shaken young wife clinging to the foot of the bed.

"What was *that*?" she started to ask, but her question was drowned out by another strike of the bell. They both moved back into the kitchen where it was just a shade quieter.

The keeper noticed Mom's face. "Don't worry. It's not so bad when you get used to it."

It wasn't only the bell noise that disturbed her. There were strange shudders in the structure when the bell struck. She was to learn the reason for that in a short time.

This first Oakland Harbor Light had been placed on eleven piles driven into the bay. They had not been treated against action by the marine worms, and in no time at all the worms had done great damage. They chewed away happily, weakening the whole station, even causing it to oscillate, as reported in the *Annual Record*.

> **Annual Record, 1894,** *Oakland Harbor, entrance to the Oakland Harbor, California—the stability of the piles supporting this structure was increased and further oscillation was prevented by filling the space under the building with 2,000 tons of stone. This was quarried on Goat Island and was transferred to the station in schooners. The depth of the water being 13 feet, the slope of the rock filling carried the footings out so far, the boats could not readily land at the existing steps. The difficulty was overcome by extending a platform from the gallery out over the rock and putting up a new ladder.*

The station didn't oscillate any more while my parents lived there, but it swayed with the wind, shook from the bell, and exhibited other sinister motions from time to time. Things were never

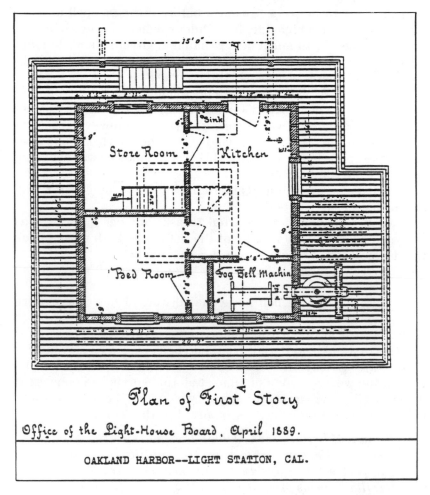

Floor plan, Oakland Harbor Light Station. Storeroom had been made into second bed-room before my parents' arrival. *National Archives.*

quite still, for the floor always jiggled under their feet.

Questions and answers flew across mugs of hot coffee. Mom worried about the scanty food supply and began making a long shopping list. Dad was eager to learn his new duties. Mr. McCarthy was happy to relinquish the kitchen to Mom and overjoyed to have a strong young assistant.

For that first evening, the keeper had prepared a simple, wholesome dish—lamb stew. Its aroma filled the little room and the three sat down with relish to a fine hot meal.

After supper Dad urged Mom to put on her coat and step outside. The fog had lifted a little and close by streamed a constant parade of brightly lighted ferry boats, traversing San Francisco Bay. The sounds of laughter and conversation drifted across the water. An occasional wayward yacht, late in returning to Oakland, sounded a relieved toot as it passed. The sight of the little light always meant a safe ending to a sea journey. This Oakland Harbor Light was a well-loved sentinel, guiding deep-sea liners, bay scows, schooners, yachts and ferries. Mom glanced up at the light housed on top of their dwelling. Such a small thing to do such important work. Just around the corner of the platform stood the freshwater tank, braced solidly against the winter gales. Below the living quarters was an ample storeroom reached by an inside ladder. She looked back at my father, and leaned against his short stocky figure, content with her new life. They continued to watch the movement in the harbor until the increasing chill drove them inside.

Back in the bedroom, Dad helped Mom unpack. There was a closet with a few rough shelves and some hooks screwed haphazardly into the wall.

"I think I'll get a little rest. I've got the watch from midnight on. Let's finish the rest tomorrow." Dad pulled a pillow from the bed and placed it on the floor. In a minute he was stretched out on his side fast asleep. Throughout the years of his life, he often chose the floor as a spot for a quick nap. We could only guess it was a habit acquired in his early life aboard sailing vessels.

My father was born in the Free State of Danzig, 1869, and was a happy school boy of fourteen until Prussian officers entered this independent city. They tried illegally to impress young men into their military service. He wanted none of this, and without a word to his parents, rushed down to the harbor to sign aboard as cabin boy on the first ship to leave port.

The rough seas were far removed from the quiet of the classroom, but this first taste of adventure opened new vistas. Dad experienced all the joys, fears, and wonders of a sailor's life, working from a cabin boy up to an able-bodied seaman. New adventures beckoned in South America, and he spent a year doing hard work on a rubber plantation in Brazil. That was too far away from the sea, and he journeyed over to the west coast to the port of Callao, Peru. He enlisted in the U.S. Navy, and entered the service just in time for the Spanish-American War.

Later with his enlistment completed, my father was discharged in San Francisco, found a job in the Union Iron Works, and settled down to enjoy this wonderful city.

From his boardinghouse, he caught sight of an attractive seventeen-year-old young lady next door. Although her family did not approve of this friendship, within a year Dad had wooed and won my mother and rushed her off in an elopement to Reno. There was enough courage and love in this young bride to sustain Mom through all the coming hardships, and these attributes fully matched Dad's sense of adventure.

Now, in this strange honeymoon cottage they had acquired, Dad's snoring brought Mom's thoughts back to the present and the work at hand. She did the best she could with the limited space, left the rest of the clothes in the suitcase, and sat down on the bed to rest.

The next morning the haze remained, but the day grew warmer. My parents resumed their settling in and Mr. McCarthy took off for Oakland with a long shopping list in his hand.

The month of November was blessed with unusually good weather, the days being interrupted only occasionally by rain or fog. The men busied themselves with routine work at the station and jetty lights—cleaning, painting, or refueling. Mom worked in the morning—cleaning, washing, and baking, but she tried to free herself for some afternoon fun outside. All it took was a line and baited hook dropped over the side. Before long up would come a protesting halibut, and sometimes even a fighting striped bass. Cut into thick steaks, the fish were a gourmet's delight.

If the fish were reluctant to bite, there were the passing vessels to watch. Ocean liners, bound for foreign ports, steamed by sailing ships as they moved through the "Gate." The constant stream fascinated my mother and she never tired of watching. In daylight hours, great white sails billowed out with the strong westerlies, and long lines of smoke marked the paths of the steamships. This parade was etched against the hills of San Francisco, an everchanging scene to enjoy. At night the running lights of the few vessels underway about the harbor gave life to the dark expanse of water.

Huge ferries carried passengers across the bay to connecting coastal railroads, north and south. These were no little riverboats, but great hulks built to carry the heavy weight. Skilled captains maneuvered these ferries back and forth from San Francisco to Oakland, and through the channel close by the Oakland Harbor Light. Some of these magnificent craft were the same ones that carried my parents on trips as well.

In the middle of November, my parents left the station for the

Oakland channel bay beacon, *National Archives.*

first time. There was a brisk breeze blowing, ruffling the surface of
the water, but Mom dressed warmly and looked forward to the trip.
Their landing was a quarter of a mile away at the ferry slip. Here,
railroad engineers who serviced the trains and who were on the alert
kept their eyes open for Mom and Dad. When the lighthouse skiff
loomed in the offing with two occupants, the engineers stood by to
help. There was no suitable landing. An old rickety ladder could not
be used. As Dad brought the boat alongside, the men reached out
and grasped Mom firmly, setting her easily on the wharf. Low tide
made it more difficult, but somehow they always managed. I've often
thought that Mom must have looked like a daughter of Neptune arising from the deep. These trips were pure joy for her. She loved the
sea.

Just a few steps away they boarded the ferry for San Francisco.
In good weather, these trips were delightful outings, and the railroad
men enjoyed being in the little circle of the conspirators who kept
the secret of "the family member living at the lighthouse."

When the barometer reading dropped, Dad rushed my mother
ashore out of danger. There was never any surety that the station
would remain upright in gale force winds that could sweep the bay.
Late in November an ominous mass huddled on the horizon. Clouds
scudded across the sky and whitecaps slapped sharply at the station
pilings. Mom gathered up a few bits of clothing for her stay ashore.
Dad snugged her down in the rowboat and draped an old blanket
around her shoulders for extra warmth and protection. The trip to
the landing was a bouncy one on the choppy waves, but they reached
the landing still dry although a bit wind-whipped. Gusts had loosened
the hairpins of Mom's carefully arranged hair, and light brown wisps
framed her happy face.

They reached the ferry slip, and the engineers were on hand as
usual. Mom and Dad hurried to the hotel where they had a simple
meal before it was time for Dad to return to the station. He lingered
a little longer than he had planned and when he stepped outside,
the wind was gusting harder and there was the smell of rain in the
offing. The oncoming gale had already blackened the dark evening
sky. The boat banged against the landing, and the first drops drove
into the water.

It would be a stiff row back, but my father was an excellent boat-
man. He and the keeper rowed daily to the beacon and jetty lights
a mile away, and made frequent trips to the mainland for fresh supplies. Dad settled down on the thwart, placed the oars in the oarlocks
and pushed the boat away from the pier out into the open channel.

Wind and tide battled him and the angry waves slopped into the boat, soaking him in cold sea water. The storm increased in intensity the farther out he rowed, but he feathered his oars against the wind blasts, dug them a little deeper, and at last arrived at the station, cold, stiff, and very tired. There was just time to change into dry clothing, swallow a reviving cup of hot coffee, and go on his duty watch. He became a better weather-watcher after that, but no less a romantic seaman.

The steamer *Newark*—no engine driven steering mechanism. Four men were needed to handle the manual steering. Note the 42-foot paddle wheels, largest on any ferry-boat. *National Maritime Museum, San Francisco.*

2

The Shake-Up

Fog is a frequent visitor to the San Francisco Bay area, and when a heavy blanket settles down, it makes the traffic in the bay difficult and hazardous. Years ago, most ships remained at anchor or tied up at wharves, but the passenger ferries still plied their way back and forth from San Francisco to Oakland, keeping to their regular schedules. The railroads depended upon them to be on time. Skilled captains knew the strength and directions of tides and winds. They piloted ferries regularly and safely in any kind of weather, always looking to the friendly Oakland Harbor Light to guide them through the channel.

There were other vessels on the move in the fog, ones that steamed up the Sacramento River with supplies and passengers to the inner regions. They were small, slow, and when heavily laden, difficult to handle in a strong current or stiff wind. Passenger and freight demands kept these craft going day and night.

The last day of November ended in a blur of haze. All through the foggy night the bell at Oakland Harbor steadily warned the mariners to keep clear. Mom arose early December 1, 1900 to prepare a good hot breakfast for the tired men who had kept their monotonous vigil hour after hour, tending the light and winding the clockwork of the bell at regular intervals. The table in the kitchen was loaded with mugs of hot coffee, plates of crisp bacon and sunny eggs, and a platterful of golden pancakes. The men relaxed onto their chairs and swallowed deep gulps of the strong coffee. After they had a good start, Mom sat down to her breakfast. There was dreary fog outside, but good cheer filled the little room.

Dad spoke soberly, "I hope they give me a transfer to a shore station soon. It's too dangerous out here for you. This old place is shaking more every day."

Mom raised her eyebrows, "Maybe you should have taken that job in the U.S. Mint. That would have kept us on dry land, and we could have been a little more comfortable. I could be riding down-town on a streetcar instead of bouncing around on the bay in a little boat." Her tone was not too serious. Dad had been a sailor too long, and she knew he would never be happy away from the sea.

But Dad winced a little when she reminded him of the ninety-nine percent score he had made on that exam for the Mint. The momentary silence was broken by the keeper's request, "Mrs. Engel, could I please have another cup of that fine coffee you brew?" He was nearly seventy years old and had been at this station a long time.

Mom reached for the pot and filled all their mugs. Dad looked up with a tentative smile and the awkward moment passed. She sat down to continue her eating, buttered a piece of toast, and had it halfway to her mouth when she calmly remarked, "Look what's coming."

The two men turned and stared in disbelief at the approaching hulk headed directly for them.

"Freda, you sit right there."

They leaped from their chairs and scrambled outside shouting and waving their arms. The ship's lookout had already spotted the lighthouse, but his warning to the helmsman came too late. Slowly, slowly, the steamer began to turn away, but not soon enough. With only slightly decreased speed, the heavily laden craft plowed toward the station. It smashed into one side of the structure, breaking a pil-ing, knocking others askew, and splintering braces. Oakland Harbor Light reeled. The water tank rocked back and forth, sloshing out most of its contents. The clapper on the bell struck and let out a faint protest. The vessel finally came to a halt and the little dwelling gave a last wobble and settled down with a sigh.

While most of the yelling and confusion went on, the captain appeared on deck, prefacing his conversation with the keepers with language salty enough to blister the paint on his ship. He had not yet fixed on a scapegoat for the error in navigation, so decided to blame the station for being in the path. When at last he had run out of both breath and expletives, they all surveyed the damage. Details on the time, place and damages were listed, as well as the fact the light and fog bell were both in proper operation. When the keeper was satisfied he had enough for a full report, the Newark backed off and proceeded on a corrected course, leaving the station even more unstable. Dad and the keeper made a more detailed inspection and returned inside.

Mom had righted things on the table and started a fresh pot of coffee. "Is everything all right?"

"Well, not quite. There's some damage and there'll be repairs to do as soon as I get this report to the office." Mr. McCarthy waved the sheet of paper with the notes he had scribbled. "I'm sorry, Mrs. Engel, but you'll have to leave until the work is done." The keeper was a sad man. He'd miss the good cooking.

That afternoon Dad rowed my mother over to the ferry terminal for a trip to San Francisco. Her family would be happy to have her visit for three weeks.

U.S. Lighthouse log entry:
Dec. 1, 1900. The steamer Newark struck SE side of the lighthouse. Broke one pile and brace of platform.

U.S. Lighthouse log entry:
Dec. 19, 1900. The railroad company finished the work on the piles and braces and made a good job of it.

Within three months after this, Dad was notified of his transfer as third assistant to a land station. It was Point Bonita, a fog-bound, wind-battered promontory jutting out into the cold Pacific, across from San Francisco. My parents did not know that it was such a rough assignment that in the 1850's, nine keepers had resigned in seven months, a pattern that was to be repeated to a lesser degree all through the years. They were to find out why later, but for the moment it was to be another step in their eventful life in the U.S. Lighthouse Service.

Part Two

Point Bonita Light Station
1901-1914

The original lighthouse was constructed back on the hills of Point Bonita and went into operation April 30, 1855. It was 300 feet above sea level and often shrouded in the typical high fogs of California, while the lower region remained clear. The guiding light was thus blocked from the view of passing ships, and often the fog signal could not be heard.

To correct this situation at Point Bonita, a new lighthouse was built at the extreme tip of the point, and became operative February 1, 1877. It is still in full operation making the northeast hinge of the "Golden Gate."

A large area adjacent to Point Bonita has been designated the Golden Gate National Recreation Area, and offers to the public a beautiful rugged space for camping, sightseeing, picnicking and beachcombing. It is worth a trip!

The Engel family, left to right: Ray, Mom and me, Dad, and El.

3

Back on Dry Land

Dad held the official letter and read aloud, "I inclose a communication from the Treasury Department, transferring and appointing you Third Assistant, Bonita Pt. Light Station, California, at a salary of $500 per annum."

There it was, after almost five months of happy times at the Oakland Harbor Light, my parents were to be stationed on dry land. The Lighthouse Service had kept its promise.

Today, Point Bonita is a headland of eroded thinness, thrusting out from Marin County, and across the bay from San Francisco. One end of the Golden Gate Bridge is anchored deep in its side near Sausalito.

Through the years, wind and storms on the ocean side, and mighty tides and currents on the bay side have gnawed relentlessly away at this vulnerable area. At one point this peninsula opens up to a ridge only as thick as a man's arm. At another section, the twenty-foot guard rail that once gave some measure of protection to my father as he hiked to his duty station has crumbled away. Replacing it is a one hundred sixty-foot suspension bridge with a one hundred eighty-foot drop to the rocks and waves below. Erosion goes on today.

The first Point Bonita Light was built high back on a hill and away from the water's edge, but it was later shifted to a point where it became more visible from sea. Construction of the new lighthouse began in the 1870's at the extreme tip of Point Bonita. It was an area of crumbling black earth and almost impenetrable rock. The strange mixture was completely unpredictable. Huge chunks of land fell suddenly. The first workers lasted only a few days before walking off the job. It became increasingly difficult to maintain a full crew. Eventually a narrow trail was cut in the rugged hills, but in certain places it could hold only two men at a time. The work went very slowly, but after many stoppages the new station was finished. The

hazardous trail was left behind to be used by the keepers on their
trek between dwellings and light, a mile of cold windy, dangerous
and altogether miserable way to work.

And so on a chill spring morning in 1901, my parents rode the
ferry from San Francisco across the bay to the little village of Sausalito. From here a rough road led them up and down hill and close
to treacherous cliffs and finally to their new home. For those three
miles, a wind-driven fog enveloped the region and biting cold hurried
their steps.

At the end of their journey, a scattering of old buildings came
into view. One was to be my parents' dwelling, but it would not be
of their choosing. As was the custom in the Service, the lowest man
in rank was assigned the poorest housing. Dad had hesitated to say
anything about the building they would occupy. He had been over
a day earlier to clean up. It had disheartened him completely. Now
here they stood, hand in hand, before an ancient, weathered structure, sadly in need of a coat of paint. It sat on a bare piece of land,
looking hopelessly uninhabitable, an 1856 relic of stone and brick.
Before they could enter, the door opened and a sturdy smiling
woman stepped out.

"You must be Mrs. Engel. I met your husband yesterday." She
looked at Mom's drawn face. "Did you walk all that way from Sausalito? You're tired. Come on into my place and get warm. I'm Mrs.
Cobb, the second assistant's wife."

They followed her through the common doorway that split the
building into two family quarters, and entered the room on the right.
In this single room they saw a stove, sink, table, chairs and beds.
A few clothes hung against the wall.

"Yes, I know. It isn't much, but it's all we've got. The tiny room
above is not fit for anyone. Besides it's warmer down here anyway."
Mrs. Cobb caught Mom's look of shock at the contents of this one
room.

The stove sent out a welcome blanket of warmth and the kitchen
glowed with the beginnings of a friendship that was to last a lifetime.
Mother and Dad sipped their hot coffee quietly and watched Mrs.
Cobb take two bubbling apple pies from the oven.

"I made two. I want you to have one when it cools a bit." She
fanned the fragrant steam away from her face.

Dad arose in a little while and spoke, "I think we'd better get
started on our own place. Thank you for the coffee."

"Here, let me fill your cups and take them with you, and here's
your pie." Placing a folded towel beneath the hot plate, she handed

Dad the delicately crusted pie. "And let me know if there is anything I can do to help."

"Freda, you stay here a little longer. I want to get the stove going and the room warmed. I don't want you to catch cold." He left with his cup and the pie, but was back in a few minutes. "I've got a good fire going. I think you'll be all right next to the stove."

Thanking her once more, they left and crossed the space that held the common stairs to the attic, and entered their room on the left side of the dwelling. Dad settled Mom in a rickety chair near the heat. While she finished her coffee, she viewed the bare room. Remembering the warning her new neighbor had given about the room above, she began to plan for making the lower one cheerful and livable. The outside measurements of their share were twenty by fifteen feet, but with stone walls almost a foot and a half thick, it reduced the inside area to a much smaller space. The rough walls and cracked ceiling reflected the age of this ancient abode. Dad could easily paint the drab interior, but as for the rest, she shook her head in despair. Only one small ugly room, and a baby on the way. She began to look around again and visualize the furniture in place. It would be a tight squeeze with all that golden oak. But there would be time to worry about that when the furniture arrived.

Closets had not been constructed on this floor. Dishes were washed at the tiny sink. Cold water was piped in from the windmill about a mile away, but the daily log entries indicated that the strong winds had the windmill flat on its back most of the time, and that meant hauling buckets of water by hand. Water was heated on the coal stove for dishwashing and bathing, and the old wooden tub would make its appearance once again.

The quarters lacked an inside toilet. An outside privy stood a regulation distance from the dwelling and was shared by the two families. And according to strict lighthouse rule, this important structure had to be moved to a new spot every three months. Rain, wind, or fog, the hardy souls made their way an uncomfortable distance to use the two-holer.

Dad later ventured to try sleeping in the little alcove above, but as the Cobbs had said, it was unfit for anyone to occupy. Over the years, dampness had crept in through the roof and stone walls, even into the chimney bricks. Fungi grew and spread, invading the attic. The air was foul and the one time Dad slept there he became ill, and use of the room had to be abandoned. The door was closed to shut off the bad air. The Service tried once to remedy the difficulty, but the old place resisted all attempts at improvement. For years before the arrival of my parents, this recommendation appeared early in the *Annual Record:*

> *The dwelling occupied by the assistant keepers, built in 1856, an old stuccoed-brick structure of one and a half stories does not afford adequate accommodations for the keepers and their families. Plans and estimates for a new double dwelling to cost $6,000, have been approved. The Board recommends that an appropriation of this amount be made therefore.*

And year after year this same statement, except for minor changes, appeared in the *Annual Record*. A tiny addition was built to each side of the quarters, but it was only large enough to be used for storage. There didn't seem to be any hope of my parents ever getting into a decent home. But along came the San Francisco Earthquake and that changed the *Annual Record* at last and a new statement was finally written in the year of 1906. It was 1908 before my mother and father and their two little boys moved out of this hovel and other makeshift housing into new quarters—after seven long years!

That first night a batch of sliced onions and potatoes steamed together and a golden mound of scrambled eggs made a hearty meal. Freshly brewed coffee, done in a bleached muslin bag, brought forth the finest filtered brew. Dinner dishes were easily done in a bucket of hot water, and after a quick trip outside, the two tired souls were ready for bed. This first night old Army cots had to suffice. It was then that Dad informed Mom she would have to go back to Sausalito the next day to see that the furniture was taken from the ferry, placed aboard the hired wagon, and carted safely to the point. One of the other assistants was ill and it meant Dad would have to stand extra duty the next day. Mom sighed at the thought of that long three-mile walk again so soon.

"I know you're tired but there's no way we can get hold of the driver, and the furniture is set to be shipped tomorrow. But I do have some good news for you. Mr. Cobb is going to hitch up the light-house buggy, and his wife will drive you over to Sausalito," Dad added hopefully.

The last remark brightened the room with good humor. Mom was looking forward to a nice long chat with her new neighbor. There was a lot she wanted to know about this station. That night even the hard cot could not keep her from a restful sleep.

In the morning my mother awoke to a blazing stove, hot coffee,

Original dwelling at Point Bonita, typical of many along the Pacific Coast. Two families shared the little space. *National Maritime Museum, San Francisco.*

and pieces of crisp toast. Dad had already left on the mile-long hike down to his watch duty. A glance out the window gave promise of some sun for the day.

At mid-morning, Mrs. Cobb knocked on the door and poked her head in when she got an answer.

"Can we leave about eleven o'clock? There's a little place we can have some lunch in Sausalito. If your things are coming over early, I know you'll want to be at the ferry slip when your wagon gets there."

"Oh, I'll be ready any time you say. I want to get settled."

"Good, I'll see you in a little while." Her neighbor ducked out.

Promptly at eleven, the two women climbed aboard the two-wheeled buggy and settled themselves for a leisurely ride to Sausalito. In the bright light of the sunny morning, Mrs. Cobb pointed out the surroundings. Behind them separate trails wound down to the station and to the two little piers on the bay side. Across the busy harbor loomed the fabulous city of San Francisco, with its Market Street, Barbary Coast, Nob Hill, and cable cars.

They passed the old rock quarry where granite had been dug to use in building Army gun batteries. Just outside the lighthouse fence, the lifesaving station popped up with its lookout tower, and beyond that hills of green pastures. Cattle dotted the surrounding fields, and here and there a few Army mules lifted their heads in curiosity. Mom turned to look back at the huge swells rolling in at the "Gate." How strange it all was—the primitive world she was now in and just across the bay the bustling metropolis.

The old lighthouse horse plodded slowly along while the women filled their trip with talk and laughter, and with periods of silence to enjoy the life around them. The area was almost overwhelming in its harsh beauty.

In Sausalito, Mrs. Cobb left the horse and buggy at the only livery stable, and with Mom in tow, headed for the little cafe. Sometimes San Francisco pastry appeared on this side of the bay at this eating place. A pleasant lunch hour passed. They walked about the small shopping space until they heard the toot of an incoming ferry, and hastened over to the landing. There stood a wagon and driver, and he looked furious. Ferries had come and gone, but none with the furniture. Mom hoped this one would bring it. The late afternoon sun sought a pathway through a few breaks in the clouds, but the cold, dreary fog had already begun to gather overhead. It would be a miserable ride home in the fading light, made more uncomfortable by a sour driver and darkening sky.

"Couldn't you have been here sooner?" Mom asked sharply.

She received an equally sharp answer from the glowering man. "Well, ma'am, I was here, been here since before noon, but it looks like your furniture just now came in on this ferry."

He pointed to some tarpaulin covered objects on the deck of the docked ferry and hurried over to check the freight. It was the golden oak. Satisfied that Mom would soon be on her way home, her friend headed for home in the buggy.

With the help of a deckhand, the golden oak went aboard the wagon. It took time to handle the heavy wood, and a good one and a half hours still stared them in the face. The oncoming dark did not appeal to either Mom or the driver. But with the last piece safely on, the wagon started on its way and for the first few hundred yards along a fairly smooth level road. That luxury quickly evaporated into a narrow, rutted roadbed. At times the wagon wandered perilously close to the cliff edge. Just enough good light remained for Mom to see just how close. Strange, she couldn't remember the ride over being so bumpy or scary.

She looked at the driver in doubt, "Have you made this trip before?" she asked.

"Only once, in the—," he didn't get a chance to finish his sentence.

"*Stop right here*!" Mom had seen and heard enough. She hopped off the wagon, marched past the mules, and managed to lead the way home.

Dad had been keeping a sharp lookout for Mom and when he spotted the wagon down the road and Mom on foot, he hurried to meet them. The wagon pulled up with its load by their quarters, and Dad helped with the unloading while Mom lay down to rest. Only then did she realize how truly exhausted she was. It had been a long hard hike, but she was thankful the precious cargo had come through safely. It was not the last lighthouse trip the golden oak would take in its lifetime.

And many times my mother said to me, "Those years at Point Bonita were the happiest in my life." And that included seven years living in one room. What inner strengths my parents possessed!

Point Bonita: showing shops, dwellings, life-saving station. *National Maritime Museum, San Francisco.*

4

Settling In Again

M om was the worrier. She worried about everything that concerned the welfare of her family. For the moment, careful planning was needed for the most efficient placement of the furniture in that one small room.

By the time Dad had returned from his morning watch, she knew exactly how the room would be arranged: the table and chairs next to the stove and sink, the bed next, and farthest away the dresser and washstand. When all was set, an extra boxed object still remained.

"What's that? It doesn't belong to us whatever it is. Someone must have gotten it mixed up on the ferry. I wonder what it is?" Mom puzzled.

"Guess we'd better take a look and get it to the right owner." Dad turned the box around to look for an address or name. A big smile came over his face. "Here it is . It's to Mrs. Hermann Engel."

"What? What on earth?" She tried to peek through the cracks in the wood. "I can't see a thing. Hurry! Open it."

Dad pulled a hammer from his toolbox and pried off one of the crate slats. He pulled one or two free. "Now you can take a look."

"It's a sewing machine! A beautiful sewing machine! And you knew it all the time." Mom gave Dad a big hug.

"Yes, your mother thought you would need one and had this put on with the other furniture." He gave the foot treadle a little touch and the machine whirred quietly. "Where do you want me to put it?"

"Over there by the side of the table. There's just enough room for it." Grandma had sent a machine that nearly matched the rest of the golden oak. It seemed to be right at home. Mom was busy pulling out the drawers, finding packages of needles, spools of thread and extra bobbins. Grandma always did things right.

Along with the present she had sent colorful yardage, some of which was quickly transformed into bright curtains for the two small

windows. Contrasted with the dingy walls, the vivid colors served
only to emphasize the drabness of their dwelling. In the next few
days, when he had some spare time, Dad walked over to the keeper's
house, thence to a small supply shed, and back home packing a big
brush and two cans of white paint. Late into that night he swung
the brush, moving the furniture out of the way as he worked.

At last my mother threw up her hands. "That's about enough.
You can finish the rest tomorrow," she ordered as she sniffed at
the paint odors and glanced about the walls. There remained one
wall and the ceiling to finish, but the smell was getting stifling, and
Dad was beginning to teeter on the ladder from exhaustion. He nodded his head in agreement and stepped off the bottom rung of the
ladder in relief.

"I'll just take this stuff outside and get cleaned up." Dad picked
up the paint bucket and brush, rags and a bucket of hot water.
Before long he was back, face shining from a vigorous scrubbing.
"I'll finish it tomorrow, after I get off from the morning watch. Let's
leave the door open for a while. This paint smells awful."

Mom turned from the stove and poured a relaxing cup of coffee
for them both. It helped to take some of the pungent smell away.
She soon learned that the stove had a nasty disposition, heating up
in uneven spurts, throwing out intense heat at one time, and lan-
guishing idly the next. But she finally tamed it, and in the following
days, cracked the whip when it became recalcitrant.

With the approach of warmer days my mother began to picture
a garden filled with fresh, green vegetables. The Army commissary
provided a limited selection, but rarely truly fresh produce. Mom
finally rebelled at the sight of the wizened vegetables. She longed
for a choice corned beef brisket accompanied by a head of fresh
green cabbage, not cabbage that had wintered in a musty cellar or
warehouse somewhere.

On one of her frequent trips to San Francisco to visit her mother,
Mom returned laden not only with a huge bagful of fresh vegetables,
but also packets of seeds. The next few days she labored digging up
a small patch of ground near the house. Dad shook his head and
scolded her, and then finished the job by breaking up the big clods.
To the fairly smooth earth, he added fresh manure from the stable,
and during the next week, mixed earth and fertilizer. Mom studied
her packets of seed, reading the directions over and over again.

A clearing sky after a soft spring rain determined the great day
of planting. The soft bed of loam was now ready to welcome the
seeds.

"Come on, give me a hand," Mom called to the Cobbs. "Let's go out and start a garden."

My father laughed at her enthusiasm, but he must have been worried too. Mom was in her fifth month of pregnancy, and he did not like to see her doing any heavy work. On this dreary station it was hard to find much to be cheerful about, unless you found happiness within yourself, and he did not want to spoil her fun with the garden.

Carefully directed by Mom, the Cobbs and Dad selected their packets of seed, and with elaborate ceremony placed their offerings in neat rows. In fifteen minutes all the seeds were tucked away, smoothed over with earth, watered, and left with a hope for quick sprouting.

"Freda, now all you have to do is keep these poor little things warm," Dad said as a cold, warning wind sprang up.

But my mother's good spirits could not be squelched. "They'll grow. Now come on in. I made a batch of doughnuts this morning." And they all trooped into the little Engel kitchen, happy to have done something different.

Occasional warm sun battled with the wet fog and chill winds. The tender sprouts did a hesitation waltz in responding to the erratic weather, spreading themselves to the warmth, or cowering from the cold. Some plants finally struggled to questionable maturity. The crops were gathered with as much fun and laughter as they had been planted. And so with this initial success, the little garden patch was enlarged. It stretched out from the house and down a slope, where vegetables and wild flowers mingled happily. Good harvests were made all during the summer, and by that time Mom decided she was somehow endowed with the power to prolong the growing season. But Dad urged her to curtail her energetic activities in the garden. The warm days were receding and the cooler winds blew in from the Pacific. She spent much of her time sewing baby clothes and chatting with Mrs. Cobb.

Dad was never an ardent gardener, but to please Mom he kept up the work. The only crop he chose to plant was the potato. While others sowed and harvested their crops, his always turned out pitifully small, in both the size and quantity. It seemed such a scant return for all the effort he put into the planting. Repeatedly following all the directions and adding extra loam did not change the results, and Dad was made the butt of many jokes at the station.

But one day he spied four little urchins gathering around a small fire far down on the beach. He used the binoculars for a better look.

The boys were pulling huge baked potatoes from the hot coals, and stuffing the charred goodies into their mouths. So that's where his potatoes had gone! After a short conversation with the younger generation, a compromise was reached, and it was agreed that henceforth, all the boys would be limited to the very smallest "spuds," leaving the large ones for Dad to harvest as they were needed.

Near the end of September a fast moving rain storm blasted in from the Pacific. The fierce gusts tore the smaller plants from the ground. Mom fortified herself in the damp kitchen by poking extra wood and coal into the stove, and returned to washing dishes, still feeling that creeping cold. Rivulets of rain poured down the window. She was glad that the Oakland Harbor Light was in the past. That little house on the bay would really be shaking in the wind like this, and it certainly would not be the place for a woman about to have a baby. In the midst of her reverie, a twisting mass of green caught her eye. The early fall winds had shriveled most of the last planting, but the hardier ones, large leaf cabbages and cauliflower thrived after the initial shock and grew into healthy heads. Nothing seemed to daunt them until this onslaught.

And there in the garden spun the cabbages and cauliflower, around and around, like whirling dervishes, their large leaves flapping in the gusts. The wind at last died down, the feverish dance ended, the plants flopped over on their sides. Mom stared in amazement. Later that day, Dad gathered the usable vegetables and stored them in the cold cellar for future use, and understandably there was more than the usual number of corned beef and cabbage dinners for a while.

October moved in quietly enough but on October 6, 1901, Mr. Cobb, the second assistant, rushed out at 5:30 a.m. for an Army doctor and nurse; it was not until 5:30 p.m. that my older brother finally made his appearance. It was a long and painful period of labor for Mother, and it had come so suddenly and unexpectedly that there had been no time to get to a hospital in the "City." Ray was born in that 1856 relic. Lack of hospital facilities and adequate obstetrical care left Mom in poor condition. As soon as possible she was taken to a hospital in San Francisco for treatment. Dad took as much leave of absence as he could, while the thoughtful other assistants stood his watches and did his share of work.

When Mom left the hospital she was still in a weakened condition and not able to do much except care for her baby. Her neighbor stepped across the hall every day to help in any way she could, and soon Mom regained much of her spent strength and good spirits. The little room seemed to grow ever smaller with the addition of a child, and on August 30, 1903, when my other brother Elmer joined the family, it really became crowded.

Fortunately Nature was free with her bounty. When my brothers were old enough, they hiked over to the pastures and hills to gather mushrooms and wild berries. After a rain and a few sunny days the fields would be dotted with creamy white mushrooms, ready for the picking. Mom liked to use them in her cooking. The task of gathering was always a pleasant one, especially when accompanied by large slices of chocolate cake. The boys combed the pastures first, just looking for the largest ones, then if their sacks still had a bit of room, they went along the base of the nearby hills. Unfortunately they usually had a joyous romp on the way home, shoving and jostling one another, forgetting the fragile contents of the sacks they carried. Too often my brothers reached home with a soggy mess. A few mushrooms were usually salvaged for a bit of flavoring. But then the next storm would replenish the fields and perhaps the boys would be more careful.

A dime tossed into the frying pan was used as a test for the edibility of the mushrooms. If the coin turned black, that was evidence of poisonous toadstools. If the coin retained its silver sheen, then all was well. In all the years this procedure was carefully followed, and the dimes never changed color. I didn't know about the fallacy of this test until I was grown. I am very grateful that my brothers were reliable pickers.

The gathering of wild berries took more time and effort, but the boys kept them in good condition. Berries went into the making of delicious pies! They picked just the best ones, placed them in double layers in small cardboard boxes and walked home in good order, their mouths all set for a piece of berry pie.

The seas surrounding Point Bonita were filled with turbulent waters and rocky shoals. The surging tides and violent winds joined forces to sweep ships off course and perilously close to danger. On stormy days, the keeper on watch sometimes witnessed the desperate struggles of the sailing ships to stay on course and away from the shore. Sometimes we could watch too, as vessels strained to make headway into San Francisco Bay, hulls and sails disappearing in the trough and then rising on the crest of a wave. Each time the ships seemed doomed to disaster, but they were built to ride out fierce gales, and their sailors had the strength to handle the hard work. To us there was nothing more beautiful than a ship under full sail running before a wind.

Cannon used as fog signal at Point Bonita, fired once every hour. At one time, an ex-gunnery sergeant fired the old gun for three days and nights with just two hours rest. When finally relieved, he resigned on the spot. *The Bancroft Library, University of California, Berkeley.*

Entering San Francisco Bay did not necessarily ensure a safe end to a long arduous journey. The powerful tides funneling in and out of the harbor, and the strong prevailing winds taxed the navigational skills of the seamen. A ship could come to a disastrous end inside the bay as well as on the high seas. The fogs that swept through the "Gate" shrouded the channel in a blinding mist that led more than one ship astray.

Late one stormy winter morning a small schooner rounded the point and headed for shelter. Waves were washing over the hull and ripping at the deck cargo. The storm had loosened some of the lashings and although the crew strove to snug everything down, some of the load was lost. The vessel had no choice but to continue up the bay, leaving barrels, kegs, tubs and boxes in its wake.

The keeper on watch sounded short blasts on the foghorn to alert the lifesavers. Word was quickly passed along and within minutes the eight-oared whaleboat was in the water and headed out of the bay. The schooner had since passed into safer water. But the men still pulled their sturdy craft out into the rough waters following after the passing ship. Here they gathered up as much of the floating cargo as they could before getting into danger themselves. Box after box and barrel after barrel the men pulled aboard until their craft was loaded almost to the gunwales.

That evening, the lifesaving crew, smiling broadly, hiked up to our house lugging a huge load of tub butter, canned huckleberries, and barrels of fresh cranberries. The next Saturday, Mom thanked the men by frying great batches of tender, custardy buttermilk pancakes for their breakfast. We were always well supplied with a variety of things when cargoes fell into the sea or were washed ashore. Saturday night became a traditional "doughnut" feast time, as the assistants' wives all pitched in and made great batches of doughnuts for the hardworking keepers, the Army engineers, and the lifesavers—all who were so good to us. The weekly gatherings brought respite from the hard work that burdened everyone.

Retrieving goods that washed up on the ocean side proved more difficult. The area to the north was a region of steep and dangerous cliffs. Along this stretch however, a few little coves reached back into flat areas, and we always headed for one of these when the weather cleared. On one of Dad's rare days free, Mom packed a large picnic basket and we were all off on a picnic. When we reached the beach, she found a safe place for the food, out of the sun and away from any curious sea birds. Then while Dad and my brothers combed the beach for lengths of lumber or scattered railroad ties, Mom and

I searched for bits of carnelian—a colorful, reddish mineral. The timber was sawed into sections that would fit on our crude sledge. The old mule we often borrowed from the Army hauled the load along the beach to a wagon, where it was transferred. After two or three sledge trips, the wagon held as much as the mule could haul, and the animal was given a well-deserved rest with a nosebag of oats as thanks. And while the mule ate his lunch, Mom spread our picnic. By the time our leisurely eating had ended it was usually time to pack up and head for home. The late afternoon chill never failed to blow in from the Pacific; the wagon would have to be unloaded and the mule returned to the Army stables.

But there were other days when no one but the keepers ventured outside, and they were the days when we could expect the unusual to happen.

Several of the Bay cities were then using the garbage disposal system so common to many of the coastal communities. Collected garbage was hauled to the bay front and placed aboard engine-driven scows that took the refuse out to sea to be dumped. These low-slung barges were always heavily laden, but considered generally seaworthy. Their powerful engines drove them through the heaviest of seas, but no one envied the crew. The barges were held in contempt by deep sea sailors, because the craft didn't look, handle, or even smell like a ship.

While on watch one morning, Dad noticed a scow headed out the "Gate." The wind had been blowing fitfully, but a heavier blow was in the offing. Even now the leaden skies promised no easy trip for the awkward vessel. Out past the "Gate" it slowly plowed its way, keeping a steady headway against the increasing winds and high breaking waves. The garbage had to be dumped far enough at sea so that the tides would not bring it back into the harbor, nor the surf scatter it along the San Francisco beaches. My father kept his eyes on the scow, using his binoculars to follow its progress.

By now the seas were buffeting the craft with almost gale force. And then the one thing that the crewmen feared happened! The engine quit. At the sudden loss of power and forward way, the barge swung helplessly around until it was broadside to the sweeping combers. Dad didn't wait to see what he guessed might happen. He rushed to the fog signal and blew short rapid blasts on the horn. Even as he pulled the cord, the heavy scow turned turtle. The men were swept into the raging waters. There was no help the lifesavers could offer in time and all hands were lost.

Despite the dangers that lurked in these rough northern waters, small fishing boats manned by a crew of one or two went out on their daily runs for catches of salmon, halibut, and crab. The boats were such gallant little craft, most about twenty-five feet long, broad of beam and round of bottom, with a free board of two to three feet, and often driven by just a reliable one-cylinder engine. They were called Monterey or crab boats and were stable in almost any kind of sea. Only the severest storms kept them in the harbor. These boats were so constructed that they went with the sea, rolling and pitching easily and dropping into the troughs or riding the crests with seemingly little effort. Many people felt safer in them than in larger vessels. Many of these still sail out of San Francisco harbor and tie up at Fisherman's Wharf.

Near Point Bonita was an area called the Potato Patch, a place of rocks and shoals. A strong wind or storm always drove the water here into a mass of white foam, like heapings of mashed potatoes. More than one ship had come to grief here with its load of potatoes from Bodega Bay. Tragedy seemed to hover over this spot.

The great gray whales sometimes wandered into San Francisco Bay on their way to the warm southern lagoons of Mexico. We enjoyed watching these gentle creatures swimming along, surfacing, spouting and taking in fresh air before the next dive. They harmed no one as they went on their way, but their very gentleness made them easy prey to any predator.

We hated to see the Potato Patch churned into an unnatural froth. It meant that killer whales were on the attack. They often drove helpless and confused whales into the shallows, tore viciously at them, seeking the tongue and underbelly. Large triangular fins sliced the water among the thrashing flukes as the giants struggled to escape. The sea had become a battle ground with the outcome already determined. The whales never had a chance. The sight sickened those who watched. There was nothing anyone could do to help.

Telegraph Hill burning after the 1906 earthquake. *The Bancroft Library, University of California, Berkeley.*

5

The City Falls

Official Log Entry: April 18, 1906, 5:12 a.m.
"Terrible earthquake occurred at 5:12 a.m.,
doing considerable damage to the assts.' quarters.
Shaking the gable ends out, and cracking it so badly,
that it was with difficulty that the families were
taken out without injury to their persons, the chim-
neys were shaken to pieces, the keepers' quarters
were given a terrible shaking. One chimney shaken
off at the comb of the roof and others broken off, but
still stand, the doors were all jammed, so the keeper
had to take his family out the kitchen window. The
tanks at the signal were cracked about one inch,
starting them to leaking but was stopped. The chim-
ney to the signal was broken or cracked around
about 6 feet from the bottom but it still stands. The
old tower is nearly ready to fall being cracked
badly."

Instinctively my mother scrambled out of bed, picked up her two small sons, grabbed at blankets and a robe, and rushed for the outside. The first massive shock was enough to wake her out of a deep sleep. The third assistant keeper was first at the outside door.

"It's an earthquake," he gasped. "Let's get out of here. The whole place is coming down on us." And as he spoke the earth groaned and shook with another sharp tremor.

They stumbled away from the crumbling building with its falling bricks and stones. Great portions of the walls toppled, leaving ragged outlines of what was once their home. The chimneys and walls soon lay upon the ground in a mass of rubble.

They all stared in shock, frozen at the sight of the leveled structure. Dust clouds drifted slowly away. The assistant made sure that the Engel family was not injured and then dashed off to the keeper's home to find out what he should do next.

Mom wrapped El and Ray more securely in the blankets, pulled on her robe, and then tried to quiet and reassure the boys. And there the three stood, on a barren hill of Point Bonita, wondering what to do. El answered that question.

"Mom, I gotta go," he said.

"I might have guessed," she sighed, "and just after I have you all bundled up."

So they all walked over to the official U.S. Lighthouse privy, still staunchly upright.

By the time the operation was concluded, they saw the lifesavers heading towards them on the run. The lifesavers were well aware of the poor construction of the assistants' dwelling and feared there might have been loss of life. They counted noses quickly and were relieved to learn that no one had been hurt.

Dad was on watch down at the light station and he would have to remain there until the relief watch came on duty. He was worried too, but the telephone lines were down; he just had to wait. In a short while one of the lifesavers hiked down with the good news that everyone was well and being cared for at the lifesaving station which had withstood the tremendous jolt.

Clad only in their nightgowns and wrapped in thick blankets, Mom, El, and Ray had been carefully escorted down to the lifesaving station where temporary quarters were readied for them. While the homeless ones ate a hot breakfast, one of the men set up cots. The little boys felt better after eating, but they were still excited and full of questions. Mom managed to get El and Ray to lie down and in a short while both of them were sound asleep. Mom sat by their cots, her mind filled with thoughts of Dad, and all her relatives and friends, until she, too, nodded her head and fell asleep in sheer exhaustion.

The short nap proved restful and quieting, and after awakening Mom moved over to stare out the window. Men were bringing down things they had recovered from the demolished quarters, their arms loaded with as much as they could carry. They placed everything in a box and brought it to Mom. She returned to a chair and began sorting the clothing—underwear, overalls, stockings and shirts. She found enough to start the day for her husband and the boys, but found herself short of undergarments. She washed and dressed with what she could assemble, and sat down by the boys again to get some more rest. There was nothing else she could do until my father came back from his watch. She thought about the others on the point, but even as she wondered, she felt they were all right. Questions crowded her mind. Was her husband safe? Had the fog signal and light tower collapsed or fallen into the sea? What had happened to her mother and stepfather? And what of her friends, the Cobbs, who were now stationed across the bay at Fort Point? Were they all safe?

One of the lifesavers came in quietly and broke into her thoughts. "Don't worry, Mrs. Engel, you can stay right here until things get settled. There's plenty of room and I've brought some more of your things too."

The young man flashed an embarrassed grin at her. Sticking out from the stuffed box were a number of pieces of a woman's under-garments. Mom smiled and nodded her thanks. She hoped the corset with its steel stays would be in that pile. When she was seven years old, she had fallen through the skylight of a two-story manufacturing building and landed on machinery below. There were severe injuries to her back, and a steel brace was fitted to her in order to give her back added support. Mom's hand reached down to the bottom of the box and she sighed with relief when she felt the familiar stays. More sorting and the job was finished. She leaned back in the chair again and closed her eyes.

Someone gave her shoulder a gentle shake, "Freda, are you all right?" It was her husband.

Mom opened her eyes, blinking against the light. "Oh, yes, but I've been so worried about you. Are you all right? What do you think has happened to the folks in the city? Isn't there some way we can get word to them, so we can find out if they are safe?" She clung to her husband.

"I'm afraid we can't get over there for a day or two. There's so much to do here at the station and I don't know about transporta-tion. Just as soon as someone goes over there I'll find out all I can. Here, drink this. It'll help." The hot cocoa warmed and comforted her.

The two talked quietly for a few minutes, then Dad hiked up the hill to survey the damage to their home. It was beyond repair. The chimney had fallen in through the rotten roof, and wide cracks appeared in the little remaining sections of the walls. If anyone had been sleeping in that tiny cubicle above, he would surely have been injured or perhaps even killed. But the floor had broken the impact of the falling material and Mom, El and Ray were all spared from being buried under stones and bricks.

Dad gathered a few more needed items, spent a little time talking to the other keepers whose newer homes had suffered much less damage, thanked the lifesavers who were removing the golden oak furniture, and returned to the lifesaving station. There he finally persuaded Mom to lie down and rest. He stretched out on the floor nearby.

By now the lifesavers had borrowed a large tent from the Army post to house the keepers' furniture. They set it up near the ruins of the old dwelling. Most of the furniture had escaped with little damage, except for a covering of dust. By the time Mom and Dad awoke the job was finished.

A room big enough to hold four cots had been set aside for the family. It was to be their home for a few days. Later in the day the whole family walked up the hill, glad to hear that no one on the point had been injured. Mom and Dad retrieved a few small items from the rubble. There was little use in hunting very much. They would have to see what the lifesavers had managed to rescue for them. As they turned back to the path down hill they met some neighbors. Without a word they all stopped to stare at the city across the bay with its broken outline. The ground shook again. Even the air seemed to envelope them with a strange oppressive feeling, and for the rest of her life when there was humid weather, Mother would always say, "it's earthquake weather." The little group broke up after commenting on the smoke beginning to arise from San Francisco. Gas from the broken pipelines fed the increasing fires.

As evening approached, the first flames could be seen shooting skyward, smoke swirling in the wind. After dark the destruction became more evident and created a greater worry for Mom. There was nothing she could do but wait.

At supper time the family gathered around the well-stocked table and enjoyed a hot meal that revitalized their spirits. Even though they were all tired, the conversation with the lifesavers went on for hours, punctuated by continuing aftershocks.

Early the next morning the lifesavers worked hard to clean up the goods stored in the tent. Mother, Dad, El, and Ray came out from their breakfast to find the lifesavers finished with the cleaning and preparing to move the goods into a dry Army building. None too soon. There was a threat of rain in the air. The Army engineers had checked out of their small office and offered it as a temporary shelter to my parents. My parents were grateful for any roof over their heads. They felt sure the Service would soon construct new quarters for them.

The office was a very small building, bare of everything except a pot-bellied stove, with just enough space on top to hold a coffee pot. But there was a bathroom, containing a toilet, bathtub and washbasin. The rest of the area was just a room with two shelves, and in all even tinier than their old home. Mom and Dad discussed the placing of furniture, and something had to be done about providing cooking facilities. The pot-bellied stove had to be replaced. But rather than start late in the day, they decided to wait until the next morning. Dad had arranged with another keeper to take his watch for the day. The boys weren't sure what it was all about, but along with the other children were having a good time watching all the "goings-on."

In the days that followed the two dispossessed keepers moved into their makeshift quarters, the third assistant into the old signal tower long out of use, and my family into the engineers' office. The signal tower had a few cracks in it, but had withstood the earthquake in good shape. Once cleaned and provided with a cooking stove, it would make fairly decent quarters.

The engineers' building lacked space and a usable stove also. The lifesavers and Dad had a hard time trying to fit the furniture into the little space. Finally it was jammed in. The pot-bellied stove proved more of an obstacle than a help and was removed when the men scrounged up an old condemned cooking stove. It was warped and full of grime, but a shade better than the damaged one in their old home. That one had been deluged by stone and brick, and until it could be repaired, the condemned one would have to do. At least it would provide some heat and simple cooking. At the time my parents were just happy to be alive with everyone safe. Happy, too, that this new abode was constructed of wood and would hold up under further shocks.

By the time the afternoon had rolled around, there was some semblance of order again. A few of the unbroken dishes were placed on the shelves, and hooks were hammered into the walls from which to hang the clothes after they had been washed free of the dust. Some of the washing would have to wait. It was important that the family have beds ready for the night.

One of the other keeper's wives came over to see if she could help. She knew of the back problems my mother had, plus the serious operations from which she was still recovering. The keepers and their families were a close-knit group, always ready to help one another. This good friend put aside her own troubles to work with Mom. She gathered up the curtains and gave them a good shake. The two of them did their best at covering the windows. The curtains were not the right size, but with the shades still in place there would be privacy.

The stove presented the real problem—rusty, filled with soot and grease, and just out of the junk heap. But they rolled up their sleeves and set to work wirebrushing and scraping until their arms ached. A final scrubbing removed most of the remaining dirt. It didn't look much better, but they both felt a great deal better.

"Freda, let's call it quits for a while. Come on over to my place. We'll have a cup of coffee and I'll freshen up some San Francisco coffee cake. It's going to be a long time before we get any more of that."

As they walked along they turned now and then to gaze across the bay. Everything they saw just pointed to greater devastation. At the old signal tower the boys were running around and around, driving the assistant crazy as he tried to make some water pipe connections. Her friend wasted no time in quieting the youngsters. Glasses of milk and cookies did the job. The two women rested their weary backs and sipped hot coffee with the cake, talking quietly about the strange twists in their lives. With a refill in hand they went outside to look again. There still had been no word at all from any of their relatives or friends.

"The whole city must be on fire. Look at that flame and smoke!" The woman could have bitten her tongue as she saw my mother's face tense with anxiety. "I'll get the shoe polish. Let's finish that stove so you'll feel better when you look at it. Maybe it'll even do a good baking job."

"I'm still so worried about my folks," Mom replied.

"Thank goodness, I have a few supplies for a while." Her friend tried to change the subject. "I don't imagine we'll be able to get much from the city." She was mentally tabulating her staples and supplies, planning to share with my mother. Their best source of supplies would be from incoming ships. The lifesavers would be ready at the San Francisco wharves to help the keepers obtain foodstuffs.

With clean rags and a tin of black shoe polish they walked back to the office. "Oh, I hope we can get a good fire going. Everybody is going to need a good hot meal tonight." Mom was tired and held little hope for the ancient cast iron relic. She followed her friend into the temporary dwelling.

They each took a rag, wiped a bit of black shoe polish on it, and went to work on the top of the stove. The lids soon lost their dullness and began to gleam. Over the rest of the top and down the sides the two women rubbed and rubbed, stopping occasionally to wipe the sweat from their faces. The sharp odor of the polish filled the air, but in an hour, the condemned hunk of metal took on a new stature, even an air of respectability and possible usefulness. They gave one last swipe with the rags and stepped back to judge their work.

"Now, I just bet you won't have any trouble with this stove."

"Oh, do you really think so?" Mom had to have a test run on the old stove before she could believe that.

"Sure, Freda, you could bake anything, anytime."

"Thank you so much for helping. I don't know what I would have done by myself." She gave her friend a quick hug.

"Well, it looks like you're in pretty good shape now, but I can see how tired you are. Come on over to our place for supper tonight. I have a big pot roast on the stove, already cooked. How does that sound? We'll just have some beef sandwiches with lots of gravy. Then you can put the boys to bed early and get a good rest yourself."

"That's wonderful. When you go back to your place will you please send my boys home? I think Elmer could use a little rest. He is not so strong after that rheumatic fever."

"Of course, now you get some rest." Her helper left with a cheery wave of her hand.

As soon as El came running in, she tucked him in bed for a little rest. Ray was too lively to settle down, so she let him continue playing with the other boys. Mom made up the double bed and lay down to rest. She ached all over from the hard work. Her eyes closed swiftly in a deep restful sleep.

The persistent shouts of four-year-old Ray roused her with a feeling of panic. "Mom, Mom, look what I got from the lifesavers." His little hands held out a covered plate. "Can I have a piece? It smells so good and I'm so hungry."

It was then that my mother realized it was late in the afternoon and she had gone without lunch. Ray probably had a bite to eat at one of the neighbors, or he would have been in earlier asking for something. "Let's both sit down and have a piece right now. I don't think it will spoil our supper." Mom filled the coffee pot with water and pushed it over to the fire side, and lit the kindling wood and paper she had placed in the stove. "There, it will be hot in a minute, and here's some cool milk for you."

The warming stove livened up the shoe polish smell again but in a little while the odor subsided and the air cleared. It was still strong enough to make El cough and awaken. The little two-year-old joined them at the table, his eyes glued on the covered plate.

Mom ground fresh coffee, placed it in the bleached muslin bag and waited for the water to boil. When it did she put the bag into the coffee pot and waited for the brew to form. In an instant the aroma took over the room. It was fragrant and clean and erased the other odor of polish.

Ray lifted the cover from the plate and grinned at his brother. There, in all its chocolate glory, sat a big three-layer cake, begging to be sliced. Mom started to cut a piece when Ray took the knife from her hand and cut a large swath for himself. It wasn't a very neat job. The cake was so tender and light that it crumbled from his hand on the way to his plate, and El intercepted a luscious bit of frosting that fell by the wayside. Ray glared but he was too late. The goodie had already disappeared down his brother's throat. My mother quickly quelled the impending quarrel by shooing Ray over to the other side of the table and giving El his bit of cake. She cut a slice for herself, and put the rest aside to take to the neighbors for supper. The hard times of the next twenty-two months had just begun.

The ensuing days brought good news from the city. Families and friends had escaped serious injuries and most homes were still intact, although some were in the paths of the spreading fires and the dynamiting that was to follow. Mother's family was blessed with no harm at all. Their home was far removed from the fire area, and it was not necessary to blow up any of the structures in their region. A great burden of worry was lifted from Mom's mind and now she could turn to making a comfortable home for her family.

"Comfortable" was stretching it a bit, for the place was not even adequate. As miserable as the old place had been, this substitute dwelling was a mockery. For the next twenty-two months, water was heated on the stove, and dishes washed in pans on the table. There was no sink or drainboard, no laundry porch or laundry trays. Day after day found Mother on her knees scrubbing clothes on a washboard in the bathtub. The government did not get around to tearing down the old dwelling until December of that year, and did not let a contract for new quarters until 1907. The hopes of having quarters suitable for human habitation loomed far in the future.

Repairs were made quickly and without question to the light and fog signal apparatus, but the keepers were left in limbo while Congress pondered the spending of $6,000 for new double quarters. The government continued to delay month after month. Keepers were the last to be considered. The physical hardships took their toll on my mother.

New dwelling for assistant keepers, finally moved into 22 months after the earthquake.

It was hard living for a family of four in the little one-room space, but the friendships with the other keepers and the lifesavers and the sharing of common miseries helped them all through the rough days. After nearly two years of waiting the promise of new housing was finally realized, and the two families moved joyously into a fine large double dwelling, complete with bedrooms, bathroom, kitchen, pantry, laundry porch, and even a dining room. Down below all this had been carved out a beautiful cellar, with shelves and all. To the families it was a dream house. Everything was new. No more balky stove, no more lifting pails of hot water for the washing. Next to the stove stood a splendid hotwater boiler, that would ensure all the hot water they'd ever need. To Mom and Dad it was a dream house. My mother was happy beyond words. She was already pregnant with me. No little baby girl was going to be born in an old engineers' office. So the San Francisco Earthquake accomplished what the keepers had been waiting for many years, a way out of that 1856 miserable dwelling.

Point Bonita lens—note its size compared with ladder at left. Made by skilled workmen in France and shipped around Cape Horn in a sailing vessel, this lens still guides ships through the Golden Gate. *National Maritime Museum, San Francisco.*

6

Three Bags Full

With hungry young mouths to feed, my parents discussed the purchase of a cow, but the idea was soon dismissed and the daily three-mile hike to Mason's ranch for fresh milk continued.

Mom's two serious operations had plunged the family into deep debt. Doctor Turner, a compassionate surgeon, had instructed my parents to pay what they could, but only after the family had been properly fed. On a forty-two dollar monthly salary, the bills stretched out for a long time.

A little nest egg of sixty-six dollars and sixty-two cents still rested in the sugar bowl untouched. The amount had been sent to my father as a bounty for his participation in the Spanish-American War, as a gunner's mate in the U.S. Navy. This handsome windfall was tucked away for future use. Both my parents were determined to keep this small amount intact, and chose to struggle through the bills without touching the bounty money.

In these first years of marriage, my mother had learned to expect the unexpected from her impulsive spouse. And sure enough, one Tuesday afternoon, she saw Dad hiking home from Sausalito leading a strange object. What had her husband done this time? Following him reluctantly was a small, scrawny cow. A heavy bag of milk swung under its belly, forcing the animal into a lurching and unsteady gait.

After making sure my two brothers were tucked safely in bed, Mom went out to meet her reckless spouse. As he approached a nagging thought plagued her mind. Where had he found the money for this outrageous creature? Even she knew enough about cows to realize that no one knowledgeable in animal husbandry would have ever given this thin bag of bones a second glance.

"Hermann, where did you get that?" Her stern tone erased the smile from his face.

"I spent some of the bounty money for it." Dad blurted out the disheartening news, and then stood quietly while the few neighbors who had gathered quickly conducted a critical inspection of Dad's purchase, pointing to the prominent ribs, broken horn and patchy hide.

"They told me she's a good milker. Just look at her bag." Dad gestured to the strained udder. Milking was long overdue. The audience stood goggle-eyed. How could that little cow even stand with that bulging appendage, so greatly out of proportion to her small frame?

"Gosh, she's gonna bust wide open," observed one of the little neighbor boys.

"Yeah, yeah and who's gonna milk her?" questioned another.

"Oh, I'll do that." Dad was confident. "Her name is Alice." He patted Alice on the rump as though to establish his authority. "I've watched Ingersoll do it. I don't think it's much of a job." He glanced at Mom, still waiting her approval.

Mom sighed as she thought about the unpaid bills. Well, maybe this would work out all right, and her husband was so pleased with himself.

"When are you going to do it? I could use some cream this evening." There was still a little sharpness in her voice. Many months would pass before savings could possibly add up to that amount of money again.

"Oh, just as soon as I change my clothes. You boys go get a pail and stool, and put some feed in a bucket. I'll be right out."

My mother's blue-eyed stare made him uncomfortable and he hurried past her to the house. Alice stood calmly where she had been tied, chewing on a bit of cud, while a few more of the curious had come out to take a look. They just shook their heads in disbelief.

Dad emerged to an expectant group of onlookers. It was no problem to urge Alice closer to the fence where he tied her line more securely. She dipped her head into the feed bucket the boys had placed in front of her, but spared a moment to eye my father warily. There was still nothing in the cow's behavior, however, to indicate anything but a well-mannered bovine.

Dad placed the milking pail in position and settled himself on the stool. Alice swung her head around once more for another look and watched as my father reached out, both hands grabbing clumsily at the udder. Bang! At the first touch of his cold hands, the indignant cow lowered her head, kicked forward with her left hind leg, knocked over the milk pail, swept her tail around and slapped the offender smartly in the face. To complete the job, she shook her head menacingly and let out an earth-shaking bellow. No sailor ever climbed a mast faster than Dad scrambled to the top of that fence, there to perch and wonder what had gone wrong.

"Gee, I don't think you did it right." Bill, the keeper's son, was sympathetic. And he ran off to get his father.

The rest of the gathering bent over in convulsions of laughter watching my father edge farther along the fence in utter defeat. Bill came back shouting, "Pa says he'll be right over. He'll milk her for you."

When Keeper Ingersoll arrived, he first mixed up a bucket of fresh feed, and then sent the boys to the house for a bucket of warm water, all the while patting Alice on the side and talking softly to her. He took slow care washing the udder. Alice seemed to approve of the procedure.

Everyone watched closely as Mr. Ingersoll readied himself for the milking. He blew his warm breath upon cold hands and went to work. A beautiful white stream immediately spurted into the pail and everyone cheered. The cow's tail swished gently to and fro, and she took her head out of the bucket long enough to cast benign eyes upon her benefactor. The rich Jersey milk beat a rhythm into the pail. It foamed to the top and a second pail was started.

"She doesn't look like much now, but clean her up and get some good feed into her. You'll have a fine milker if you do that. All the cow needs is better care," Mr. Ingersoll advised as he finished and gave Alice a final pat.

Mom had watched intently, and at the remark she smiled. Now it was time to get all this milk into the cool cellar. Here the warm liquid was poured out into large shallow white enamel pans for the cream to rise to the top. When my brothers were old enough they learned the fine art of skimming. They sneaked down spoons in hand to poach some of the rich layer.

They had an excellent routine. The boys ran their spoons around the edge of the pan, lifted each spoonful to their mouths and let the cool sweet cream run over their tongues and down their throats. It was nectar. Then they skillfully pushed the remainder of the cream around, doing a fair job of covering the bare areas. Mom knew what they did, but why spoil such harmless fun?

Alice created one more frustrating and awkward situation. After a rain storm, she wandered into the fields and gorged on wet alfalfa, and ballooned to an enormous size. Again Keeper Ingersoll came to Dad's rescue. In the absence of modern veterinary knowledge or medication, the keeper placed a sturdy stick crosswise in the animal's mouth, tied a heavy twine to each end and looped the rest of the line around the horns, thus keeping the cow's mouth open. Then he told Dad to walk the poor creature.

Around and around my father led the suffering cow, giving her an occasional good whack on the side and jumping at every cavernous belch that arose from her interior. Dad was embarrassed, and Alice was indignant and in pain, and matters only grew worse when Alice began to roar at both ends. Dad kept his distance at the end of the lead line. Mercifully, relief finally came to both. The cow deflated to a more normal size once again, and she was placed in a stall to rest and recuperate. Dad retreated to the kitchen for a cup of hot coffee. Neither my father nor Alice were to forget that incident.

It took a while for Dad to establish a working relationship with Alice, and even then he occasionally received a tail in his face as a reminder of past grievances. He never became a skilled milker, but through the cow's patience and his persistence, he managed to empty her bag daily. And true to the keeper's prediction, there was milk in abundance. Dad sold the surplus and the cow more than repaid her initial cost. The savings in the sugar bowl grew day by day.

In time Alice gave birth to a weak heifer with such horribly misshapen legs and hooves that it seemed best to destroy the young thing. No one had the heart to do the evil deed, and the animal was given very special care, with special emphasis on physical therapy. Monkey was given the best fodder and choice oats, daily rubdowns, particularly along the legs, regular daily walks over even ground, and much hugging and loving. It didn't surprise my dad at all to watch the heifer outgrow its early physical handicaps and become the best milker on the point. She had certainly inherited her mother's genes, and the family's debts lessened with each milking.

There was no pasteurization of milk at the point. It was all used in its natural raw state, and when the government inspectors ordered, all cows in the vicinity had to be tested for tuberculosis. Many of the nearby ranches supplied milk to the military.

Official Log Entry: June 15, 1909:
All milk cows to be examined for tuberculosis. This order was received from Fort Barry.
June 16, 1909
Keeper kept cows up all day for inspection.
June 18, 1909
Gov. Inspectors inspecting all cows near lighthouse.

GENERAL APPOINTMENT

Department of Commerce and Labor
OFFICE OF THE SECRETARY
Washington

May 10, 1904.

Mr. Hermann Engel , of California, is hereby appointed

First Assistant Keeper of the Bonita Point Light-Station, California ,

in the Light-House Service ,

at a salary of Six Hundred dollars per annum,

this appointment to take effect May 10, 1904. or as

~~soon thereafter as oath of office is taken.~~ *taken about June 4-1904* vice George D. Cobb,

transferred. (By promotion from the position of Second Assistant Keeper

of the same station, at $550 per annum.)

Lawrence O. Murray
Acting Secretary.

Date of oath: , 190

The Light-House Board.

MAY 23 1904
Forwarded
Commander, U.S.N.
Inspector.

F
D
L
MAY 13 1904   792   RECEIVED

A promotion and raise ($4.16 per month) for Dad. The poor pay and insufficient transportation provided keepers made it necessary for some families to board their children out of the home so they could attend school. *Official letter, U.S. Lighthouse Service.*

June 19, 1909
*Completed inspection of cows 2 lighthouse cows con-
demned.*

Monkey passed the tests with flying colors and grew into a
treasure.

Last to arrive on the bovine scene was Maggie. Alice and Monkey
had been greatly appreciated, but Maggie, offspring of Monkey, was
the grand prize. She was a charismatic, affectionate, good-natured
and intelligent milk producer. She did not resemble her mother in
any way except in coloring. Maggie was large and well-built, but with
not a single infirmity or physical blemish, and endowed with a
remarkably sweet disposition.

From her early days she decided to bestow all her affection upon
Mom. The gate to our yard was frequently left open, and Maggie took
every opportunity to wander in and station herself near the kitchen
door. Here she serenaded my mother with soft pleading "moos."
When Mom opened the door, Maggie stuck her head in for a handout.
She had a passionate appetite for the unusual—sourdough, pumper-
nickle, ice cream, or peanuts. As long as it was handed out the door,
it was accepted. She became quite a pet of the family, and we in
turn received the loyalty of a happy animal. Her fine qualities
included a magnificent bag of milk every day.

Our four-legged friend did not even flinch in the face of scarlet
fever. My brothers and I were in different stages of convalescing
and all of us were in some bit of whining, fussing, crying for attention, or begging for a change in the deadly monotonous routine of
having to stay in bed. We were used to roaming the hills, combing
the beaches, and being with our animals. There just had to be happier
days somewhere.

"There's a visitor here to see you. How about it? Feel like seeing
one of your friends?" Dad poked his head around the corner of the
doorway.

Before we could answer, there came a strange clop-clopping
down the hall. Mom entered first, and right behind her, coat shining
from vigorous brushing, red ribbon tied in a bow and dangling from
a floppy ear, and warm brown eyes looking inquisitively, came our
friend, Maggie. The stopper went on all the whining and fussing.
We all hopped out of bed and hugged and patted Maggie and laughed
with our parents over the strange sight of a cow in a bedroom. It
proved to be wonderful medicine. The visit lasted only a few minutes. Maggie was not the ordinary household pet, and although she

had the manners of a lady outside we had no way of knowing if she understood the proprieties of visiting inside. But her good manners never failed, and the hall continued to resound with strange clop-clopping until we were all up and about again. How we all loved Maggie!

When Dad transferred to Ballast Point Lighthouse in San Diego, we left Maggie behind with good people knowing she would receive excellent care. But it was a sad, sad day for us when we said our tearful goodbyes to our special four-legged companion.

Dangerous walkway built by the workmen who were constructing the second Point Bonita light station. Later used by keepers going to and from station. *The Bancroft Library, University of California, Berkeley.*

7

You Can Get There from Here But It Isn't Easy

I t required a broom handle, a pair of sturdy legs, an excellent sense of balance, and a dedication to the U.S. Lighthouse Service to shepherd the keepers safely from their quarters back on the hill down to the fog and light station. The brave men struggled back and forth over a hazardous trail in the worst kind of weather. Only small strips of the walkway were protected from the wild winds by some high ground. Other sections were exposed to fierce gusts blasting through the gaps, sometimes violent enough to sweep a man off his feet. Unsteady railings set at intervals on the crumbling earth offered little aid in passage over these dangerous lengths of trail.

The men devised their own special but simple means of protection against the unpredictable elements. Each new assistant quickly realized the value of a broom handle. When heavy storms buffeted the point, anyone going down to stand watch grabbed his trusty stick and carried it to work with him. When he approached any treacherous area, the keeper used the handle as an additional support. With the winds blowing across the trail, the slim prop pushed into the ground often supplied that little margin of safety so badly needed.

Each worker was assigned a regular schedule for standing watch, and in order to maintain a happy station, everyone tried to be prompt. Extra time had to be allowed for the unexpected event. The trail ran through a narrow dark tunnel, and frequent occupants were small furry black creatures with broad white V's on their backs. The little animals claimed it as one of their favorite gathering spots, defying anyone to rout them from this place of shelter. My father encountered them only occasionally, and sidled carefully along the side away from the skunks, leaving them to huddle in peace. Now and then a bit of pungent scent served as a reminder that this was no place for humans to linger. Dad was lucky and never had any trouble, but then he was cautious and also fleet of foot.

Even with all the danger and discomfort attached to traversing the trail, it was far better than being assigned to the only dwelling constructed near the light station. It had been built atop steep rocky cliffs and on very uncertain land. The surroundings shook with the force of the winter winds and the air reverberated from the hoarse bellowing of the fog signal. With transportation already a problem even for those living up on the hill, those housed below had the additional long hard hike up and down the trail whenever they went on leave.

For a long time, only single men occupied the quarters, but the inevitable had to happen sooner or later, and everyone viewed with alarm the arrival of a new assistant, accompanied by a wife and small children who were all sent down to occupy the isolated quarters. Horror grew as the families of the other assistants helped move some of the household goods into the dwelling. The wives and children stared unbelievingly at the wild surroundings.

The house did have a fenced yard, but over the years the damp earth had crumbled away, leaving holes large enough for any child to slip through. As soon as the Martins were settled, the new keeper walked around to survey the situation. The children could not be cooped up in the house all the time. They would need to get out to play in the good weather. Mr. Martin promptly solved the problem. The Lighthouse Service always had a good supply of manila rope on hand. When the rope became weathered and worn, the harsh fibers wore off and the rope softened. Martin cut sections of small diameter, fashioned two crude harnesses for the young children, and whenever they played outside, the little ones were secured by the harnesses and lines of rope, cumbersome but effective.

This family never lost a child but there were times when the mother almost lost her mind. She arose each morning in a constant state of worry. One wash day she stepped out to hang clothes only to find a taut line under the fence and over the cliff side. There at the end of the line dangled a very unhappy youngster sending up wails of distress signals. His mother hauled him up quickly but carefully, hugged him tightly, looked for any sign of injury, and then sat down to recover from her fright. When the terrifying moment was over, Mrs. Martin was determined to ask her husband to resign from the Service and move the family to some place where she could breathe more easily each day. But because of the turnover of personnel at Point Bonita, they were soon able to move up to different quarters on the hill where the children could run around safely and enjoy

Another view of Point Bonita—showing house on edge of cliff where assistant keeper had to tie ropes around children for safekeeping. *National Archives.*

the companionship of others their age, and where Mrs. Martin could join in on the daily chatter of the other wives.

Some time later my father took me down to the station and we stopped at the poorly placed housing. I can still remember how frightened I was as I looked around the yard and saw how close the cliffs were by the old rickety fence. The dwelling is no longer there. The earth beneath it finally crumbled away into the sea. Only a small bare piece of land marks the spot.

While hiking up and down the trail to the station was a necessary part of the life of the keepers, transportation for the family members to other areas posed almost equal problems. Children journeyed to Sausalito for schooling—three miles by foot, buggy, boat or occasionally by an Army mule wagon or any combination of these. Travel by water was usually ruled out except in good weather. It was the most unpredictable because of changing conditions, with fog, rough water, and even engine failure often leaving the passengers stranded. My two brothers chose a miserable day to return home from school by hiking to Fort Baker and there taking the Army tug. But when the boat approached the pier at Point Bonita, waves and swells were running so high the boat could not land and returned to Fort Baker. By that time even that area was dangerous and the craft finally made a safe landing in Sausalito. That was the night the boys arrived home at 10 p.m.

My family enjoyed their rare outings in the city of San Francisco. There was still the three-mile trek to Sausalito, but the ride to the city on a regularly scheduled ferry brought us back into the world again. The Sausalito ferry was reliable but possessed limited hours of operation.

The Army tugs that landed at Point Bonita were given to fits and whims of crossing, and never sure of making port in a storm. So if one was to go to the city and back in a day, it meant being on time for the return ferry crossing or there would be nothing but an empty slip in view.

Mom cherished her monthly visits to the city to spend precious time with her mother. It brought relief from the hard life at the point, and the invigorating bustling air of San Francisco renewed her spirits. Besides there were the fragrant pastry shops to be enjoyed.

But one day either the clock moved too swiftly or Mom lingered too long over selecting a mocha cake. By the time we reached the bay front, the last Sausalito ferry had gone. The Army tug was not listed for an evening trip and there we stood on the pier. I held tightly to her hand. She could not hold me in her arms; they were full of gifts from her mother and one box of pastry. Well, there was always a trip back to Hampshire Street for an overnight's stay. Dad wouldn't be worried. Transportation problems had arisen before but Mom wanted to get home. She looked around for help and saw only the empty ferry slip. Without a word she pulled me by the hand and we were off again, hurrying along the line of piers. We halted at the end of one and she looked down its length. There bobbing up and down on the choppy waves was the lifesavers' boat. Mom whooped and hollered as she spied the men clambering into the double-ender. The men spotted us and waved back. Telling me to hang onto her skirt, we ran to the end of the pier, my little legs stumbling along. Strong arms lifted us both aboard. The crew pushed the boat away from the pier and with an even sweep of eight oars, we were safely on our way home. This was even better than the ferry, for the lifesavers' landing sat down below our quarters. It did mean a stiff walk up hill.

Blades cut deep in the water and the rowers pulled the boat steadily across the bay. Wind blew in fitful gusts kicking the water up into little whitecaps, and scattering salt spray over us. One of the men covered us with a light tarpaulin, leaving our heads uncovered. I was never afraid if I was with my mother or father. Mom always loved the water, never feared it, but never learned to swim.

San Francisco had given the lifesavers a holiday from hazardous work and they were still in high spirits. Nevertheless, a straight course was steered across the bay and we landed easily at the little pier. As a fitting conclusion to a fun day in the city, we were escorted up to our home, bags and mocha cake carefully carried by one of the men.

Later another little pier was built directly below our quarters which promised to ease the way to the city and back by eliminating the long haul from Sausalito. But only small boats could dock here, and their use was also limited by the condition of the weather. The huge swells that rolled in around the point made it too dangerous to discharge either passengers or freight. To make it even more difficult the landing led to a rough, steep path up the hill, which discouraged all but the hardy.

A flatbed funicular bore freight up the incline by cable. Regulations forbade any passengers, but after the freight had been lashed on, there was a scramble for the best spot on the tram. There were those who preferred a trip up the almost perpendicular cliff to a hike up the hill. The choice spots were at the front where one could get a good grip on the forward edge of the car. Others had to cling to the lashings and hope that there were no "granny" knots to pull loose. Up, up the flatbed crawled, agonizingly slow. There was no jumping off place. The cliff was too steep for that. The fifteen minutes it took for the platform to gain the top discouraged many first riders from a second attempt. Only once did the cable snap, scattering boxes and barrels down the precipice. There had been no passengers aboard.

There are other stories to tell about going to the city, like the time Dad came from Sausalito and was chased by coyotes. He spent that night in the limbs of a friendly tree. But the best of all times was when our whole family, back from an outing in San Francisco, walked the three miles from the ferry landing to the point. It was never a hike. It was a family stroll with fun and laughter and happiness along the way, with our family all together.

Mom and Dad walking three miles home from a May Day celebration in Sausalito.

8

Nellie Was a Lady

The U.S. Lighthouse Service buggy exploded into kindling wood as it crashed on the rocky beach. The Service had provided the small two-wheeler, a horse, barn, and large corral for its employees' use. The shortsightedness of the government was apparent in its selection of the conveyance. It held only two passengers and had no space to carry food and household supplies. With families that had two or three children, the little buggy was rarely used. Single keepers did not like to use it either, for had any damage been incurred, it would mean endless correspondence back and forth to the superintendent's office.

The mystery of the demolished buggy was never solved. The horse was still in the barn. Someone, during the night, had spirited out the buggy and rolled it over the cliff. An investigation proved fruitless, and after a great deal of correspondence, the matter was closed. The buggy was not replaced, but the keepers still had to care for the horse and paint the barn.

For years Dad struggled to pay off the hospital bills that continued to accumulate. He conscientiously maintained a payment routine, and gradually the heavy bills lightened and he had a little breathing room. Into the sugar bowl went some savings week by week from the sale of the rich Jersey milk. The small amount of money gradually mounted to a sizable sum. Spending it for anything frivolous was out of the question, even when it became a veritable treasure. It just seemed so good to be a little money ahead.

The lack of adequate transportation for the keepers wishing to go to San Francisco really became a major problem. For Mother it was doubly difficult in those early years at Point Bonita because of her slow recuperation from two serious operations.

She was surprised, then, when just after their trip to the "City" the day before, her husband suddenly decided he had urgent matters in San Francisco that demanded his immediate attention. My mother did not want to accompany him on this tiresome trip. Fog and dampness filled the air and El had come down with the sniffles and needed bed rest. Dad and Ray left together, Ray bound for school in Sausalito, and Dad to catch the ferry to San Francisco. Strange that he hadn't mentioned what kind of business and strange that it had come up so suddenly. Mom hadn't asked him about it. She was still too exhausted from the long walk home, but she didn't complain. Dad had seen the lines of pain and weariness on her face, and it worried him.

Time flew by on her busy hands. There was the daily baking and the house cleaning with no time to sit down and wonder about business trips. El coughed and snuffled down his lunch of hot soup, and Mom tucked him in for a little nap. He was always an uncomplaining patient.

She busied herself until late in the afternoon, chopping up fresh garden vegetables for the stew, braising the meat, and adding all to the big iron pot on the hot coal stove. Then she spared a moment or two to keep Elmer company for a while. When he dozed off, she hurried out to gather some fresh parsley. The wind-driven fog quickened her return to the house. At the top step she turned and glanced down the road to Sausalito, hoping for a sign of her husband. Only a strange carriage in the distance, and her first thought was, "here comes the superintendent on an inspection." And she began to panic. Where to start on the cleaning? Why did her husband go off and leave her on this day of all days? The carriage squeaked and groaned its way nearer and Mom began to hear familiar voices. The clop-clopping of the horse's hooves close by awoke El. He pulled himself from bed and ran to the window.

"Hey! It's Pop! He's got a horse!" This was enough to induce a complete and instant recovery for El. He dashed into the kitchen in his nightgown, grabbed Mom and hugged her, and started for the back door.

"You get right back into bed," Mom scolded and pointed to the bedroom.

"Oh, gee, Mom, I feel fine." And he looked at her with those teasing blue eyes.

"All right, but you dress warm."

My brother ran back to his room, pulled on his shoes, wrapped a coat around himself, and headed for the outside before Mom could get a good look at him. Ray was just stepping down from the carriage. Dad alighted from the other side and tied the reins to the fence. His smile could have lighted all the lamps in San Francisco.

"Boy, that's really something. Is it ours?" El wanted to know.

"Yes, now go get your mother. It's a surprise for her."

But Mom was already out the door and rushing to the carriage. Her eyes widened with amazement. "Hermann, where did you get that horse?"

"Oh, I had a little extra milk money, and I put aside some left over from that war bonus, and here we are. You won't have to walk to Sausalito any more." He was so happy to see her bright smile. "This will be fine for all of us, and we'll be able to pack groceries in it too."

"It's beautiful, but can we afford it?" Mom was ever mindful of the few debts that remained. With happy tears in her eyes, she walked around the carriage with admiration. The horse stood quietly during all the noise from my brothers.

Ray and El were entranced by this new acquisition. They envisioned gallops to and from school, or to the Army post.

Dad intercepted their thoughts. "Now there'll be no fooling around with this horse. It's for your mother, and you kids are not to ride unless you ask me first."

Well, there wasn't a direct instruction not to ride, so my brothers were content. They knew Dad would relent.

"Her name is Nellie," he added, "and you are to take good care of her." To them she was a handsome animal and looked like a real bargain. Dad started to lead Nellie into the corral.

"Hey, where are you taking her?" Ingersoll was on hand early this time to view another one of Dad's bargains. He went on, "You can't leave the carriage in the corral, and what's more the horse can't be here or in the barn either. You know it's against the Service regulations."

"Regulations or no regulations, I'm going to give this animal some protection from the weather." And Dad walked on toward the barn.

The rest of the small group of onlookers lingered for a little while, discussing the possibilities of difficulties arising for our father. Keeper Ingersoll walked beside him into the barn. He had been examining Nellie while Dad was unhitching her from the carriage. From time to time he had shaken his head. Dad remembered the keeper had done the same thing when he brought home the scrawny cow. He just hoped he would be as lucky this time.

"Before you put her in the stall, I want to show you something. Have you looked at her legs and hooves? She's an old race horse, probably been used by a cabbie too. Her hooves are cracked. You may be in for some trouble. Walk her up and down a bit. I want to see if she favors any leg."

Dad's face fell at these remarks. He knew and respected his

friend's opinion, and realized he should have taken Ingersoll to check the horse before it was purchased. But Dad was so worried about Mom that he just took off in a hurry to try to do something that would ease her pain.

"Well, she doesn't seem to have any bad areas except for her legs and hooves. Your horse seems to be pretty sound, just a little old. Most of all she needs attention to those hooves. Pulling a cab around the San Francisco hills will break down any animal. She's a pretty good-looking nag. Give her some fresh hay and a bucket of oats. She could stand a good rubdown. Her coat needs it. You might just as well begin learning how to take care of a horse. You've done pretty well with your cows. And by the way, don't worry about keeping the horse in the barn. And when you are through here, come over to my place and I'll give you some salve for those sore spots on her sides. We'd better go over the harness too. You don't want your horse running off, leaving the carriage behind." He left giving Nellie a pat on the rump. Before he was out of sight he turned and called back. "Better rest her up for a bit, and then you can take her over to the Army post and have her shod."

For the first time Dad gave a close look at the horse's legs. The knees were knobby and her hooves were a mess. Dad hoped that Ingersoll's judgment was again correct. Nellie enjoyed the rubdown, but most of all she enjoyed the rest inside and away from the damp air. Nellie had all the lines of a thoroughbred, but now they were just a little bit blotted out by too many years of racing and too many hills to climb in the "City." She was a tall horse, coal black, with a neck that showed signs of arching, eyes dim with age, but still aware of their surroundings. Despite her hard life, Nellie appeared to be very tractable. Dad heaved a big sigh, took another look at his new possession, and headed for the house. His family was waiting for him, all wreathed in wide smiles. He felt better right away. After dinner, they all walked out to take a second look. The boys watched as Dad poured some more oats into the already empty bucket, and forked more hay down from above. Nellie ate like a lady, and it was plain that the good food was a real treat to her. She nosed the oats a bit, and then blew a snort of contentment. She wasn't such a bad-looking nag after all. As though on inspection, she made a feeble attempt at arching her neck, flicked her tail, and whinnied softly Some of the other Service people had come back, too, and offered to help in repairing the harness or painting the carriage. There was no more to be done that evening. Around the table talk flew back and forth. Nellie's possibilities seemed endless.

The rising sun greeted my brothers as they dashed out to the stable to see if Nellie was still there. She was, happily munching away on the last bit of hay as though she had never stopped during the night. They put a halter around her neck and led her to the watering trough, and then turned her loose in the corral. Nellie stood still for a moment, savoring the peace and quiet of her new home, then with an unconcerned glance at the outside world, paced slowly back to her stall. There were more important things on her mind, like oats, hay, and just resting.

Dad answered the knock on the door. Mr. Ingersoll was ready to conduct a more careful examination. Dad and the keeper walked over to the stable, my two brothers close behind. They didn't want to miss anything. Nellie continued eating while the checkup went on. My father followed every move. When it was over, Ingersoll advised, "Rest her for a couple of weeks. It'll do her more good than anything. Better yet, turn her out in the corral or in one of the pastures, some place where the ground is soft. Her hooves will mend faster. She's good enough for what you want."

"I should have had you go with me." Dad shook his head in chagrin. "I didn't think there was much to buying a horse."

"No use worrying any more," answered his friend.

For the following three weeks, Nellie had the freedom of the nearest pasture, but she never wanted to get too far away from her oats. It was easy to approach and pet her. Her hard life had not made Nellie mean. The first few days' rest brought remarkable improvement, and our horse perked up a bit. Once or twice she broke into a tentative trot. By the time the third week had rolled around, Nellie was ready for a new set of shoes. The Army blacksmith was a man skilled at his craft. He removed the old worn shoes, muttering to himself over the sloppy job done previously on the horse. Hooves were cleaned and filed, and then the smithy spent a long time deciding on the weight and shape of the shoes. With the fire roaring, the new shoes were shaped and at last fitted to Nellie. She walked with a new pride on the way home.

During the weeks that Nellie was recuperating, the carriage and harness were put back in good working condition. The assistant keepers helped in painting the carriage a shiny black while their sons got mixed up with the axle grease. They repaired the harness and let the younger generation rub it with saddle soap. The wives fussed about making some cushions for the sagging seats. Wheel spokes were strengthened, and for a final touch, someone had waterproofed a section of light canvas to fit over the old top. When Nellie in her

Mom and her offspring on the beach at Point Bonita.

new health and the carriage in its new splendor finally merged, they dazzled the eyes.

The first warm Sunday that Dad had free, the family and Nellie took a trial run down to a small nearby lake. Mom had packed her usual tasty picnic lunch and Dad brought along a couple of home-made fishing poles. The morning promised a sunny day of fun and rest. When they reached the lake, Nellie was unhitched and left to enjoy the fresh grass. Mom and Dad laid out a piece of canvas and an old Army blanket to relax on. Mom stretched out and was asleep in a moment. Dad sat for a bit, then decided to do some fishing. The boys had been teasing him a great deal about what a poor fisherman he was, and Dad had had enough of that.

He grabbed one of the lines, baited it with a freshly dug wriggling worm, and tossed it into the quiet water, then waited all of five min-utes for a bite. Dad was not the patient angler and as the time wore on, he became disgusted, tied the line to his right foot, and lay down to nap. El and Ray had gone over to one of the hills to gather mush-rooms, interrupting that chore with chasing some cottontail rabbits. There was nothing to break the serenity of the day, except for the occasional shouts of the boys ringing against the hills. Dad and Mom slept peacefully, and Nellie still munched contentedly.

"Hey! Hey! I've got a fish!" Dad scrambled to his feet and bent over to untie the line he had wound around his foot. A glistening steelhead leaped out of the water, fighting the hook in its jaw. "Somebody help me." Dad was still hopping about, struggling to free the line, ignoring the advice of his offspring who came running back.

"Never mind your foot, Dad. Pull in the line before it gets away," yelled Ray.

Mom laughed and clapped her hands. It was one of the few times she had ever seen her husband in a situation that he had trouble in handling. El grabbed the line and started to bring in the fish.

"No, you don't. That's my fish. You've all been making fun of me and I'm gonna finish the job." He finally yanked the line free from his foot, and with a complete lack of finesse hauled in a beautiful five pound steelhead. It was big enough to grace our supper table with enough left over for the next day's lunch. Dad never fished again, but that ended the teasing about his lack of an angler's skill.

And so the days settled down in a not-too-vigorous life for Nellie. Dad was happy to have the assistant keepers use her for a ride to Sausalito, where they promised to place her in a livery stable while the keepers and their familes journeyed to San Francisco. Nellie received the much needed exercise, and the families were spared the long walk home from the ferry landing. On weekends our handsome steed and carriage were rented out to some of the lifesavers who were off duty. The men were fairly quiet on the way to Sausalito, and when they returned from their recreational activities on the Barbary Coast or from visits with the families, Nellie would be waiting in the stable. The crew was never hard on the horse, but sometimes she was exhorted to a faster speed than her regular walk. With whooping encouragement, Nellie sometimes broke into a spritely trot on the way home. But in a while the sleepy souls let Nellie relax to her own pace and find her way home in her own time. We soon learned that this old steed could navigate in the thickest fog. On our trips back to Point Bonita, Dad would just loop the reins loosely around the whip handle and let her go. We always arrived home safely.

During the work week, there were few calls on Nellie's services and she was turned loose to roam about in the pastures, letting the warm sun ease her old bones. The grass was green, the air was fresh, but for the first month or two the horse never wandered far away from the oat bucket. She had an excellent sense of timing and soon learned that her oats would be ready as soon as one of my brothers returned from school. We never had to go to the pasture to round her up. Nellie would be standing patiently at the corral gate waiting to be let into the barn.

On the day that military maneuvers at the Army posts ended, their mules were turned loose to graze and our Nellie became "Queen of the Hills." The mules caught sight of her and moved over en masse to look more closely at this beautiful interloper. There is no accounting for the strange attachment they formed for her, but it was in unquestioned evidence. Nellie responded to this by holding her head a little higher, and taking a few mincing steps. When she had their full attention, Nellie turned for home, and in her wake followed a band of Army mules. The lighthouse gate was open and through it went our horse, her newly acquired admirers close behind. She reached the corral gate and waited for someone to open it. The mules milled around in a cloud of dust, vying for a closer glimpse of this four-legged enchantress. The disturbance brought Dad to the kitchen door, coffee cup in hand. He gazed flabbergasted, and then chuckled, "Freda, come here and have a look at this."

"For heaven's sake, what are all those mules doing here?"

"Well, I'm not sure, but it looks like they followed our horse home. Where are the boys? We'll have to get these animals back to their pasture."

El and Ray had already seen the commotion from where they had been playing in the old rock quarry and came running to the back door where Mom and Dad were.

"Wow! What are they all doing here?" asked Ray.

"They followed Nellie home, I guess, but I don't know why," Dad replied. He couldn't figure it out. "Come on, let's get them back where they belong."

El led Nellie into the stable, while Dad and Ray drove the mules back to their pasture. When the job was finished nobody thought any more about it. The mules were given the freedom of the Army pastures and Nellie grazed on the fields inside the fenced lighthouse area. It was only when someone failed to close the gate that Nellie wandered farther away, and it was on those occasions that our bell-wether horse appeared with her long-eared entourage. My brothers were usually home in time to get things back in order, but sometimes a cursing Army squad came to retrieve the strays.

For the next four years Nellie performed her regular duties with good grace, taking the Engel family on happy rides over to Sausalito to catch the ferry for San Francisco, down to Jolley's ranch for a picnic, or to the shore for beachcombing. Warm days were rare at the point in the face of the prevailing westerly winds and hovering fog, and when the sun rose in a clear and friendly sky, and the fog had backed off, that was the signal for an outing. Most of all Nellie was a blessing to my mother who no longer had to face the hike to Sausalito.

But one summer day in 1912, Nellie failed to return from the pasture. It puzzled us because she never failed to show up at the corral gate ready for that treat of oats. We could almost set our clocks by her regularity. When early evening came and still no horse there was deep concern about her whereabouts. The sun had already dipped behind the bank of fog, and in the face of the darkening sky, it was decided to wait until morning to search for her. If she had gone through the gate into the wide expanse of military pasture land, there was no telling where she might have roamed. We were worried.

At the crack of dawn, El and Ray set out to locate the missing horse. Dad had the early watch and could not help. The boys passed through her favorite grazing areas and near a scattered herd of mules without sighting Nellie. That was strange, because where Nellie was the mules congregated. No one at the Army post volunteered any information. The soldiers questioned were very reticent. The boys searched all day long without any success. There was the thought that one of the soldiers might have ridden Nellie to Sausalito, but there were no happy answers to our inquiries. By nighttime the family felt sure that something had happened to our horse.

It was days later that a keeper who had been down at the beach returned with the sad news. Nellie's crumpled body lay at the foot of steep cliffs. There was never any satisfactory explanation for her fall, and no one ever volunteered having seen the horse go over the precipice, but our family always felt that she had been driven to her death by some of the disgruntled soldiers who hated to round up the mules that wandered off after her. We had no proof of such action, but there was enough quiet talk to verify our suspicions. So we lost Nellie. We had loved her and were sure she held us in high regard. She had given us many years of faithful service.

After that we borrowed an Army mule to pull our carriage. It wasn't quite the same. There was a certain grace lacking in the plodding mule. Dad was hoping for a transfer to a better station and put aside the thought of purchasing another horse. Probably none could take Nellie's place in our hearts anyway.

Department of Commerce and Labor
LIGHTHOUSE SERVICE

OFFICE OF INSPECTOR, 18TH DISTRICT
CUSTOMHOUSE
SAN FRANCISCO, CAL.

January 20, 1914

Mr Hermann Engal,
    1st Assistant Bonita Point Lightstation,

    1.   In accordance with your acceptance you have this day been recommended for transfer and promotion to Keeper of San Diego Bay Lights, Cal., with pay at the rate of $720 per annum, effective upon entrance on duty.

    2.   Upon notification of your appointment, in the course of a week or ten days, you will receive orders to transfer.

Rhodes
Inspector

Through the Keeper.

After offers as far-flung as Hawaii, Dad happily accepted the Ballast Point assignment in San Diego. It was one of the most sought-after stations on the Pacific Coast. *Official letter, U.S. Lighthouse Service.*

9

Headed for Ballast Point

The bedroom door burst open and my mother stood in the doorway, a letter clutched in her hand.

"It's here—the letter. I'm going to start packing." And I just had time to glimpse the happy tears in her blue eyes and the sweep of her long skirt disappearing around the door.

I just sat wrapped in a warmth of gladness. My father and brothers had left January 1914 for Dad's new assignment at Ballast Point, San Diego. Now in early March, his letter said it was time for us to journey there too.

I had missed my father so much, the loving twinkle in his brown eyes and that quick smile across his tanned face. I could see his swinging seaman's stride, bowed legs appearing to cave in under his huge barrel chest. He was a short muscular man, and I well knew the strength of his arms whenever he grabbed me for a quick affectionate hug. I would be so glad to see him again.

Dad and my two brothers had gone on ahead in order to make our new quarters completely habitable for Mom and me. Cleaning and painting had been sandwiched in between the hours of hard work demanded by the regular lighthouse duties. That hard work included complete upkeep and refueling of the twelve harbor beacons, ocean buoys off Point Loma, the light and fog signal at Ballast Point, a launch, quarters, wharves, all ground areas and outer buildings, in addition to standing watches, six hours on and six hours off. And this station was manned by only two men. It is no wonder that the letters from Dad put off our departure for three months. A perfectionist, he did not want us to set foot upon the station until everything was in spotless condition. That short letter finally arrived: "Freda, we are ready for you and Norm. Write and let us know when you will be here."

That letter meant the new home was now shipshape, freshly painted, linoleum scrubbed and waxed, stove shining with newly applied black shoe polish, fireplaces stoked with coal, and windows so clean they seemed devoid of panes. With my dad's usual thoughtfulness, the pantry would be stocked with the staples Mom required most to feed her hungry brood, a five-gallon can of honey, leaf lard, dried Navy beans, aromatic slab bacon, flour, sugar, and on and on.

After calming down, Mom rushed out to purchase tickets on one of the coastal steamers, and we were lucky to get almost immediate passage. Then she penned a short letter to Dad to let him know the time of our arrival. The great adventure loomed ahead of us. We had been on many small boats, and even the old Army tug Harris across San Francisco Bay and had ridden the ferries, but to steam majestically down the coast on the speedy liner was something to be anticipated with wonder. The three days' wait snailed by. On the fourth, a bright sun rose in an unexpected blaze of fog-free warmth presaging a good beginning to our journey. Never were suitcases packed so quickly, but then we didn't have much to pack. The noise and bustle around my grandmother's house grew by the hour, and I withdrew to the front room window where I could catch first sight of a horse-drawn carriage.

"Go to the bathroom and hurry. Don't forget to wash your hands!" Another admonition from Mom.

"Hurry, hurry, Norm." This time Grandma banged on the door.

I opened it and found myself propelled down the hall, out the open front door, and into the waiting carriage. No fine royal parade from house to carriage, no grand display of departure to be observed by the bay window peekers, and only a brief opportunity to say good-by to my friends. I felt a little cheated. My mom and grandmother pushed themselves in beside me, and the horse pulled away from the curb. Down Mission, and then along busy Market Street accompanied by the unharmonious cacophony of clanging streetcars. The driver dodged around the scurrying pedestrians and eventually deposited us at the end of a long pier. A porter appeared out of nowhere and tipped his cap.

"Going aboard the Harvard, ma'am?" He addressed himself to my mother who looked so splendid in her black and white checked suit, with its collar of white satin trimmed in braid. Atop her head was the hat I loved best, a velvet one with its ostrich plumes waving gaily over the crown of her brown hair. She was indeed a lovely picture. She nodded her approval to the porter, and we all marched off along the pier, Grandma with her long steps easily keeping up with my mother and the porter. I had that same feeling again, that most of my young life was going to be spent in trying to catch up with someone or something. Instead of the usual damp fog, the warm sun filled the air and made me squirm in my heavy coat and knit cap.

"What's the matter with you, Norm? Stop wiggling around so."

Mom had her mind on more important matters.

"I'm hot, Mom. Can I take off my coat?"

"I know it's warm, but can you wait until we get aboard? It'll be just a couple of minutes."

"Guess so," I answered and regretted the words the minute they left my mouth. Perspiration rolled down from under my cap, and my clothes were sticking to me all over.

The porter carefully placed our luggage near the foot of the gangway and lifted his cap in thanks to the good tip. "Thank you, and a very pleasant journey to you." His wish matched the beautiful day.

Curls of smoke rose lazily from the ship's stack. The sleek white vessel, narrow of beam, and built for fast coastal service, lay alongside the pier like a leashed greyhound. I stared in awe at its size. A line began to form and we found ourselves funneled into it. Mom and Grandma who had been engaged in quiet conversation, exchanged teary-eyed looks while I tugged at Mom's sleeve.

"Mom, Mom, we'd better get on now. Everyone's going up the gangplank."

"Yes, I know. 'Bye, Mama." She gave my grandmother one last hug as we made our way along. Grandma didn't come aboard with us for a visit. She stood alone on the pier, a tiny figure looking very forlorn. Our movement was interrupted by a steward who had taken charge of our bags. "This way, please," he directed after having a quick glance at our tickets.

Down, down, down, deck after deck, through narrow passageways and down steep companionways. The deeper we descended, the warmer it grew, and the louder the subdued throbbing of the harnessed engines. We stopped far below the level of the main deck. Here the steward dropped our luggage just inside the cabin, looking none too hopeful for a generous tip from such a poor passenger, but Mom was ready. She was relieved not to have carried the bulging suitcases through such small spaces.

"Not very big, is it, Norm? Well, we'll be here only a short time," she said. "Here, let me get those warm things off." While she pulled off my coat and cap, I took stock of the cabin. There were two narrow bunks, one above the other, and a small wash basin nearby. There were no chairs. Another suitcase would have filled this cabin to overflowing. I knew I wouldn't be spending much time in this little coop. I breathed a sigh of relief as Mom finished with me.

"Now, let's go up on deck and wave goodby to Grandma." She headed me out the door.

A sharp blast of the ship's whistle signalled the raising of the passenger's gangway, and the dock tenders threw off the remaining lines. The graceful ship backed slowly away from the pier. Grandma became a tiny figure in the distance still waving that white handkerchief.

Out in midstream, the liner turned and pointed her bow for the Golden Gate, a last series of whistle blasts splitting the air of the clear blue sky. We milled around by the rail with the rest of the passengers trying to decide which side of the ship to be on for a last look.

"Come on, Norm, let's go over to the other side. We can see Point Bonita from there." I held tightly to her hand as she led the way through the throng. On the starboard side only a few curious souls stared at the rugged peninsula that projected into the Pacific. The Harvard picked up speed rapidly and our old home faded to a dim outline on the distant horizon. Mom never said a word, just held my hand more tightly, and I wondered what her thoughts were.

A brisk breeze blew across the water, slapping up white caps here and there. Nothing on the horizon, not even the trailing smoke of a slow moving freighter or the gray hull of a Navy ship. Far, far in the distance we thought we could still see a trace of land through the haze. This we both loved—ocean, clear sky and a wide, wide horizon. No time for conversation, just pleasant restful rail leaning. The gong roused us from our quiet reverie.

"Last call for lunch. Last call for lunch."

"I'm hungry now, too," Mom said.

Already seated was a friendly elderly couple, the Maiers, a snowy-haired gentleman with a ferocious, bristling mustache, and a wee little old lady. Across from me was a couple, obviously honeymooners. Mom and the Maiers lapsed into easy conversation. The two lovebirds ate quickly, giggling, sometimes staring quietly at each other, and leaving before dessert was served, an action that was beyond my comprehension. Content to be thus abandoned by all, I happily restricted my activities to consuming as much of the food as my small stomach would hold.

After lunch the Maiers invited us for a stroll on the deck. It was certainly better than a stuffy cabin and had the additional bonus of keeping Mom from being so homesick. The air buzzed with lively chatter and banter, Mrs. Maier chirping up now and then. I ran off to join some other children in a game of hopscotch, especially good for settling a full stomach. When this palled we started a game of tag; up and down the passageways, in and out of the bathrooms, and around the deck chairs we galloped, followed by the hostile glares of the adults. It was not long before complaints poured in, and we were firmly shepherded to a spot amidship and given a stern command to remain there and play a quiet game. Nine energetic youngsters with fertile imaginations, we planned our revenge on the oldsters.

By now the Harvard was rolling, rolling gently but rhythmically to the heavy swells, rolling barely enough to stretch the esophagus, upset the balancing ear fluid, and bring on some queasiness in the stomach. As the first distressed adults began swaying toward the bathroom, they passed our play corner, and tried not to hear our loud conversation about the dinner menu. By the time we had gone through the list of items such as cream soup, fried pork chops, and chocolate pudding, anyone else seated near us had a touch of *mal de mer*. We were content. There wouldn't be many around to complain about us for a while. But this fun began to wear off, especially when some of our group became victims of their own plot and hurried away. The rest of us removed ourselves to a small section of the lounge. One of the stewards soon appeared with two sets of checkers, enough to keep us out of mischief for the rest of the day.

That evening as Mom and I walked the deck, we felt the definite change in the weather pattern. Scattered dark clouds huddled on the southern horizon, and the wind had turned damp with gusts kicking up now and then. My mother shivered and pulled her coat tighter. We both loved the moods of the sea and stayed out until our dinner gong sounded.

"Come on, let's get washed up for dinner." She pulled me away from the cold rail. The wind was picking up. Off in the distance clouds began to look shredded and full of rain. I hoped we were in for a good "blow."

The passageways seemed strangely deserted later as we made our way to the dining room. Here it was a barren waste, except for a few courageous souls and the attentive stewards who stood by their assigned tables. The ship groaned inwardly as it plowed into the unexpected foul weather. Our tablemates were in fine fettle and had good appetites too, and we downed an excellent dinner with gusto. Back in the cabin it was difficult even getting undressed, and once in my bunk, I rolled from side to side. Only the side rails prevented me from being tossed out. After a period of listening to the loud protesting from the ship's hull, I fell asleep.

Gale force winds and driving rains awoke us in the early morning. Rain splashed in from the open port and Mom pushed it shut. Then she helped me down from the upper bunk.

Breakfasters were even more noticeable by their absence, and it was a very quiet dining room. That morning two officers joined us at a larger table to which we had been directed.

"Mrs. Engel, you and your daughter are very good sailors in this weather. Tell me, have you made many ocean voyages?"

"No, just a few trips across San Francisco Bay." My mother was embarrassed by the question. "My husband is a lighthouse keeper. He was stationed at Point Bonita, but is now at Ballast Point in San Diego."

"Oh well, that explains it. You're used to rough seas. I'm glad you could join us this morning." A new tone of respect filled the first mate's voice. He knew how much the lighthouses and their men helped to make the seas safe.

"Mom, if I wrap up good, can I go out on deck for a while? I'm hot."

"Well, I don't know. The wind is pretty strong. What do you think?" She directed her question to the officers.

"Please sir, I'm tired of just sitting inside."

"If you wait just a minute until I finish my coffee, we'll both take a turn around the deck. Run and get your coat," answered the first officer.

"Oh, gee, thanks."

I was back in time to see him swallow the last bit of coffee, and waited impatiently. He finally arose, grabbed me by the hand and we plunged out onto the windswept deck. The first blast from the gale threw us against the bulkhead, and almost knocked the wind out of me.

"Hey, are you all right?" He looked down anxiously. "Maybe you'd better get back inside."

"No, it's fun out here, and I like the rain."

"Okay, let's go then. I have to check and make sure that everything is secure out here."

Up and down the deck we reeled, clutching at support along the way, until finally I had to beg for a rest.

"Thought you wanted to walk," he chuckled.

"I did, but your legs are longer than mine."

"Sorry, but I have to go on watch now. I'll take you back inside."

"I'm gonna stay out here for a while."

"Well, I don't know about that, but you seem to have pretty good sea legs, but no more than five minutes, and you stay close to the door." He was late for his watch. "I'll send someone out for you. I think you'll need some help getting back in."

"Yes sir!" The prospect of braving the storm on my skinny six-year-old legs challenged my imagination. I would be the skipper of my own vessel, pacing the decks, facing the storms with the greatest courage, and keeping all passengers safe. I gripped the outside rail and stood fascinated by the wrath of the angry seas. Waves crashed over the bow of the ship as it plunged into the deep troughs, setting the decks awash with sea water. It swirled around my feet soaking my shoes. Rain dripped from the lifeboat above, soaking me from head to toe. I shivered with excitement, a solitary figure thoroughly enjoying the "wetting down." My dreams were cut short abruptly.

"Hey, young lady, what are you doing out on deck by yourself?" The deck steward making the rounds to see that the deck chairs were all folded and secured, spotted me. "You're soaked. Do your parents know where you are?"

"Yep."

"Won't they be worried?"

"Nope."

"Well, I think you've soaked up enough salt water for now. Better come in and get dry."

Inside the wind and the rain were shut out, but the rage of the storm still made itself felt in the ship's struggle to keep on an even keel. The howling gale could not drown out the complaints emerging from the battered hull, whenever it bucked into heavier seas. Only a lonely passenger appeared here and there, the rest groaning miserably in their bunks. Even my playmates were strangely absent.

"Mrs. Engel, I found your daughter out on deck by herself. She's very wet." The steward frowned at Mom for her neglect, but it passed unnoticed. The Engel offspring had long since learned to handle such situations. Mom's greatest worry was always about our catching a cold.

"My goodness, Norm, how did you get so wet?"

"It's raining real hard."

The few others still at their tables were horrified at the news that a small child had been out on the deck alone. They didn't know how Mom and I had earned our superior "sea legs" in the many crossings of San Francisco Bay, in large craft or small, in fair weather or foul.

The rest of the voyage offered no change in the weather, and the battered vessel crept into San Pedro harbor hours behind schedule. Inside the shelter of the harbor, white caps reminded us of the storm on the ocean. The Harvard edged slowly toward the pier, pushed by strong little tugs. It was a delicate task for the wind was still strong, and a ship not under good control could easily crash into a pier and tear out pilings.

Heads poked out of the portholes, but were quickly pulled back as new onslaughts of rain pelted down. Many passengers collected in the lounge, where they tested their legs once more. Mother and I were glad we were arriving before dark. It would make it much easier to locate our cousin in the crowd huddled in the warehouse doorways. We had already packed our bags, informing the steward where we would be on deck, then worked through the excited voyagers to the main lounge. There was no point standing out in the rain while the gangplank was being lowered. The moment it rested on the dock, relieved travelers scurried down like rats deserting a ship, anxious to once again set foot on a firm stationary surface. After the first wild rush, we stepped out and made our way quickly to the shelter of the adjacent warehouse with our steward not far behind. Mom soon located the tall figure of Cousin Letty and they rushed into one another's arms in a tearful embrace.

"This is terrible, getting you out in this storm. Oh, I wish I was back at Point Bonita," Mom said.

"Now, you're just tired out. Wait 'til we get some hot coffee and food in you and a little rest. You'll be just fine again." Letty reassured her. Then she picked up our suitcases in her strong arms, and motioning to us to follow, hiked off into the furies, leaving us to trail behind. When we caught up with her, she had one foot firmly planted on the runningboard of a taxicab, ready to defy anyone who stood by about to "jump her claim." Water was gushing down the street and over the sidewalk, piling up at the drains which could not handle the flow. We sloshed into the cab and were back in motion once again, rumbling over the slippery streets, too weary to say anything. Letty kept up a cheerful line of questions, that became an endless monologue to which she supplied all the answers.

"Have you heard from Hermann? Of course you have, or you wouldn't be on your way to San Diego now. Was the trip bad? Well, it couldn't have been very pleasant. Have you had enough to eat? They never give you much on these trips."

Letty tried so hard, but we could only let our heads joggle on our weary shoulders. We tumbled out of the cab, when it came to its jolting stop and scrambled onto the porch, leaving Letty to take care of the fare and bags. Mom glanced down at the ever-widening pool of water at my feet.

"Norm, you take off your wet shoes and coat before you go in the house."

A stentorian bellow from the street countermanded that order. "She'll do no such thing. Both of you get inside right now!"

Inside we dripped meandering trails of water from the front door to a fragrantly warm kitchen. Here we shed our sodden outer clothing. Letty came buzzing down the hall, snatched a big coffee pot from the stove, poured out three mugs of aromatic brew, lacing each generously with brandy. "There now, get that in you first, then a good hot bath and you'll be as right as rain." She laughed heartily. Nothing Letty did was ever on a small scale.

I sipped the hot liquid, burning my tongue. The brandy fumes rose in a pungent fragrance and the liquor warmed me all over when it hit my stomach. The kitchen seemed to sway a bit and I almost expected the mugs to start sliding around. Things around me faded into a blurred haze.

"Come on now, a hot bath for you." Our hostess took me in tow to the bathroom, expertly stripped off my clothes and helped me into a pool of forgetfulness. "Now you just soak there a bit." And she left.

I drifted off into a short nap that was interrupted by Letty's arms lifting me from the tub.

"Out you come, lazybones, let your Mom have a chance."

What a rubdown, skin aglow, tiredness relieved, then warm clothes and off to the kitchen again. Over bowls of hot soup, we told the story of our hectic passage down the coast.

"We are leaving on the train tomorrow," Mom announced.

"Oh, Freda, I thought you would stay with us for a few days."

"Perhaps later, right now I want to get settled down as soon as I can."

The remainder of the late afternoon passed quickly, along with sessions of eating and resting. At bedtime Mom and I closed our eyes and slept soundly through thunder and lightning, storing up our energy for the final leg of our journey.

Birds-eye view of Fort Rosecrans and Ballast Point. Perhaps you can follow the route we took on our arrival, from wharf to point. *San Diego Historical Society-Ticor Collection.*

10

Our Journey Ends

We arose the next morning hoping to see a bit of sunshine, but leaden skies paired with a bone-cutting chill wind hit us as we stepped outside to the taxi. The old conveyance waded slowly down to the almost empty depot. It was not a day for travelers. It was at least one hundred feet from the curb to the protection of the station and Mom urged Letty to remain in the cab. They said a quick goodbye. A porter had picked up our bags and started for the inside away from the rain. We splashed through the puddles behind him and I was beginning to get that waterlogged feeling again. My shoes were wet and squishing out at the sides. I wondered if I would ever be dry and warm again. The cold damp depot offered little comfort and we sat in a dreary silence waiting for our train.

Mom shook me. "Come on, Norm, it's time to go." The ever-present porter stepped over eagerly as we arose.

"San Diego, ma'am. Just follow me." And like docile children we walked behind. "Your tickets say you're in this coach." And he helped us aboard. "I hope the weather is better in San Diego."

"Thank you," Mom replied as she handed him the tip. "Take off your coat and cap, Norm, before you sit down. There, that's better. Better take off your shoes too." She bundled up my wet head in a heavy scarf, rubbing to get out most of the moisture, then squeezed out my wet stockings. I pulled on the pair of dry ones she handed to me. "Are you any warmer now?"

"Yes, Mom," and the prospect of my first train ride helped to dispel much of my weariness. I peered out the window. Only grayness, even the whistle sounded gray to match the weather, as the train pulled slowly away from the Los Angeles depot. I watched the puffs of smoke swirl upward to be broken into miniature clouds by the wind gusts. Rain dashing against the window made lacy patterns in downward streams. It was difficult to see much outside, so I just laid my head against the glass to rest. Normal speed had been cut to await repairs on the washed-out spots ahead, and the clickety-clack of the wheels measured off the miles monotonously.

The conductor passed through. "I'm sorry about the delay. This is one of the worst storms we have ever had. I'm afraid we'll be very late getting in to San Diego." His tone somehow indicated we might not get there at all.

"Mom, I'm hungry." The huge box of lunch Letty had prepared looked inviting. I'd seen her tuck in pieces of chocolate cake that would just fit into my empty stomach. I didn't know about dining cars, but my mother had worked up her courage and decided that was the place for us now.

"I think that something hot would make you feel better on a day like this. Let's try the dining car. It will help to make the time go a little faster."

Anything to remove ourselves from the damp interior of our coach. We walked along to the dining car, passing through almost deserted cars. Few hardy souls had ventured out into the storm except those traveling on urgent business. The dining car was also cool, but warmed by the friendly greetings of the waiters. It did not take long for us to make our selections, First, the hot soup, creamy and tasty barely warmed our palates before inviting plates of steak, potatoes, and green beans were set before us. We ate slowly and the hour passed quickly. The splashes of rain continued against the window, obscuring any clear view of the countryside. When we returned to our seats, time still hung heavy on our hands as we gazed wearily at the outer world.

A chill blast of wind flung the conductor through the door, bringing with him the smell of burning coal and acrid smoke.

"Whew!" he remarked as he shook off drops of water. "It's really blowing outside. Doesn't look like it's gonna let up at all. I hope you have someone to meet you."

"I'm afraid not. My husband is a lighthouse keeper at Ballast Point, and we'll have to take a boat to Fort Rosecrans. Do you know where I can catch the boat?" This was another worry to her.

"Oh, sure, right at the foot of Broadway. It's just about a block and a half from the station. Not very far except for this storm. Wait for me and I'll get you started off in the right direction." He was a friendly light on a cold dark afternoon. The daylight began to wane, leaving nothing but eerie shadows flashing past the windows.

"Next stop, San Diego! Next stop, San Diego!"

Mom roused me from my nap with a nervous shake. "Norm, put on your things. We'll be getting off soon." She gathered our luggage and looked expectantly into the bleak evening.

The train crawled the last few blocks and then jerked to a clanking stop. I stumbled along the aisle behind my mother. The last glimmer of daylight was rapidly retreating behind the high hills of Point Loma as we climbed down from the meager comfort of the train. We walked through the station to the nearly empty street where we had been directed by the conductor.

"Ride, lady?" Our first stroke of luck presented itself in the form of many cabbies eager for a fare, ready to speed tired travelers home. "Where to, lady?"

"To the Broadway Pier, please. I want to catch the boat to Fort Rosecrans."

The driver's face fell. Gone was the long ride and a fat tip. A two-block fare hardly paid for the gas. But he picked up our suitcases and stowed them in the cab after seeing us safely seated inside. We started with a lurch, rattled over the rough train tracks, went one more block and landed at the foot of Broadway. Here shadowy outlines silhouetted against a darkened sky. The driver sensed our confusion, and still in hopes of getting a good tip, helped us from the cab, carried our bags to the gangway of a small boat and shouted to get the attention of someone aboard. One of the seamen glanced out and gallantly ventured out to help us. The cabbie drove away with a grateful smile. Mom had emptied her heavy coin purse. The seaman carried our bags to a small cabin. It was empty but warm.

"I'll just set your bags here."

"When do we leave? How long will it take to get to the fort?"

"We'll leave in about twenty minutes. With this weather it will take a little longer, maybe an hour. The seas are quite choppy. Are you new at the fort?" The seaman was trying to be cheerful.

"We're new to San Diego. My husband is a new keeper at Ballast Point. I'm sure he doesn't know we're arriving tonight. He doesn't have a telephone." Mom worried about going that last stretch.

"Sorry, wish I could help you, but we'll be heading back up the bay. But I can show you how to get to the point."

Mom listened intently as he gave his directions. To me it sounded like, "get off the boat, bear left up the hill, walk along the road until you come to the post exchange building with its sign, then go down the hill to the left, bear left again at the bottom of the hill and you'll be on the way to Ballast Point."

We bumped along the bay to the fort. I huddled next to Mom. By now we were both reduced to complete weariness. The wet and cold had long ago seeped through our skins. We sat there and dripped little pools of water on the cabin floor. I tried to lie down, but that was even more uncomfortable. The friendly seaman poked his head in occasionally, hoping to be the bearer of better weather news, but every opening of the door was a blustery denial. The slowing of the vessel roused us from our watery stupor. Out of the cabin windows we barely made out the one flickering light on the pier. The launch bumped against the dock but settled down quietly. Our friend returned and picked up our bags. "I think you'd better get started right away. This 'blow' is going to get worse from the looks of it." Without waiting for an answer, he left and we followed him up the gangplank. "I'll carry these up the hill for you. I've got time for that." And he strode off again.

His friendliness, the thought of our family being reunited, filled Mom with renewed energy. She hiked up the hill in full stride after him. I half-ran, half-walked bringing up the rear. "Well, here you are. Keep right along this road. There'll be someone at the post exchange who can direct you from there. There's the Ballast Point light right over there." He pointed out a bright light in the distance, and Mom located it easily. He quickly disappeared in the darkness. We could hear him running down the hill to the pier.

"We're almost there, Norm. Do you think you can make it the rest of the way? I have to carry the bags. You stay close to me now. In a little bit we'll see your father and brothers." By now the soggy suitcases looked like leaden weights as she picked them up.

"I can keep up, Mom, but I'm sure hungry." I wondered how many times I'd said that in the last few days.

"Well, if your father has a few eggs, some bacon, onions, and potatoes, as soon as we get there we'll have a feast. Now let's get started."

We slopped along the muddy road, trying to maintain our balance against the growing wind. At times our headway seemed at a standstill, but at least we hit level ground as we passed some large buildings, and the sound of men's laughter guided us to the post exchange. It was deserted on the outside, but my mother had a "full head of steam," and she never wavered in her pace, not even to stop to ask questions, but marched right on by bearing to the left, down the hill toward the beach. She kept her eyes on the light at Ballast Point, making sure it did not recede in the distance. Tall eucalyptus trees on our right formed a momentary windbreak but that ended when we struck the open beach. The sound of angry waves crashing on the shore warned us of a rough walk ahead. But there through the gloom shone the light of home.

"Come on, Mom." I tugged at her hand.

"Let me catch my breath first." She set the bags down for a moment and patted me on my head. "You've been a good girl, but I hope you haven't caught cold. Are you ready? We'll start and we won't stop until we're there."

"Do you want me to go on ahead and get Dad?" I really wasn't that brave.

"No you don't. Hang onto me and keep your eyes on the light. That's where we'll be in no time at all."

We plunged into deep Stygian darkness as we left the few guiding lights of the fort. No paved road existed, only two ill-defined wagon ruts now obliterated and awash by the storm's violence. Fierce gusts of wind and drenching rain tore at us. We found ourselves slogging in wet sand or wading in the rising waters. If my mother was afraid she never showed it. Broken logs, slippery kelp, and puddles of sea water blocked us every inch of our painful progress. After a few more shin-barking steps, Mom stopped dead in her tracks and broke into tears. "Oh, I wish I was back in San Francisco, It wasn't like this up there. Just wait until I see your father." The angry outburst spurred her on. There was a new purpose in her step that promised an interesting meeting between my parents.

Stumbling over the few hundred yards of debris finally led us to a smoother surface, and to a narrow boardwalk. It was hard to stay on it in the darkness, but it brought us to a gate and thence to a dwelling. We hoped we stood at the right door. Mom rapped sharply and waited. The door opened a crack and my brother El's face appeared. His eyes bugged and the door swung wide.

"Hey, it's Mom, it's Mom!" And for an eleven-year-old he exhibited prodigious strength as he literally grabbed her off the top step and swept her into the house, leaving me standing between two suitcases. There was a rush of steps to the door. Dad and my other brother, Ray, gathered me in their arms and I joined the happy family inside.

"*Gott in Himmel,* Freda, why didn't you tell us you were coming today?" Dad's eyes filled with shock as he realized what we must have been through.

"Hermann, I did write, but, oh, this weather. I guess the mails are even delayed." All thoughts of scolding Dad had vanished in the warmth of our homecoming.

"Boy, you must have had some trip. Did you get sick?" Ray was curious.

"No, but almost everyone else did," I answered proudly.

"Freda, you and Norm, get out of those wet clothes. I'll show you your room. Then you can inspect the rest of the house later." Dad chuckled as he spoke, for inspect, and minutely, Mother surely would. Dad carried a small kerosene lamp to light our way as we went up the flight of stairs. Halfway up, a bathroom was set apart next to the landing as the stairs took a turn.

"Here's the bathroom." We turned and followed up the remainder of the stairs. "Norma, here is your room, and Freda, here is ours."

I had been given the best bedroom in the house, with windows facing south and west. The cool wind billowed the white curtains, and Dad went over to close the windows more. He knew I loved the fresh salt air. My white iron bed had an extra blanket, and over on one side was the golden oak dresser and a straight chair. I followed my parents into their room. There stood the beautiful golden oak bed and the accompanying washstand gleaming softly in the dim light. Mom ran her hand over the lovely grained wood and sighed, then broke into quick action.

"Norm, get those clothes off. Hermann, will you open the bags, please? I do hope there are some dry clothes in them, but I doubt it. We'll change and then I want to see what you have in the kitchen." El and Ray stood close by, grinning. Now they would *eat*!

The opened suitcases revealed a mixture of very damp and soggy clothing. Deep down she found one dry sock. The old reed suitcases had really soaked up the elements.

"We'll just hang these up tonight by the stove to dry." Mom busied herself around until she found two extra blankets. Then she sent my brothers downstairs to stoke up the fire and peel potatoes. She didn't bother to ask them if they had had supper. Knowing the hollow legs they possessed, they'd probably eat again.

By now I was standing in a cozy woolen blanket. Mom had wound it around me efficiently, and I was practically immobilized. It was inevitable that I come up with the common complaint of young souls who fail to plan ahead.

"I gotta go to the bathroom."

"Oh, no," Mom cast a chagrined look at me and then at Dad. "Here, you take her. I'll get into something dry and be downstairs in a minute."

"All right," said Dad and he lifted me in his arms and started for the bathroom.

"Make sure she doesn't catch cold."

"Oh, she'll be fine," Dad laughed.

Into the bathroom we hurried with my father grabbing one end of the blanket, unwinding it like a matador, as I turned round and round, until I stood like a little cold puppy before him. He deposited my hindside on the cold toilet seat, and waggled a finger at me. "Call me when you are ready to come down to the kitchen." Then he left taking the blanket with him.

From where I sat, I could see one side of the keeper's house and the Ballast Point light itself. What a strange watch tower. I wondered what my new home would be like in the daylight hours. I didn't linger. The chill of the unheated bathroom discouraged any lingering. Such a strange place for one, halfway up the stairs and no heat. I washed my hands and opened the door to be enveloped in a toasty blanket from head to toe. It was all I could do to keep my eyes open to thank the thoughtful one.

"There, how's that?"

"It feels good," I answered Dad as I fought to stay awake. He packed me downstairs to the kitchen where I was greeted again by my brothers with raucous war-whoops. The table was against the east wall. My brothers sat on one side, Dad at the head and Mom and I on the other side.

Wrapped in Dad's bathrobe, Mom was already busy slicing potatoes and onions into an iron frying pan. Diced bacon was added and the cover put on, leaving it all to steam in fragrant juices. Golden eggs drifted lazily in a big bowl, ready to be beaten into a happy froth. Fresh coffee and a pan of hot cocoa added their aroma.

"Boy, that smells good," Ray sniffed appreciatively.

El inhaled deeply too. "Mom, will you make a cake for us tomorrow, if you're not too tired? Dad's a good cook but his cakes were always lopsided."

"Yeah, and one time he even burned the boiled potatoes, but we ate them anyway," Ray added. As long as I can remember we never allowed my father to forget the burnt potatoes.

"Now, your father's a good cook." Mom defended her husband.

"Well, he sure makes swell baked beans," Ray helped out.

"Are you all ready to eat?" Mom's question had us ready with our plates.

She placed the pan of steaming potatoes and a huge platter of scrambled eggs before us.

"Here Freda, you and Norm help yourselves first. The boys have had their supper." Dad warned my brothers off with a look.

My overflowing plate challenged the capacity of my small stomach. But miraculously, Mom seemed to know my exact limits, and in a few minutes my plate was empty. I had swished it clean with a "pusher," a thick slice of wonderfully crusty bread from the fort bakery. By the time the last bite had gone down, and the last swallow of cocoa had left my cup, my eyes were too heavy to remain open any longer.

"Better get her up to bed," Mom said.

Dad carried me upstairs, wrapped me in one of El's long nightgowns and tucked me in. I curled my toes in the soft flannel and went to sleep. Home at last!

As you have guessed by now, food was an important element in our family, but for much more than providing nourishment. There was no radio for us in the early times, and our kitchen became the communication and entertainment center. Here we lingered over supper to relate the day's activities and plan for the next day. With all the events at school, at the fort, in the harbor, and at our station, there never was any lack of topics for discussion. And if we could get Dad started on one of his sea tales, all the better. We could sit for hours listening to him.

Mom's good cooking made these times all the more enjoyable. It made us children happy to know we were also good providers, for when Dad's meager income stretched beyond the limit for the month, my brothers and I would stock the larder with fresh catch from the sea. We all pitched in to help provide and prepare our meals. It was all just a part of the intangibles that create a close-knit family.

All the Engel children grew up to be taller than their parents, we were so well fed.

Part Three

San Diego Historical Society-Ticor Collection.

Ballast Point Light Station
1914-1931

It nestles like a jewel in the sparkling clear waters at the entrance to San Diego Bay. Just above sea level, Ballast Point extends eastward from the high sheltering peninsula of Point Loma, and separates the calm bay from the vast Pacific Ocean. Here Juan Rodriguez Cabrillo first set foot on California.

Many years ago, sailing vessels when too lightly laden with California hides, stopped here to take aboard cobblestones to act as ballast on the way back to the East coast.

From this spot whalers set out in longboats to harpoon the gentle giants of the sea, and our point became a rendering area for whale blubber.

The Spanish established Fort Guijarros in the 1700's to guard against intruders. Excavations are now taking place on the site of that old fort.

During his years of Navy service, my father came to know San Diego and Ballast Point. This idyllic spot stuck fast in his memory. After joining the Lighthouse Service, he refused many offers of assignments until a vacancy became available here. With three school children, this was the assignment Dad accepted. For the next seventeen years we enjoyed an extraordinary life at Ballast Point.

And through all the years the main function of this light station has remained unchanged. The light sends out its guiding beam, and the thrust of land forms a steadfast bulwark against the ocean. And as Dad always said, "Rio, San Francisco, and San Diego, are the three most beautiful harbors in the world." And we were fortunate enough to live by two of them.

N.B. From the observation point at the Cabrillo National Monument, you can look down upon Ballast Point, a small spit of land stretching out from Point Loma.

The family takes Grandma for a ride in the old launch, "Useless."

11

Home Again

A gentle touch awoke me early the next morning, and my mother bent over me with a concerned look on her face. I opened my eyes and blinked at the morning light.

"I didn't want to wake you up, but I was worried about your catching cold." She reached out her hand and felt my forehead. "How do you feel?"

"Hungry!" I rolled over and started to get out of bed, but my aching muscles sent out protests, and slowed down my progress abruptly.

"Are you all right?"

"Yeah, Mom, but gee, I'm stiff all over."

"I guess you've had enough traveling for a bit. Get dressed and I'll fix you a good breakfast. Dress warm." She sounded relieved.

Getting dressed took but a minute. The bathroom stop was made in record time, and I took a flyer down the smooth bannister, sailing off at the bottom and landing in a heap on the floor.

A right turn led me into the huge kitchen alight with a reluctant sun and my mother's smiles. Against the east windows sat the golden oak table, on the north an ample cupboard for dishes, against the inner wall a magnificent stove complete with hotwater boiler. The other wall filled out with the usual small government sink and short drainboard. And around the corner—a big pantry. There was a place for all with room to spare. While Mom fixed my breakfast, I wandered around the rest of the lower floor. Underneath the stairs a small space housed brooms and mops. Across the hall and opposite the kitchen were the dining and living rooms. The dining room would be our nightly gathering place. An old battery operated radio sent out its raspy programs along with the acrid smell of the bubbling "B" batteries. The long table became our favorite spot for doing homework. We rarely ate here except for company. The living room, facing the north, was an antiseptically clean uninviting one with its furniture carefully arranged and freshly dusted. Mother wanted no young intruders here unless there happened to be a very special occasion, and then we had to sit properly and quietly for a short spell in the presence of guests until a nod from Mom released us.

I finished my rounds and returned to the kitchen with its warmth, fragrant aromas, and Mom. She turned to me and pointed to a place next to the window. "That is your place. I've made some French toast for you." She opened the oven door and there in custardy richness sat a stack which was quickly transferred to my plate, slice after slice, each one drowned in a slab of butter and spoonsful of golden honey. To help it all go down was a cup of steaming cocoa.

Mom sat down beside me with a cup of coffee in her hand and watched unbelievingly as each piece disappeared. At the sight of the empty plate, she laughed quietly. "I'm sure you're all right. Now before you go outside, put on a sweater. It's not raining any more, but the wind is still a little cold."

"Where's Dad?"

"Your father's in the carpenter shop and your brothers are down at the pier cleaning the rowboats for the fishermen who will want to rent them tomorrow. Why don't you go out and say good morning to them all?"

I needed no second urging to see the rest of my family again, especially my dad. He was always so full of fun and so patient. Mom had thoughtfully hung some of our clothes to dry next to the stove and the warm sweater felt good. The cold air swept into the kitchen as I opened the door, so I closed it quickly and stepped outside. The sky was still sullen and gray clouds moved in a ragged pattern above. The air lacked that bone-chilling dampness of Point Bonita. Everything else was so different too. This station was situated on a flat area just a couple of feet above sea level. I wondered what things would be like in a storm. Used to the violent northern gales, I couldn't believe it possible that we could go through a winter without being swept into the sea. I stood for a moment longer to look around. The flatness stretched out forever, except for Point Loma to the west, which rose like a huge wall to protect us from the prevailing westerlies.

Even the grounds around our house differed. Instead of a verdant garden we had inherited a yard full of cobblestones, all shapes, all sizes and monotonously gray. Interspersed were strangely flattened stones of varying diameters, wonderful for skipping across the water. Sometimes we could get one to skip four or five times on the surface before diving below the water. Some were small and filled with holes which made them excellent sinkers for fishing lines.

Others were so big they could be used as anchors for our rowboats. It seemed ridiculous to fence in a yard of cobblestones, but that's what the government had done. In the coming months we were all going to busy ourselves packing out these stones and unloading them onto the beach. It wasn't just the surface we had to clear. In order to have a good garden we had to go down at least two feet. The yard was large. It took us months to do the job.

The banging of a hammer sounded from the building at the end of the sidewalk. I hurried along to see my father. Absorbed in his work, he failed to hear my approach. With his usual concentration, he was trying to repair a rung on an old ladder. I came up to stand close beside him and put my hand on his arm. Dad turned quickly, flashed that warm smile of his, and hugged me. Then he sat me up on the workbench where I could watch.

"How do you feel this morning?" he asked.

"Oh, I feel fine, just kinda stiff."

"Well, that'll wear off in a day or two. Now, why don't you go out and take a good look around at your new home. This isn't a bit like Point Bonita. The weather is so good here you'll be playing outside most of the time."

I didn't move from the bench, content to watch my father go back to his task. Having the family back together again made everything right, even if I did have to stand for my brothers' constant teasing. Dad finished the ladder repair in another ten minutes, and turned back to me. "You still here? Come on, I'll show you around myself. It's getting near lunch time anyway."

Dad lifted me down from the bench and we walked outside to find the sun breaking through the remains of the slight overcast. We walked along the narrow boardwalk that stretched from the shop out to the little pier. On the right we passed the woodchopping block, on the left the broken foundation remains of an old warehouse, and farther along a large inverted water tank being used as a home by one of the civilians working at Fort Rosecrans. My eyes popped wide when a man exited from an opening in the tank side to throw out a basin of water.

"Good morning, Engel. Is that your little girl?"

"Yes, this is Norma. She and my wife got in late last night. Norma, this is Mr. Tyler. He works at the fort where they are putting up more buildings."

"Hello." I managed to get out a stunned greeting.

"Sometime, when you're not so busy, stop by and have a look at my place." He waved and went back in.

Dad tugged at my hand, and we continued our walk to the wharf. In the distance across the cove, appeared the outlines of Fort Rosecrans nestled against the bay side of Point Loma. Two wharves jutted out from the shoreline. One of those docks must have been where Mother and I disembarked the night before. I tried to trace the route we had taken from the boat along the road, past the hospital and barracks, the recreation building and down the hill to the beach. Near there I saw huge mounds covered with cement slabs. These were the ten-inch gun batteries, positioned to be able to fire at any enemy vessel attempting to enter the harbor. The quarter-mile long spit of sand and rock began at the foot of these gun emplacements. There along the narrow strip of land were the kelp, logs and debris we had clambered over in the storm. Waves crashed restlessly on the beach, some still splashing over the dirt path. But on the sheltered side of our cove, only small whitecaps kicked up a little fuss.

A few fishing boats bobbed up and down in the quiet inlet. Some were the Monterey type and it was good to see familiar objects. We reached the start of the pier and Dad paused to unlock the door of a tiny red structure no more than four feet high and four feet square. He peered inside and then closed and locked the door. Later he explained it was the top from an old bay beacon. On the other side of the wharf stood one which my brothers used for their fishing gear. My two brothers took time off from swabbing the boats to greet me. Fishermen would start arriving early the next morning demanding a boat to rent. Dad always made sure of a number of things, that the boats were clean and properly equipped, that the men could swim, knew how to row, had some knowledge of the tides, and in general, were good sportsmen.

"Hi, Norm, wanna help?" El held up a grimy rag.

"No, thanks."

Dad steered me over to a corner and pointed down. There in lath crates crawled a batch of brownish creatures, the delicious Pacific lobsters.

"We'll have some tonight. I've already told your mother not to cook dinner. Don't you tell her about these. It's to be a surprise for her. Look around by yourself for a while. I won't worry about you here. You can't fall off any steep cliffs in this place. And stay out of the boats. You'll have to learn to swim first."

With that admonition, I got another hug, and Dad climbed down the ladder into one of the rowboats and rowed out to a little launch.

"Gee, is that our boat?"

"It's not a boat. It's more like a submarine, always ready to go under," Ray laughed. "Dad's had it up on the ways twice and on the beach a lot trying to plug up the holes in the bottom. But the hull is so old and rotten, it doesn't help very much."

"Why don't we get a new one?" I still had a lot to learn about government foot-dragging. My father battled to keep that little launch afloat and its tired engine running for almost all his years at Ballast Point. Such a waste of money. It was constantly in a state of repair, and a burden of work to Dad.

I was never surprised to hear him say, "I'm going out to work on the launch."

Dad disappeared into the cabin and after a moment or two the engine sputtered, coughed and wheezed a puff of dark smoke, and fell silent.

"That darn old engine quit on him yesterday when he was coming home from the beacons, and the Navy towed him home. I sure wish the Lighthouse Service would buy him a decent boat." El knew almost as much about boats and the sea as my father. He was always around the water, one way or another, and usually in a boat. The pilots often invited him along for a ride when they went out to bring in a ship. And he became as frustrated as Dad over the hours devoted to the upkeep of the old launch.

I stood for a while watching my brothers finish their job of cleaning, and retraced all my steps along the wharf, peering over the edge at the sea life below. Small green crabs scrambled over the rocks and tiny fish darted back and forth in the shallow water. Gulls stood arrogantly on the shore, their eyes peeled sharply for an easy lunch, and pelicans sailed lazily. A clearing sky sharpened the distant objects. Point Loma now towered clearly above us. It stretched southwest into the Pacific Ocean, enclosing and protecting the harbor of San Diego.

A short stroll led me to the chicken yard. Here big fat Rhode Island hens fluffed their feathers and settled themselves comfortably in the dust. Occasional squawks arose from the chicken coop. The peace of the day shattered suddenly with a strange gobbling and excited barking. From behind the bushes near the chicken yard emerged an angry turkey, half running and half flying, pursued happily by our lovable collie. The outraged bird finally became airborne and landed atop the water tank, there to stare malevolently down on the frolicking dog.

"Come here, boy." I received the full welcome I had missed last night, wagging tail, and all. Rover stopped his bouncy jumping and joined me in a romp on the ocean side of the spit. Here we found a long line of sand to run on. Up and down we went, Rover chasing the gulls, and I getting some of the travel kinks out of my still weary muscles.

A familiar shrill whistle brought us to a stop. Lunch! My brothers were already on their way, and waved at me to hurry. Rover bounded away at the first sound of the whistle. I tried to get up to top speed, and barely made it to the old stable on the run. I slowed down to take a closer look at the old barn, a leftover from the building of the fort, it was now in a state of disrepair. Earlier the barn had held as many as sixteen horses. I wished they were still there.

Lunch was lively with conversation and laughter, but Mom looked tired. In her efforts to get everything shipshape, she had already done a day's work in just the morning. A huge wash swung idly in the breeze soaking up the sun, and the kitchen had an extra shine. This was my mother's domain.

We sat down to bowls of hot vegetable soup, with boiled potatoes and shortribs on the side. Sighs of contentment filled the sunny room. Life was back to normal again.

Later Mom and I went upstairs to rest. In a little while I could hear gentle snoring from the other bedroom.

My restful nap was broken by my brothers' excited voices and Dad's low tones. I got up, tried the short length of bannister to the bathroom landing, got around the curve at the landing, and swooped down the last lap successfully.

I stuck my head into the kitchen and what a sight! A big washtub stood on the stove with bright red feelers sticking out from under the cover. Inside were boiled lobsters.

A simple array filled the table with plates, knives and forks, sliced sourdough bread, salad and a bowl filled with tub butter. Dad made a final inspection and then turned to me. "We're ready. Go call your mother."

All three of us shoved and elbowed our way upstairs, making such a racket that there was no need to say anything to Mom, but we did anyway.

"Surprise!" We all yelled and ran back downstairs. Dad stood proudly at the table when Mom made her entrance and waited until she sat down. Then he pulled a very red lobster, still steaming and dripping water from the tub, and took it to the drainboard where he pulled off the upper section of the body. With a sharp knife he cut through the center of the tail and pulled the halves apart. There in beautiful tender goodness lay the white meat. It didn't take long for Mom to have a taste. She liked fresh seafood. With the first bite, a smile of appreciation appeared. At that we all pitched in. No need to dunk the meat in butter or any sauce. We just ate as is and enjoyed the sweet flavor of the young lobsters. The salad and bread were somewhat ignored. We all stopped our feasting at last, groaning at the sight of the remaining shellfish.

"They'll be just fine for a salad in a day or two. Oh, Hermann, they were so good, and I was really hungry." Mom thanked Dad for his thoughtfulness.

Later that evening we demolished the walnut cake, and all went to bed with good thoughts: Mom and Dad of being together again, Ray of finding some buried pirates treasure somewhere near, El of being a sea captain, and I just content to have our family united, and as a side issue, hoping I wouldn't have to go to school right away.

San Diego Harbor—taken from the city, 1928. Note mud flats, ill defined narrow channel. Dredged material from these mud flats later formed Shelter and Harbor Islands.
San Diego Historical Society-Ticor Collection.

12

School Daze

The hope was short-lived. Within three days my brothers hustled me off to school with them as though eager to have me share in their misery of confinement.

In La Playa, one small building housed the kindergarten and first grade, and an older structure the other grades in two large rooms, with teachers teaching multiple classes. Assigned to kindergarten for the remainder of the session, my most vivid memory is that of learning the alphabet and those long black and white strips of letters that still stare at me from their place above the blackboard.

Fort Rosecrans supplied a mule wagon which made regular trips to and from school but we had more fun on foot and made much better time than the old plodding mules, particularly at the end of the school day. With a few pennies in hand the only village general store lured us to the candy counter with its licorice sticks and whips and the five-cent grab bag.

Hiking along the same road, still in use today, provided the most fun, with hills to climb, canyons to explore, and spring flowers to gather, while now and then we caught up with the wagon to hop aboard for a little rest. Ours was a conspiratorial group bent on daily mischief and never failing to find some.

By the time I reached the fifth grade, my parents decided to send me to school in San Diego, along with my brothers who would be going to high school. It meant travelling by boat to the Broadway Pier and then walking a ways to school. We could still go by way of the "Tunaville Trolley" but it meant a longer trip. Two boats tried to maintain a regular schedule from the fort to town: one was the De Russey and the other a large tug from San Francisco, our old friend, the Harris. It was a welcome sight when it first steamed by our station into San Diego Bay.

The De Russey measured forty feet long with an extremely narrow beam. The designer must have been thinking in terms of speed and not comfort or safety, but the engine that was installed fell far short of propelling the launch at even a moderate pace. It was a potentially unseaworthy craft and assigned only for use around the bay. Its instability, however, inspired a delightful game, playing tag along the side rails of the boat. The step rails were very narrow and made movement along them slow. The crew used the rails to go fore and aft on the boat. Atop the cabin were hand rails to cling to as we inched around and around the De Russey. We chased one another, gave the skipper gray hairs and worried the passengers. None of us ever fell in, and I wonder if the captain might not have been a lot happier if we had, as long as he didn't have to pull us out. The passengers did not complain of our antics too often. They were happy to have us outside the cabins. However, one time a whole group of us gathered on one side of the boat, clinging to the rails. Our weight was too much and the De Russey took an unexpected list to the starboard side. By the time the crew had us back on even keel, the cries of the frightened passengers had changed to those of outrage. Happily for us, the son of the commanding officer at that time was an eager participant in the hilarious activity. All complaints fell on deaf ears until concerted anger brought our fun to an end. After that children were assigned to the forward cabin and adults to the one aft.

The sanity of the fort inhabitants remained intact upon the arrival of a larger vessel, the old tug Harris. It had a top deck which contained the officers' cabin and two cabins on the main deck, all ample in size, capable of holding many passengers. Along with the De Russey, the Harris was to make regular runs to San Diego. But both were so old that the scheduled trips often found the two tied to the wharf undergoing repairs. A water taxi making a run to the fort with a load of soldiers sometimes was available, but this was rare.

We found a joyful amount of room on the Harris. The top cabin was reserved for the officers and their families. Aft on the main deck stayed the enlisted group, and the forward cabin held a motley group, some crewmen and teenage boys. My brothers found a certain questionable manly pride in playing penny-ante there, but to me it was only a place of strange jokes, smelly spittoons and cheap poker.

With the De Russey and Harris frequently out of commission, we had to resort to the old mule wagon for a lift to the streetcar line, and then on to the long slow trip to town. We were usually late to school those days. One morning a small group of us gathered at the wharf. We hadn't been informed that neither boat was running, and most of the other children had gone on to the car line. It was a cold foggy morning and I suspect both skippers were glad not to make the run. Tied alongside the wharf was an old water taxi. Its small low cabin and huge engine took up most of the space in the craft. It began to look as though we'd better head for the "Tunaville Trolley." A workman repairing some of the pilings around the wharf heard our chatter and spoke up, "I'm afraid you kids are out of luck. They're both getting repairs today." There was a sympathetic note in his voice. None of us wanted to make the trip by streetcar, but it began to look as though there was no choice.

"I sure wish there was a water taxi around. I wouldn't mind using some of my spending money if I could get a ride. It's late now and we'll all have to stay after school again. That means we'll have to walk home from the car line too," Ray remarked.

The workman glanced up, thought for a moment and then said, "How'd you like to have me take you in. My boat is just a dirty old thing. We just use it as a workboat now, but this taxi still has some zip left. I can have you at the dock in no time."

"Oh boy, that's great!" We tumbled over each other in our eagerness to get aboard. What we knew was that this old taxi could get us to school on time. No matter that it smelled of old oil sloshing around in the bilges, or that we had to sit on clumps of damp Manila rope. We had transportation. What we didn't know was that the fog was not going to lift; in fact, it would thicken. And also what we didn't know was that our skipper was a fair-weather one. He normally ran his craft on the work jobs near the fort and then only in clear daylight hours. We settled down happily, our warm coats wrapped tightly around us, and our lunch sacks clutched in our hands.

The motor started with a roar, and we yelled in delight. This was more like it, I thought. This whole trip was going to be something to talk about with our other friends. As the worker backed the boat away from the wharf, it became obvious to three lighthouse youngsters that he had not completed any course in seamanship. Instead of the slow to moderate speed foggy weather requires, our boat took off with a sudden burst that almost took our heads off. It is the primary rule of the road, that in poor visibility all craft travel at a safe speed. Not this young fellow. He had an appreciative audience and intended to make the most of it.

Up the bay we sped, salt spray whipping against our faces. We had never gone so fast in a boat before, and relished every minute of this. The workman kept up a steady pace and by some miracle we arrived at number two beacon safely and breathed sighs of relief.

We knew where we were, but we weren't so sure the skipper did. And instead of sticking to the main channel, he turned the wheel abruptly to the right and headed for the little-used inner lane between the mud flats and North Island. It was not a true plotted waterway, but small craft used it as a shortcut. There was only enough depth of water when the tide was high, an extremely narrow area—not easily navigated even in good weather, and certainly not to be undertaken during a spell of heavy fog. At high tide the mud flats were deceptively covered with about six inches of water. At low tides the exposed sand bar marked the lines of the true channel in midstream and a little lane of water we were headed for. The harbor has since been dredged and is one big deep waterway.

A slight warmth from overhead seemed to indicate the fog would be breaking up soon, but it still clouded our way. The boat moved right along, the throttle thrust forward for a high speed. We were having too much fun to think of any possible consequences. Now and then we could pick out the dim outlines of the banks of North Island, and knew we were in the inside channel, and headed in the direction of town.

Without warning, a dense wall of fog closed in on us, wrapping us tightly in a sightless world. It blotted out everything over a few feet away. At last our skipper slowed the boat, and then came to a full stop. He looked around in bewilderment, ignoring all our noisy outbursts of juvenile advice. Staying there was too logical for us, so we harangued the poor fellow until he started the engine and put it in gear. At first we edged along at a slow speed, but couldn't help wondering in what direction. As we proceeded without incident, our helmsman felt confident again and went at a faster clip. We listened for sounds from nearby craft, but all was silent except for the muffled tones of ships' bells in the distance. In those early days, not many ventured out in a pea soup fog. We stared at each other and wondered where and when this trip would end. We did not have long to wait. The skipper was determined to get us to the Broadway Pier and then himself back to his job at the fort. A bunch of frightened kids huddled in the launch, waiting for something to happen.

The jarring stop was so violent that El flew forward and hit his head on the cabin hatch. The rest of us landed in a pile on top of each other. Ray pulled himself loose and shut off the racing engine. The workman had knocked himself out, and we were stuck fast on a mud flat in San Diego Bay. The boys took off their shoes and socks, got out in the shallow water and tried to push the boat free, rocking it back and forth, but the gooey mud had it firmly entrenched. The skipper offered no help as he sat rubbing his aching head. We were left with nothing to do until the weather cleared and the tide came in.

Time dragged slowly, and we were restless for some kind of activity. Water surrounding our boat was only a few inches deep, so before long we all had our shoes and socks off and started playing a noisy game of tag, splashing up and down the length of the sand bar. Hope of getting to school within an hour dimmed. Even if we did we would not be in a mood for lessons. At times we stopped our fun and tried to work the boat into deep water, but it wouldn't budge. All the excitement and play worked up our appetites. We opened our lunch sacks, made our usual exchanges and sat down on the side of the boat to munch happily on the goodies. School seemed very far away.

Noon approached and the fog began to relent at last. Its gradual lifting revealed a few fishing boats making their way along the main channel, on the wrong side of the sand bar to help us. We hoped one would try the little waterway. We whooped and hollered for help. The warm sun had come out and we did not feel like running around anymore, so we just waded quietly about scaring the little fish and poking at mud holes. But it wasn't long before the tide moved in and we had to climb back into the boat. A little fishing boat inched its way up the narrow channel near us, and after much yelling back and forth we grabbed the line thrown to us and fastened it to the stern cleat on our marooned craft. The boys and the skipper got out and shoved while the fishing boat tugged. At last the mud released its hold and after thanking the fisherman, we once more headed for San Diego and school. By the time we reached the pier, we had cleaned ourselves up a bit but were still a mud-spattered sorry sight. The fun of telling our friends about our adventure was considerably dimmed by the assignment of extra homework we received for missing our morning studies. Thus ended another one of those lively days on the bay of San Diego.

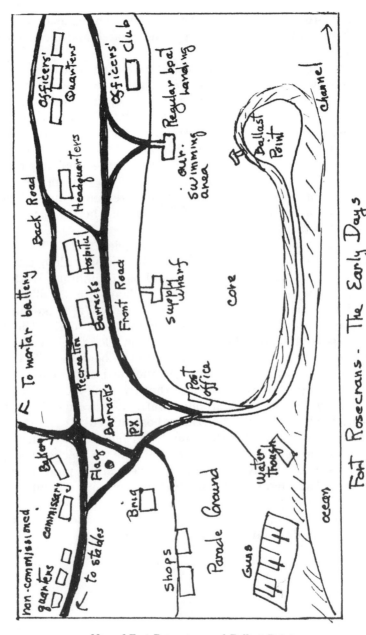

Map of Fort Rosecrans and Ballast Point

13

The First and the Last

W hen the warm waters of our first summer filled our little cove, my brothers and I stumbled over the round cobblestones into the shallow waters. There, under the watchful eye of our father, we dog-paddled around and around. In a day or two we passed the novice stage of swimming. Step two—a jump off the little pier into deeper water. We hopped off and up we came floundering and sputtering, but still in command of the situation. And when we had swum over to the ladder on the side and climbed up, Dad pronounced us ready for the *big* exam—proper use of, and behavior in the rowboats. He failed to mention upkeep of the boats.

Boats had to be secured properly, lines tied with a double clove hitch, no granny knots. Oars were to be stored under the seats, anchor lines curled, and last but not least, the last bit of water had to be bailed out.

My brothers were older, eleven and thirteen, but I was just six. They learned to handle the boats with ease. My lessons took longer but they were thorough. Dad let me use the smallest and lightest rowboat, the shortest oars, and a craft that did not leak. Rowing is a matter of both strength and good coordination. The oars had to move in unison, bite not too deep in the water, and be feathered on the return position. In moving the oar from out of the water forward to dip for another pull, you simply flattened the blade by turning the oar with your wrist. It cut down on the wind resistance and readied the blade for a smoother entrance into the water, not only a practical procedure, but a graceful one as well. Just a part of good seamanship.

Use of the rowboat opened a new world for me. It was my magic carpet (not without some effort on my part), taking me wherever I wished, floating up the bay, across to the fort wharves for play with other children, drifting out to the open ocean, or seeking out the best places for good fishing. My magic carpet carried me to the limits of my strength and endurance, and was governed by only two family rules:

1. Mother and Dad had to know where we were going.

2. They needed to know when we planned to be home.

With such freedom and trust it gave my brothers and me endless opportunities to enjoy and explore our sea world.

Sometimes, on a warm summer day, I managed to coax Mom away from her kitchen and take her for a row on the quiet little bay. Dad never failed to warn me, "don't get funny with Mom in the boat." His meaning was clear. No fooling around or showing off, nothing that would put her in any danger. Mom did not swim. She had been born in San Francisco, and Dad had communicated his love for the sea to her. It was easy to understand why there were no swimming lessons in the chilly waters of the north.

But one fine summer morning, Mom marched down to our little pier. My brothers and I were working in the skiffs bailing and cleaning. Dad was in the launch near us, struggling with the worn-out engine.

I stared. Mom was wearing her long flannel bathrobe. Something was wrong for she had been fully dressed at breakfast. But before I could ask, she pulled off the robe and stood quietly, a graceful figure in her homemade bathing suit, covering her from neck to toes. So that's why the old treadle sewing machine had been whirring so much in the late evenings.

I called to Dad, "Hey Dad, look at Mom. She's going swimming."

He popped his head up over the edge of the pier and almost fell back into the launch, recovered enough to look again and ask, "Well, well, what's all this?"

"Hermann," Mom directed, "I'm going to learn how to swim and I want you to help me." The tone of her voice was unmistakable. When Mom made up her mind she became an immovable force. It happened rarely but we respected her wishes on those occasions, for they were always with good reasons.

We cheered her on. We wanted her to have as much fun swimming as we did.

"Well, uh, fine." Dad was still recovering.

"Will you show me now if you're not too busy?" Mom asked.

We didn't want her to be discouraged at her first try. We remembered how our first few minutes went. The boys and I stood by her.

Dad moved to help her. "All right, we'd better get a rope around you first. I think I've got some old soft manila line in the launch."

He disappeared over the side for a moment and returned with a piece of line. "Here, let me tie this around you." And he made a loop of rope to encircle her waist.

"Don't you think I ought to wade in at the beach first?"

"Nope, those rocks are slippery and I don't want you to lose your balance and have a fall. Now you just go down the ladder and step off into the water. I'll hold you up by the rope and you'll be safe."

My ever-trusting mother followed his directions, feeling her way gingerly down the ladder, hesitating a bit before easing herself off into the water. For a moment she hung half in and half out of the water, and then Dad let out a bit more of the rope.

"Move your arms and legs," he shouted.

Arms flailed and splashed, but there was only slight movement from her legs. "Kick your legs," Dad yelled. But for some strange reason she seemed almost paralyzed from the waist down. Her mouth and eyes were clamped shut, as she vainly tried to make some headway, but her efforts just made her more frantic to succeed.

"Stop for a minute. I'll hold you up a bit so you can rest." Dad heaved in the rope and pulled her far enough up so she did not have to work so hard at keeping afloat. There was a desperate do-or-die look in her eyes as she glanced up. "Okay, here you go. Now try again to kick your feet." He lowered the rope a bit. The same results, lots of flying arms, but not much leg work.

By this time we didn't know whether to laugh or cry. Mom wanted so much to learn to swim, but it was becoming very clear that the desired results were not immediately forthcoming. There was another spasm of arm flailing, and Dad got to laughing so hard he accidentally let some of the line slip and Mom sank below the surface. She came up quickly, sputtering and gasping for breath and fighting mad. It was at that moment that Dad had an inkling he was not the best swimming coach in the world. My brothers and I leaned unhappily over the rail, scared but fascinated. This was not exactly developing into a good family situation.

"Boy, is she mad." El made the understatement of the day.

Dad immediately pulled Mom over to the ladder, holding the line steady as she caught hold of a rung. Silently she climbed up, stepped out of the rope, threw her bathrobe over her shoulders, and stalked off toward home, blue fury in her eyes and rage in every step.

"Do you think she'll want another lesson, Dad?" Ray had to ask.

"Whew, I don't know. She probably thinks I let the rope slip on purpose." He looked troubled. We had never seen our parents in a serious quarrel, and this seemed to border on one. We were all worried as Dad walked home dejectedly. My brothers and I stayed away from the house until lunch time. Hoping there was strength in numbers, we all slipped quietly into an atmosphere of cold, stony silence. Dad tried to brighten things up a bit, but all his efforts fell on deaf ears. We didn't linger over our food. None of us wanted dessert and when I nobly offered to help with the dishes, a shake of Mom's head dismissed me from the kitchen. It was the only time I had ever seen my mother so angry. She had decided that her dunking into the briny deep wasn't that much of an accident.

That evening we all climbed the stairs to our bedrooms without the good nights, or hot cocoa and cake we all enjoyed so much. The silence hung heavy about us, and I felt very helpless.

Dad took refuge by sleeping downstairs as he so often did on foggy nights. There was no fog that night, just a thick chill in the air from the direction of Mom's bedroom. Morning brought no change. Dad diplomatically had eaten breakfast early and taken off in the lighthouse launch for a trip up the bay. Mom kept her back to us as she fussed with some dishes in the sink. We hurried through breakfast and left the kitchen. My brothers and I wondered how long this cold war was going to last.

Nothing was much fun that morning. We puttered around the carpenter shop, cleaned out the already clean boats, looked for fish near the pier, and kept a safe distance from home. Anything to pass the time.

Along about noon we spied Dad returning, with little "Useless" pushing her bow sturdily against the flood tide. What had Dad been doing all morning? The stationary beacons had all been tended earlier in the week, and there had been no reported emergencies of "lights out." So my brothers and I just sat down on the edge of the pier, dangling our legs over the side. Something had to give in all this tension. Maybe Dad had a solution.

The launch eased alongside the pier and we jumped to secure it while Dad shut down the engine. When he stepped up to the pier, his hands held a large bulky package wrapped in heavy white paper.

"Gee, Dad, where've you been all morning? Mom's still mad and we don't want to bother her," I said.

"What did you bring home?" El wanted to know.

"We haven't been home since you left this morning," Ray explained, "We're scared."

"Well, so am I. Now let's get home and hope for the best." Dad led the way to the house. We trailed behind him in silence, apprehensive as we walked along the planks. We followed him into the kitchen and waited as he placed the package on the drainboard.

"Just something I thought you might like today." And he backed off as Mom rose from her chair, glanced at him briefly and stepped over to the sink.

She slowly unwrapped the paper. There in all its briny glory sat a prime piece of corned beef, a huge slab of brisket. She turned the meat over slowly as though passing inspection on it, and a tiny smile lifted the corners of her mouth. She turned back to all of us and said, "I've been so hungry for some good corned beef. We'll have this for supper tonight if you children will go over to the commissary for some cabbage."

Flowers or candy might have been in order, but corned beef as a peacemaker? It was a wonderful choice. There were beautiful blossoms in our garden for the picking and no one could whip a batch of divinity fudge better than Mom.

Corned beef was her favorite dish. The butcher wagon that came to the station twice a week never carried this beef unless specially ordered and the commissary offered little choice. Dad had gone all the way down to the finest meat market in town, Hardy's, to pick out this fine brisket from the brine barrel. No wonder the ice in the family residence melted so quickly.

With her simple statement my mother had swept away all the past angry moments and welcomed us back into the warm embrace of her love.

"Here's some money. Now hurry back. Take Norm with you."

Ray tucked the money in his pocket. El whooped and dashed out the back door and my two brothers with their long legs flying leaped and ran across the narrow spit while I struggled to keep up.

We went into the commissary straight to the produce section, where my brothers studied and argued about the merits of each head of cabbage. They finally picked up the two largest, greenest ones in the bin. Then Ray generously gave them to El and me to carry home. As we hurried back, I thought how much this really meant to Mom. The meat had taken a hefty cut out of the budget money earned from the lobster sales. Dad always tried to save that for the future.

"Come on, hurry up," Ray ordered.

Mom met us at the door. How good it was to see her there waiting for us. "My goodness, you didn't have to get such big ones. But there's plenty corned beef for supper tonight and tomorrow. These are just right."

Thus ended the formal swimming lessons for Mom, a first and

a last one all in the same day. Thereafter, she would don her home-made suit, go down to a sandy part of the beach nearby, wade out and splash herself with good clean sea water. Never again did she ask for our help, and she never learned to swim. I've always felt sorry about that.

14

Feathers and Fur

Fresh air and outdoor fun gave us gargantuan appetites that kept Mom busy in the kitchen most of her time, and it took every bit of Dad's ingenuity to fill the larder every day. My most vivid memories of those early days are of Mom at the gleaming coal stove, preparing meals for her appreciative family, sometimes taking a cake from the oven, or lifting a cover to sniff and inspect a fragrant pot roast. There was always a cake for us to slice away at any time, and one reserved for the family meal. No matter how tempting, we never touched *that* cake ahead of time.

Food was plentiful. The bay and ocean provided us with fresh seafood. Our garden flourished with the finest vegetables, and we raised chickens and turkeys. The chickens wandered around the point, a few venturing to the beach. They soon discovered their legs were ill-equipped to move over the rounded cobblestones. Like inebriated souls, wings went flopping and heads bobbing as the chickens staggered to keep their balance. Some found better success on the sandy beach, where they pecked at tiny sea life, but unhappily for us the chicken flesh acquired a strange taste as a result.

Dad finally fenced an area to confine the fowl. The dismal task of cleaning the chicken roost fell to my brothers and me. We scraped and shoveled, while the hens squawked protests and fluttered from rail to rail, stirring up more feathers and dust. It wasn't a job we pursued with much enthusiasm, but when it was done the chickens went back to laying beautiful brown eggs, which Mom later used in stirring up a batch of fluffy buttermilk pancakes.

The turkeys showed more common sense. Left unconfined, they ignored the beach area, and spent their time strutting noisily, announcing their domination of the lesser fowl. They not only chased other feathered creatures, but charged at us now and then, heads outstretched, wings spread fully, an awesome sight. Our dog, Rover, was the only thing to put these birds at a disadvantage. He was a big black and white collie, and could dart and dodge around them, leaving them to retreat in frustration.

We stared in amazement one early morning when three of the turkeys took off in flight across the narrow channel to North Island. Here they wandered about in the brush, and startled the aviators by strolling onto the runway. Whatever made them initiate this trek remained a mystery to us. If they possessed migrating urges, they certainly had a compass failure, for they flew east and west instead of north and south. That first flight filled us with despair. The turkeys certainly seemed on their way to a watery grave in the channel, but they flew to the island and back safely. We never gave a thought to clipping their wings, and as younger birds grew strong, some of them joined the traveling group. What a sight! These large ungainly birds in flight perilously close to the bay, but even at that they appeared to be more airworthy than some of the early biplanes that took off in their training flights. Not a single bird flopped into the bay. Some of the planes did.

Ornithologists might dispute the ability of those turkeys to fly such a distance, but fly they did. Perhaps they thought they were sea birds, and were trying to follow their examples. We were never quite sure what they found so attractive on the island. Maybe the wild seeds were to their liking, and maybe they just liked to hobnob with the wild ducks and quail. Fortunately, enough of the domestic traits remained to impel them to lay and hatch their eggs under our protection and not on foreign shores. At Thanksgiving, one of these fine birds was chosen for our holiday feast. We were all eager to get a taste of the first slice, to relish the wonderful flavor, and then to sit around and eat until we were stuffed.

We never had any luck with ducks. They would only have rebelled against being cooped up, and when left to roam, spent much of their time on the water, swimming and picking up the habits of wild birds and indulging in some romantic interludes with them as well. They picked up miscellaneous scraps along the beach, and our first duck dinner proved disastrous. Don't ever eat a fishy duck!

El and Ray somehow managed to create problems out of the most innocent beginnings, notably the day they each brought home a pair of beautiful New Zealand rabbits. There was no comment from Dad, and Mom began to envision pots of rabbit stew. Two small rabbit hutches went up quickly and the New Zealanders found comfortable quarters. They became so tame and friendly, the boys left the hutches open during the day, and the happy rabbits gamboled about all day, returning to the hutches at night. They darted by the turkeys and teased Rover into games of tag. In the midst of all this freedom, a bit of free love found expression, and more and more little bunnies gamboled about. The boys had not yet disposed of any, and the feed bill began to soar. When we were about to be bowled over by the thundering herd, Dad issued an ultimatum. The ever-increasing population had to be reduced immediately, and thereafter kept within reasonable bounds. For a while my brothers were quite successful in disposing of the overload quickly. They sold rabbits to the families at the fort, but eventually that proved to be barren ground, and the surplus remained, leaving us to plan on fried, stewed, and roasted rabbit—at least that was the idea. This seemed like a feasible solution. We all liked rabbit, but had always bought it from the butcher. We had never eaten any of our own. They were pets.

One day after lunch, Dad suggested it might be nice to have some fried rabbit for supper. With that he instructed the boys to supply the meat, and then he left to work in the light tower. I hurried to finish my chore of shining the brass lamps. Newspapers spread on the table collected the grime. Mom washed the glass chimneys and filled the lamps with kerosene. With one last good rubbing with Brilliant Shine and a final polishing with a clean rag, the finished work gleamed until I could see my image in any of the shining brass. The chore was done for another two weeks. I cleaned up the kitchen table and with a hug from Mom, hurried out to join my father.

I loved going up to the tower. From the outside walkway I could look down on the tops of the nearby dwellings and see all around. It was a wonderful lookout spot. The light tower had been built side by side with the keeper's dwelling, so it was only a few steps up to the entrance and into the antiseptic interior. Two acetylene tanks stood snugged against the wall, ready to supply fuel when needed. Weather instruments hung from the wall.

I climbed the narrow semi-circular steps to the top. Dad had already taken down all the shades that shielded the lens from the bright daylight. In the center of the tower stood a pedestal, and atop it a round object covered by a soft dust-free linen cloth. It looked like a bird cage. Dad carefully pulled off the cloth and smiled down at me. Then he lifted me up to take a look at the beautiful lens. The prisms glistened like carefully cut diamonds. The light had been made in France and then shipped all the long distance around the Horn.

My father busied himself wiping the tiniest bit of dust from the glass, and then replaced the shades on the windows. He did not put back the cloth, but joined me on the outside, and walked around to watch my brothers who were at the rabbit hutches. While he leaned on the rail for a bit of rest, I continued to stare at the panorama which unfolded before me.

Across the channel on a sandy beach stood the front range beacon, one of the lights that ships lined up with the rear range beacon farther up the bay. As the ships rounded the bar, the range beacons helped guide them safely through the narrow waterway, past Ballast Point and up to the first turn in the bay. From there on, red beacons and buoys dotted the starboard side (right) of the channel, and black ones on the port (left). Daytime navigation should never have been a problem, and at night the contrasting lights marked the way clearly.

Dad came around to where I stood and pointed out the coal station, telling me how large ships stopped there to fill up their bunkers with the fuel. Just beyond that flew the yellow flag on the quarantine dock, reminding ships coming from foreign ports that they were subject to a health inspection. I looked back over our little entrance. Before the days when it was dredged to a deeper and wider area, ships tried to avoid passing here, blasting on their whistles to indicate their intentions. At times some ships failed to give way, and squeezed by each other with a few well-chosen displays of anger, either by gestures or wrathful pulls of the whistle cord.

Dad had other work to do, so I returned home just in time to see Mom push a large pan of sweet dough into the oven. I knew the smell of cinnamon buns before they even started to bake.

I wondered what my brothers had done about supper, and went out to join them. They were still fussing around trying to make up their minds which rabbits would be selected for the sacrificial feast. As I listened to them, I was glad I didn't have any pet bunnies.

"Well, guess we'd better get at it. Mom will be waiting for us." El picked up one of the fat rabbits.

"Yep, guess we'd better get started," Ray agreed, clinging to one of his own. Another moment passed slowly.

"Dad will be hungry."

"And sore too, if we don't do it," said El.

At that moment Mom stuck her head out of the back door and called, "When are you boys coming in with those rabbits? It's nearly time to eat."

Eat! That did it. Kill, skin, clean and eat their pets? It couldn't be done. A flood of tears began to flow down my brothers' cheeks. They carried their wonderfully warm and live pets home, opened the back door and stood silently in front of their mother.

"Mom," El started and they both held out their animals. When the words did come, they nearly choked, and it was clear there would be no stew that night. How could you eat a pet? No rabbit stew or fried rabbit, but we had one of our favorite meals, hot German potato salad, scrambled eggs and slices of homegrown tomatoes. Dad ate quietly and the boys squirmed in doubt, waiting for his comments on the lack of a rabbit supper.

After his last bite of food, he turned to his sons and said, "I think you'd better get rid of the rabbits this week. We can't afford to feed them any more. You think of something by morning."

No harsh words and there were sighs of relief. The following day my brothers had decided to take the rabbits to school to give to the other children. So they solved this problem, but knowing my brothers, I was sure another would pop up on the horizon before long.

A friend and I take a look around from the light tower.

15

Just for the Looking

Under each rock, beneath every leaf of kelp, lay an abundance of sea life. Little squirming, wriggling creatures—sea worms, tiny crabs, delicate starfish, or hermit crabs that lunged along the sand like miniature inebriates. Frightened crabs waved their pincers menacingly, threatening to nip the largest invader, but backing away discreetly at the same time.

Once in a while a small octopus lurked among these rocks looking for his delicate clam dinner, only to slither away at the first disturbance. Occasionally an oddity turned up, a small fish caught in a little pool under a rock, lying quietly, but ready to dash away when the tide came in. These small fish were protected with a natural mottled coloration and ferocious appearance that belied their timidity. They were fun to scoop up and study for a minute—only an inch or two long, but endowed with brave hearts and sturdy bodies; I never had the wish to use them as live bait. A hook piercing such helpless bodies did not seem a fitting end for such gallant souls.

In the winter months larger life came into view. The great gray whales made their down from the icy polar regions to seek the warm waters of Mexico during the breeding and calving season. Hundreds spouted their ponderous way past Point Loma, geysers of spray marking the course. Sometimes one strayed into our harbor, seeking a quiet spot. There was little ship traffic to bother them in the early days of our life at Ballast Point, and we watched for these giant creatures during the migratory period.

Seeing them rise to the surface for air, we marveled at their size. Normally they were gentle by nature, yet one swift protestation by their flukes could send a small boat flying into kindling wood.

All old whales eventually became encrusted with barnacles. We endowed one ancient visitor to our bay with the title "Barnacle Bill." He was well known for his perennial excursions into San Diego Bay. Ships and small boats moved past him with the respect due another craft under way.

Upon his arrival, "Barnacle Bill," toured the bay in slow grandeur, blowing contempt of mortal man and sounding periodically with a graceful curve of his huge flukes. A short stay and then he left our area under full speed as though suddenly reminded of more important business farther south.

Many whales entered our harbor from time to time, and there was really no way we could identify a particular one as being "Barnacle Bill." We just dubbed them all with that name. After all, they all had barnacles.

One beautiful December day Dad left early for work at the beacons. Scraping and painting, cutting kelp clumps free from the pilings, washing the lenses, refueling where needed—the tasks went on day after day.

Birds chose the tops of the beacon lights for their resting spots until Dad at last found a way to keep the lights free of droppings. He hammered long sharp nails through a board, inverted the wood so the nails stood up with pointed ends, and then fastened the device atop the light. After that birds landed only momentarily before getting the message. It reduced Dad's work considerably.

Lights had to be kept burning through the night and my father made many emergency trips up the bay and even out into the ocean to relight an extinguished beacon or buoy. Ocean buoys were in rougher seas, subject to more severe weather. When lights needed care there, the lighthouse tenders could be called on, but too often they were on other jobs and would not reach San Diego for days. This meant that vessels headed for our port would be without the guidance of an important ocean marker, so Dad always tried to remedy the situation first. He journeyed out in little "Useless," and upon reaching the buoy, had the difficult task of leaping on to it, line in hand ready for a quick tie-up. The wet surface of the base of the buoy offered slippery footing, and sometimes he had to chase sleepy sea lions from it before he leaped. That done he usually managed to put the light back in working order. Smooth seas or rough, my father never once took a dunking into the ocean waters. That was fortunate, for in those early days he had to make these trips alone.

On this particular day my brothers and I had seen a whale enter our channel headed up the bay, but we gave no more thought to its appearance until we sighted Dad returning home from his work on the beacons in our little lighthouse launch, "Useless." My brothers and I so nicknamed it for two reasons, because of the USLHS painted on its bow, and because it was so frequently out of use in need of repairs.

For a while we just looked with interest, but then it suddenly seemed as though Dad and the whale might well be on a collision course. Dad was too far away for us to yell a warning. We could only hope that "Barnacle Bill" would not surface as they crossed paths, and there was no way of determining that. The lighthouse binoculars gave us a better view of the possible impending disaster.

Dad headed the "Useless" at an angle to move against the outgoing tide, and we held our breaths as the launch reached the deepest part of the channel.

There had been no further sight of our ocean guest, but he was due to surface at any time. The binoculars gave a close-up view of the placid bay waters near the launch, waters which suddenly broke into a swirl of motion. Little "Useless" rose abruptly from the bay as though going up on an automobile grease rack. In a few seconds, the boat rested high and dry on the old fellow's back. Then without any further commotion the launch slid slowly back into the water as gently as a slow ride in an elevator. "Barnacle Bill" waggled his flukes as if to say, "thanks for the good back scratch," and on up the bay he meandered, while "Useless" chugged a wavering course homeward.

We met Dad at the wharf, and waited while he tied the launch securely, turned off the engine, and then sat down to wipe his face. After a pause, he looked back out toward the channel and gave a sigh of relief for his safe return.

"Weren't you scared?" El asked.

"I sure was. I still am." Dad mopped his forehead again.

I remember how we all laughed, but I couldn't believe that my father could ever be frightened by anything in the sea. He knew the possible consequence of a fourteen-foot boat irritating a sea monster, and I think his knees wobbled a bit on the walk to the house.

Dad had been a deep-sea sailor on old wooden vessels at the age of fourteen, and learned very early in life to have great respect for the oceans and everything they held. He tried to instill in us all his knowledge, and often brought home objects for us to enjoy.

In the winter months we watched for the whales regularly, and looked every day for their small kin, the dolphins. We called them porpoises. They are delightful, friendly creatures, playful and curious. Huge schools of them often came leaping into the bay. They frolicked about near the bows of moving boats as if to be entertaining anyone who might be watching. Though we all knew them to be harmless and fun-loving, a school did manage to scare the wits out of our swimming group one day.

We were over at the fort dock, dunking, laughing, treading water, or floating on our backs. We were all too intent upon play to be totally aware of the porpoises until they were almost upon us. At a distance they had seemed headed up the bay, but suddenly veered toward the cove. Twenty frightened kids in the midst of swimming found themselves trying to outrace speedsters of the sea. It was useless. We thought of being torn limb from limb and our bodies being dragged out to sea to be devoured. Everyone forgot for the moment the true nature of the porpoises. These gentle harmless mammals just wanted to join in on our fun and had been attracted by our splashing and noise. They dove and leaped among us, coming close, but never touching, inviting us to swim along with them. It ended as quickly as it had begun. They departed abruptly, heading once more out to sea. We thought they must be the happiest souls in all the oceans of the world. It never happened again.

But life was not always light-hearted play for them. The tragedy of the sea appeared one somber morning near our shores. Two porpoises rounded the point close to our beach, one guiding and pushing the bloated body of the other. It was a situation beyond my young mind. Why would a porpoise spend its time and energy trying to move along a dead one? The two disappeared up the bay, a heartbreaking sight. I never saw them again.

Dad was so in love with the sea. He never let a moment pass that could bring another measure of respect for the world around us.

Midnight on a warm summer evening—the moon was full and bright, casting its light on the quiet bay waters. I was sound asleep when Dad came to my bedside and gave me a little shake.

"Come on, put on your robe and shoes," he said. "There's something I want you to see."

No need to ask any questions, although my head was buzzing with them. If Dad wanted us to see something in the middle of the night, it had to be very special. I pulled on my robe, and slipped my feet into cold shoes. Why not my slippers, I wondered?

The rest of the family had already gathered at the front door whispering quietly. With a last word to move slowly, Dad led us out the front door, along the sidewalk, over the bulkhead and out to the beach facing on the channel.

There ashore on the smooth round cobblestones lay about fifteen huge creatures, bodies glistening like ebony in the moonlight. We approached as quietly as we could until we stood alongside. They were pilot whales and known to strand themselves high and dry at times, unable to move back into the water. These small whales had moved in on a medium low tide, and if all went well they could be back in their native habitat in a short while. We had never heard the stories about whales dying upon the beaches around the world. We only knew that these would soon be back swimming again when the currents brought in the full high tide.

My father pointed out their size so we could compare them with our porpoise friends. We waited for the tiny bit of spray to shoot out of the blow holes as they breathed steadily. We asked Dad why the creatures had come to our shores this way, but he had no answer for us. We stood for a while longer, moving about slowly on the rocks, listening to the rhythm of their regular breathing. That was reassuring, especially when it was explained that these were air-breathing mammals and did not need to be in the water to obtain air. They stirred very little, only an occasional movement of a tail set up some splashing in the shallows as bodies rested half in and half out of the bay.

We wanted to remain around for the next high tide to see what would happen, but it was damp down by the shore edge, and it would have been a long wait. Mom called us all in and for a little while we sat happily around the kitchen table drinking the hot cocoa, munching on buttered bread and wondering what the fate of the pilot whales would be. By the time our cups were empty we were all ready for bed once again. El ran out to take a last look and reported back that the whales were still there.

At sunrise we gazed upon an empty beach. There was no sign of our mysterious visitors. All the whales had returned to the sea with the high tide. Their safe return seems contrary to all we hear now about such occurrences, but the shoreline at parts of Ballast Point is very different from the gradually sloping shores where beached whales are usually found. Our pilot whales had come in from a sharp drop-off and landed on a cobblestone slope. When the tides are in full stride, the water moves strongly around the outer point where the whales rested. They did not have to struggle to get back into the water. Rather, it probably swept them out in strong currents that flooded and ebbed past our station. A few feet off the shore and they plunged into deep water. We were happy to have seen them and to know that they had returned to their place in the sea.

Rover, a friend, and I.

16

The Canine Brigade

From Point Bonita Lighthouse we had shipped our beautiful black and white collie, Rover. He had been acquired as a pup in payment for the many quarts of milk from our cow Maggie. Rover was a superb animal, a champion in lines and breeding, but just a pal to us. As usual, when any animal entered our household, it always gravitated toward El. No amount of food or coaxing could draw it away from my brother. We finally recognized this as a basic fact of life and gave up on trying to claim the animal's affection. And that's the way it was with Rover. He was content to play with me until El showed on the horizon and then it was goodby as Rover galloped off to be with my brother.

The 1915 San Diego Exposition in Balboa Park announced a forthcoming dog show where children could enter their pets—mutts and all breeds. Somehow El got the notion that Rover should be entered. If he thought our collie was the best in the world, that was good enough for the rest of us, so we all pitched in to help.

The day before the show, preparations started with a good bath and scrubbing. Mom even dug out her precious bottle of peroxide and applied some of the fluid to the already white ruff around our pet's neck until it was spotless and snowy white, and then worked on his four white paws and white-tipped tail. The rest of Rover gleamed like polished ebony. We took turns brushing and standing guard to make sure that the handiwork wouldn't dissolve in a wild doggie scramble along the beach in pursuit of seagulls. He remained unsullied, his tail constantly waving a question at the overwhelming care.

On that special day, Dad accompanied El to the fair, and all along the way there were "oohs" and "ahs" for our pet. At the show, what seemed like thousands of youngsters had gathered with their yapping, tugging, sniffing, and tail-wagging canines. Some semblance of order finally evolved out of this mayhem, and the show began with a rather rapid and tearful elimination. Rover survived all the initial rounds and came down to the finals, still standing quietly in his good-natured way, waving his tail and looking supremely happy just to be with Dad and my brother. The pinning of the blue ribbon on our collie just confirmed what we had all known for a long time. Rover was a champion.

As Dad and El started home, blue ribbon clutched proudly in my brother's hand, a dog fancier approached my father and made an outright offer of four hundred dollars for Rover. I know we all must have loved our father very much that night when we heard the story.

"You'll have to ask my boy. The dog belongs to him and his brother and sister," Dad informed the man.

I know now what that four hundred dollars meant to a keeper making fifty dollars a month who was trying to clothe and feed his family and provide good schooling for all his children. The gentleman turned to El, but the question needed no repeating for El just shook his head, gave Rover a few pats and started leading him away.

The man smiled and said, "I'm glad he feels that way, but I'm sorry I can't have such a fine collie."

So Rover stayed with us. Never again did the subject of his dollar worth arise, and he spent his days escorting us around, chasing birds and being a gentle companion to our feisty tomcat.

When Rover died, the whole yard seemed a vast open space with nothing vibrantly alive in it. No other dog could fill the void in our hearts, but some variety of tail wagging and barking was sorely needed. We had little money to buy another pet, so El and I decided to try the city pound for a homeless pooch to cherish. At the pound a fine looking shepherd caught our eye. He crawled to us on his belly. We thought he was just begging to be loved. Now I think he was practicing his crouch before leaping at unwary strangers, but we plunked down the two dollars and led Prince home to be our pal. He became a friend to us, but for only a short period of time, for day or night no one else dared approach our dwelling without the risk of having Prince at his throat. No amount of love could change that part of his nature, and we were in a quandary. Prince must have sensed our dilemma for he voluntarily removed himself from Ballast Point and began running with the few wild coyotes left on Point Loma. Sometimes I imagined hearing his mournful howls and wondered if he were at last happy.

Then someone gave us a cocker spaniel, brown, big-eyed, with a misleading facade of shyness. Brownie was anything but shy. He possessed a great sense of playfulness, was highly inventive in his activities and completely lacking in common courtesy.

When the boys went over to the fort, of course Brownie went along, following their every move, but always on the lookout for something different in the way of fun. While my brothers bowled in the gym, Brownie would lie down quietly and watch the balls as they rolled along. But this palled after a bit and the spaniel began to make the rounds of the fort. He was a likable animal and often lingered with the cooks in the mess hall begging for goodies, or running around the noisy barracks, or once outside giving chase to a lazy butterfly. But all this lacked a certain zest for such a spirited canine, and Brownie took to wandering farther afield.

One day he ended up at the quarters of the non-commissioned officers and viewed a sight to delight the eyes of any canine delinquent. It was a Saturday. The Army had its strict code of inspection too. Inside and outside of all quarters, the residents were in full preparation for the weekly check-up. Hung over the porch rails in the warm sun, swaying ever so slightly in the mild breeze, were the household mattresses and pillows. Brownie was entranced by the gently undulating objects. He never had any success in catching any of the birds on the beach, but here was something within his reach. At the first leap, his paws caught on the corner of an old pillow, and oh, what joy! Feathers began to emerge and drift off in every direction, wafted along the line of houses on the gentle breeze, down to the barracks like a vanguard of summer snowflakes. Not content with his first blow, Brownie continued the attack, jumping at everything in suspension, sometimes falling short of his mark, but scoring enough to churn up two or three more billowy white clouds of feathers. The cry of alarm quickly spread, and Brownie, tongue lolling out of the side of his mouth and grinning as only a dog might grin, watched the frenzied housewives as they tried to retrieve their bedding. Brownie was a typically delinquent dog in a nice way, full of endless fun, but completely out of step with the Army. Fortunately, a kind friend who lived on a ranch took Brownie off our hands, leaving us to pay for his day of fun at the fort.

It just seemed that our dog world was destined to go from bad to worse. Last in our list of canine pets at Ballast Point was Jerry, an energetic Airedale that El had paid for with his caddying money. Jerry normally behaved himself in spite of his nervous terrier background. There were three high points in his life with us. One, his perennial feud with our old huge Rhode Island Red rooster, which erupted daily either in loud barks or a scattering of feathers, depending upon which combatant had won the daily round. Second, the time my brothers and I went crawfish tramping for fish bait on the mudflats near North Island. We always took Jerry along and this time he decided to chase rabbits in the hot sun. He ended up with a case of running fits. I had never heard of them, but my brothers recognized them and used the incident for one of their fiendish ideas. They finally caught up with the wildly racing dog, placed him in the boat, tied him securely in the stern of the craft, and doused him with cold water. Then they pointed out the fact to me that we had a mad dog on our hands, and were in a very dangerous position. There was no doubt in my mind at all. My brothers could always put on a good show, and I was usually foolish enough to believe them, and ready to forgive them for we all had good laughs at the jokes we played on one another.

But this time I was really scared. I looked at Jerry's slavering jaws and glazed eyes, and knew instantly that I was going to be a victim of rabies. All the way home across the channel they kept me in a state of fright, pointing out how loosely they had tied Jerry, along with the horrible results of being bitten by a mad dog. I crept as far up to the bow of the boat as I could without falling overboard, keeping my brothers between the dog and myself. As soon as we reached the pier, I leaped out and ran for home, but my brothers just as quickly untied Jerry and here he came bounding after me. I made it to the carpenter shop and slammed the door. Safe temporarily! Dad turned from his work at the bench.

"What's this all about?"

"Jerry's gone mad and he's trying to bite me," I gasped.

"Well, you stay here, and I'll take a look at him," Dad tried to reassure me.

Dad left and closed the door behind him. I waited and waited. Then Dad opened the door and said, "You can come out now. It's all right and Jerry is fine, just a little warm yet."

Jerry sat at the foot of the steps, his tongue still hanging out and next to him a half empty bowl of cool water.

"Nothing to worry about. What made you think he was mad?" Dad wanted to know.

When the whole story came out, the boys got a good scolding from Mom, but the giggles from my brothers at the supper table were infectious, and we all laughed at the "mad dog."

And third, the most heartbreaking for me, was the time Jerry broke up my high school romance. A fine young lad had given me a carved wooden ring as a token of his friendship. I wore it proudly, but not for long. One day it was my turn to feed Jerry, and as usual he was to receive a portion of freshly ground meat. As I placed his food in the bowl, off slipped the oversized ring, plop, into the meat. And before I could snatch it away, Jerry, in one gulp had swallowed meat, ring, and romance. Now just how do you recover a ring in such a situation? I didn't—end of romance.

Jerry lived with us for the rest of our time at the point, but somehow or other no dog ever took the place of that wonderful collie, Rover.

But there were other pets to gladden our hearts, pets of a different nature as you will read about in other chapters.

The pilot boat, still in use today, which El had as his first command when he was only twelve. *San Diego Historical Society-Ticor Collection.*

El as he looked later as an officer on the Catalina Island ships.

17

The Initiation

E ntering the San Diego harbor channel offered a challenge to any skipper of any size vessel. From the wide expanse of the ocean he had to pilot his ship through the narrow waterway between Ballast Point and North Island. This passageway was only one-fourth mile wide, and of that width little could measure as deep water.

Tidal activity did not match that of the San Francisco bay, nor did the winds blow so fiercely, or fog shroud the bay so often. Nevertheless, owners of many ships preferred to have their captains use a harbor pilot rather than risk the loss or delay of a valuable cargo.

Only the doleful moan of a buoy, the harsh clang of a bell or the raucous blast of the foghorn served as guides, for there were no direction finders, radio or radar in the early days at the point. For many years the pilots kept themselves informed of arrivals only by newspaper sailing lists or by letter from a ship's company. Neither one proved too reliable as to time. Sometimes the pilots remained out at the bar days and nights waiting for a prospective arrival. The bar as we knew it was an area about two miles from Ballast Point, a beginning to the entrance to the harbor. It was at that point that pilots boarded the vessels, and the skipper turned over his command temporarily until it was safely docked in San Diego.

This tiresome waiting for ships to appear on the horizon was a source of irritation to the pilots, but when my two long-legged brothers came to Ballast Point, the problem eased. For fifty cents a ship, the boys maintained a sharp lookout on the brow of Point Loma for incoming merchant vessels. They soon became adept at identifying them. When one was spotted, whichever brother was on duty dashed down the two miles to inform the pilot. The job was sporadic since harbor traffic was light, but fifty cents now and then gave the boys some spending money and the pilots a fine bargain.

The pilots appreciated this service and often took the boys out with them on a job, at times allowing them to steer the boat or help in starting or shutting down the engine. They had the excitement of watching the boat draw easily alongside the huge ships. They held their breaths when the pilot made a leap for the "Jacob's ladder,"

and climbed up the swinging support bumping against the hull of
the ship.

One morning El posted himself near the Old Spanish Lighthouse
to watch for a lumber schooner. With a substantial lunch by his side
and the serene blue Pacific stretching endlessly before him, he was
content. All morning El lounged in the sun. One could be lazy at this
job, for ships sailed slowly, and trailing smoke usually appeared on
the horizon long before the ship hove into sight. By ten o'clock El
had eaten his lunch and wished for more. At eleven thirty a tiny
wisp of smoke rose in the distance. He waited a bit longer and then
used the binoculars to be sure it was a merchant ship and not a Navy
destroyer. Satisfied with his identification, he hopped to his feet,
and ran at top speed down the two miles to home.

Captain Johnson spied my brother running along the beach and
went below to start the engine. Then he realized in dismay that he
was alone. The other man was ill at home and unable to make the
trip. Someone had to bring the boat back. Dad had helped at times,
but he and the assistant keeper were still at the beacons. The pilot
decided to gamble on the seamanship of a twelve-year-old youngster,
who could even now handle any of the station's boats with skill.
But the pilot boat measured fifty-two feet, while our lighthouse
launch could only boast of fourteen.

As El climbed aboard, Captain Johnson asked, ''El, do you think
you can handle things? Captain Keith is sick today.''

My brother stared at the length of the boat, swallowed the lump
in his throat, and grinned in answer.

''Okay, cast off the mooring lines.''

El ran forward, untied the line and dropped it carefully on top
of the buoy so it would be easy to pick up again. A boy's dream was
unfolding before him, blotting out that cardinal rule—always let Mom
and Dad know where you are or when you go out with the pilots.
We were always taking trips out to the bar when the runs were not
extended and the weather was fair. This created no great worry for
our parents, for we could all swim and possessed plenty of common
sense around the water.

When Captain Johnson and El rounded the point, Ray waved
to El from the beach where he was gathering fresh clams for the
next day's supper. From my perch on a step at the fogbell tower,
I could see my brother standing on an apple box and steering the
boat. Well, there was nothing unusual about that. I couldn't help
wonder. I hadn't seen Captain Keith all day, and he didn't appear
topside on the boat. I left the fogbell and wandered down along the

beach on the seaward side, looking for the hiding spots of the long-necked clams as they spurted up water from beneath sandy mounds. If you were quick enough in digging you might come up with a six or seven-inch hardshell clam with a neck like a collapsible rubber tube. The necks were too tough to use but the rest made excellent bait. It provided energetic sport if you were in the mood. I wasn't.

I turned over a few rocks seeking different sea life but disturbed only a gathering of small green crabs. They scrambled off, wagging their tiny pincers. Little dime-sized starfish moved away in fear. Slowly the afternoon passed, and I whiled away the time just poking about the beach waiting for the ship to come in. It was good to lie on the warm sand watching the gulls sail lazily by overhead, while white clouds glided slowly before a westerly wind. It was a wonderful calm afternoon and I fell asleep.

The sudden blast of a ship's whistle shattered the quiet air, and I sat up to enjoy the sight of the incoming freighter. Captain Johnson was never one to fool around, and the partly laden vessel stood high out of the water revealing ancient rust spots above and below the water line. The propeller thrashed around, half in and half out, leaving a churned up sea behind. The freighter pushed on up the channel, a little "bone in her teeth," the huge propeller still whipping up a frothy wake. A short distance behind chugged the pilot boat, avoiding the waves left by the steamer.

I waved a welcome to El. As he turned past the point, I saw no one else, just my brother standing on the apple box, handling the wheel with great concentration. He saw me on the beach and pulled the whistle cord for a few short toots in greeting. I scampered home to relay the news.

"Mom, Mom, El's bringing in the pilot boat by himself! He's all alone. Oh boy! I'm going out to meet him." I didn't wait to see the look of disbelief on her face.

I ran down to the pier. It would really be something, I thought, to see him bring that big boat up to the shifting mooring all by himself, and against the wind. By now Mom had probably sunk in the nearest chair and was wondering, what next? And I wondered what kind of reception El would get when he got home.

Sometimes the pilots even had to make more than one approach to the buoy, and now my brother faced this task on his own. The boat slowed as it neared the mooring. El threw the gear into neutral, hurried out of the cabin and ran to the bow to pick up the long boathook. The boat gently nosed the buoy and El skillfully picked up the line from the mooring. In a minute the pilot boat rested safe and secure once again. With the final shutdown of the engine and closing of the hatches and cabin door, he swung his legs over the side into the rowboat and rowed happily ashore. Dad, who had just returned from the beacons, waited for him with me. I saw Mom hurrying along the boardwalk. Tears and anger gleamed in her clear blue eyes. When El stepped up on the wharf she glared at him for a moment, and then hugged him tightly. Dad stood quietly by and just smiled.

"You should have told us. It was dangerous," she reprimanded.

"Oh, gee, Mom, Captain Johnson said I could handle the boat, and besides there wasn't anybody else. You and Dad aren't mad at me, are you?" He stood there looking up at them and bursting with young pride.

"No, I'm not, son," Dad answered, "But there's more to handling a boat besides just steering and tying up. You were lucky to have calm seas. I'll see Cap Johnson later."

Dad was remembering that we all knew how to swim and handle small boats, but running a fifty-two footer in open sea demanded a new set of skills and mature judgment. He didn't want to squelch my brother's enthusiasm, but caution dictated his remarks.

Nothing, however, could erase the glow from El's face, and though he listened to his father, I wondered if he heard a word. El always envisioned himself becoming a sailor, perhaps a pilot or even master of a great ship, anything to be a part of the ocean. Dad understood how strong a lure the sea held for his youngest son. He had succumbed to that lure many years ago himself. Nevertheless, he wanted El to be aware of and prepared for the pitfalls that loomed ahead.

In the days that followed and with some special help from the pilots, everyone knew that a young seaman had earned a steady good weather job. He became letter perfect in all his tasks and the pilots breathed sighs of relief, for it meant much additional rest for them and someone close by to call on when necessary.

El continued working the daytime hours on non-school days. Most vessels timed their meetings with the pilots for morning. That whole day could then be used for loading or unloading freight. The crew would have a night's rest and the ship underway the next day. But with company schedules to be met, ships sometimes chose to enter the port at night, and the pilots began to think of El for that duty. Dad raised no objections, saying only that he'd like to go along on the first trip.

Those who are familiar with the ocean have respect for its ever-changing moods. In the day, its vast expanse of blue water may seem inviting and uneventful. But at night the full mystery of the sea expresses itself. The wind dies down. The sea becomes placid, and all appears peaceful and safe. But when you are out there alone, the daylight beauty can become a shadowy nightmare. Familiar objects vanish, leaving only a few strange lights in the distance.

On the first night trip, El trembled with excitement. This new step challenged his ability to overcome the misleading elements of a darkened sea. Dad rode out that night too, to see how things would go. Steering the boat on the way out presented little difficulty. The water lay quiet and the friendly Point Loma station beamed its guiding line of light at regular intervals.

In the distance the dark hulk of the approaching freighter could be pinpointed by the slight glimmer of its running lights. El kept his craft underway at slow speed waiting for the ship to round the bar and head in. As the ship finished its turn, El began to circle the pilot boat around to lay it alongside. Both vessels had to keep underway at a fair speed during this operation, to keep the ship from losing steerage way or rolling into the pilot boat. As the great mass of the steamer bore down on them, my brother felt his first qualm of fear. The freighter did not diminish its speed, hoping to take the pilot aboard quickly and bring the ship alongside a wharf in short order. El wavered a bit, staring out of the cabin at the huge monster about to swallow them, and thought for a moment of handing the wheel over to his dad. My father just stood there calmly, not saying a word. El made his decision. He grasped the wheel firmly, steered the pilot boat smartly close to the ship, easing it carefully into position, and keeping up a matching speed. It was a lot for him to do all at once. With a wave of his hand Captain Johnson leaped aboard the rope ladder and scrambled upward. El heaved a sigh of relief as he pulled away from the inward bound ship, and looked at Dad for his approval. He received a hearty pat on the back.

"Not so easy in the dark, is it, son?"

"No, Dad it sure isn't, but I know I can do it now." And do all right he did, so much so that in adult life he became the senior port pilot for the Long Beach harbor, handling some of the largest ships in the world, and fulfilling all his childhood dreams.

Ray, his older brother stuck to the land and became a testing engineer for the Douglas Aircraft Company. The sea never beckoned to him.

A fur seal of the type we rescued from an oil dunking. This one was found at Ocean Beach and was taken to Sea World for treatment. *Union-Tribune Publishing Co., San Diego.*

18

We Welcome a Stranger

The stench of dirty oil lay heavy in the damp October air. A thick sheet of scum coated the surface of our cove. A host of helpless birds gathered along our beaches, unable to fly with their oil-encrusted wings. They were sick from trying to rid themselves of the foul stuff by stripping oil away with their bills. So much was swallowed in their frantic attempts to cleanse themselves, it only compounded the problem. Even the little shore inhabitants suffered unless they retreated to deeper water somewhere below the oily layer. There would be no swimming, clamming, fishing or beach-combing until fresh tidal flows washed us clean once again. There would only be rowboats to scrub along their fouled waterlines. I hated the careless ships that emptied their foul bilges along our shores.

After breakfast I walked out past the carpenter shop and along the upper side of the beach toward the pier. I scanned the water. On other days there was always some movement, the splash of a playful porpoise, a noisy gull snatching at his neighbor's breakfast, or a pelican sailing serenely above, ever on the lookout for some careless fish below. Very little was astir.

I broke the smoothness of the water by skimming a few flat stones across the surface. Reaching to pick up another stone, I caught sight of an unfamiliar object near the water's edge. Many strange things washed ashore on our beach—old Navy brooms, empty paint cans, discarded mattresses, broken and seaweed-covered rowboats. This new bit of flotsam resembled an oily brown mop, but unlike a mop, it moved at the sound of my approach. I slipped and slid over the rocks, wondering what it could be. And there close at hand lay a small furry bundle, a baby fur seal. Harbor seals, sea lions, and porpoises were known to us in our daily observance, but not this helpless little fellow, and helpless he most certainly was. He was a total stranger to our harbor waters, far from his native element. The little seal stared at me, big brown eyes frightened and watchful. His body was thin and in need of nourishment, and the normally luxuriant coat was streaked and matted with the oil that had escaped from the bilges of some passing vessel.

Would he leave if I approached? Would he bite if I tried to pick him up? The starved creature seemed too weak to put up the slightest protest, but after taking another quick look I ran to get aid. Dad and my brothers returned with me, filled with doubt as to my report, but expressing complete knowledge on how to handle such a situation. Once again I moved quietly down to the water's edge and pointed out our visitor. Dad scratched his head in disbelief; Ray scrambled back up the rocks to fetch something to carry the seal in. El scrunched down and just stared.

With the old soft canvas Ray brought, the seal was carefully carried up the beach above the high tide line. We did this tenderly avoiding any contact with his sharp baby teeth. High up on the beach, Dad's hasty examination revealed no outward injury.

"He may be hurt inside, but if he is to have a chance to live, you'll have to get that oil off his coat. He needs to be cleaned up and fed. I think he's past taking milk. Try some soft clams first. And you go put on some old clothes before you start." Dad went back to his work in the carpenter shop.

Mom dug out our old clean overalls and asked, "What do you want these for?"

"We're gonna clean a seal." And El explained our new project.

Mom stared at all three of us for a moment and then reminded us, "Well, don't you come in the house until you're all cleaned up good." She was busy and waved us outside, but we knew she would come out to see for herself as soon as she had a break in her work.

If you are not aware of the essential properties of bilge discharges, you have no idea what can happen when three enthusiastic youngsters are combined with one gallon of kerosene, rags, and a slightly protesting seal pup. The oil was dark, thick and sticky, and smelled awful, but my brothers and I took turns gently wiping the mess from the little animal. After laboring for over an hour, we sat back to gaze at the soft fur, now beginning to show signs of its natural beauty, and then we caught sight of each other and whooped with laughter. Most of the oil seemed somehow to have been transferred to us. Where we had scratched an itch on our noses, there were black streaks. Where we had wiped the sweat from our faces and foreheads, there appeared dark smudges. We were now as smeared, sticky and smelly as our new-found friend had previously been. Giving the pup a last little pat, we all tramped up to the house filled with the righteous pride of good accomplishment.

"You kids can't come into the house like that!" Mom threw up her hands in horror as she gave her daily battle cry and made her stand in the doorway. Each day she prepared herself for the worst. Our vagaries into nature's wonderland caused no great distress, just constant uneasiness as she wondered what we would do next. I also suspect she enjoyed the breaks in her daily routine.

We sat on the porch steps outside and chattered and giggled, as we rubbed the dirt from our arms and faces. Dad brought us all clean clothes, and one at a time, my brothers and I washed and put on the fresh garments, making sure we left the little outside washhouse in perfect condition. Fairly clean once again, we began to plan our next step. Like all healthy children, possessed of good appetites, we thought that food and plenty of it could cure all ills. And here was this little fellow, starving to death with three humans as foster parents. He was too weak to seek his own food. What had happened to his mother? Had she been shot, or perhaps struck by a passing ship? And how did he come to be in strange waters? But no matter, getting him food was the immediate problem.

Happily, catching fish was never difficult at this idyllic spot. We all went down to dig clams for bait. The fish bit eagerly and soon we had some small bass, and we hurried back to the seal with his fresh breakfast. We dangled pieces of boneless fish below his nose, but he just looked at us unhappily. For what seemed like an hour we swung the fish back and forth like a metronome, but it evoked no response. Here was death staring us in the face, and we were helpless. I began to cry. Ray looked thoughtful, and El began to cut the fish into smaller pieces, checking carefully to see that there were no bones. Just then Dad came out of the carpenter shop and walked over to us.

"What's the matter?" he asked. "Did you remember to try some clams?"

"What's the use of that?" I blubbered. "He won't open his mouth. He's gonna die."

"Well, you just open it for him, but be careful of his teeth, and go get some clams." Dad tried to make us feel more hopeful.

Ray and El went down to the water's edge and dug up a few clams. It took but a moment to open the shells. Heroically, I stood by and gave moral support as Ray held the weak seal firmly while El quickly slipped a fat clam into its mouth. Down went that bit of food, and more and more, each time with a bit more willingness. After he was thoroughly stuffed, one of us remained on stand-by for any emergency. The only emergency, which fortunately did not arise, would have been that of an overfed baby losing its breakfast.

With the long day still ahead, problems remained. Should he be left on the beach for the rest of the day or be taken home to shelter? It was decided that "Furry" had had enough activity and belonged close to things familiar to him. So he rested undisturbed for hours. He slept quietly for a long time, and at evening he had another meal, this time without any protest. His body seemed to be filling out. Life was suddenly brighter for us all.

When the cold chill of the evening began to creep in from the ocean, it appeared only right that Furry be invited to join the warmth within our home, but Dad stopped us cold with his usual logic. "Why do you think he was born with that fur? And don't you think he would not be so frightened if he were close by the water?"

And although it still seemed cruel to us, the seal stayed that night on the beach, tucked away in the folds of the old piece of canvas.

I didn't sleep for the first five or ten minutes. Snuggled down in my own warm bed, and knowing the penetrating dampness of the night fog, I worried about our little foundling, but the soft lap of the waters upon our shore lulled me to sleep.

The next morning the house rang earlier than usual with noises of footsteps up and down the stairs. We shouted as we raced to slide down the bannister. Even the fragrance of bacon slowly cooking over the shiny coal stove, coffee steaming cheerfully, or the sign of a mile-high stack of old-fashioned custardy buttermilk pancakes, could not sidetrack us from dashing out to see Furry. Mom made one last frantic appeal. "Eat first or you'll be sick!"

"Back in a minute, Mom."

And off to see our new pet. He hadn't stirred, nor had his wistful attitude changed—still lonesome and forlorn, but heaven be praised, he was hungry. The remnants of the fish and some hastily dug clams found their way down an eager throat without any coaxing, and Furry tolerated the touch of a human hand. We took turns stroking his fur, and continued to clean him. It would be a long time before he would be free of the last bit of oil.

For three days he received our tender care and as the hours went by, he grew stronger. We doused him with buckets of salt water regularly. He wriggled happily under its impact. And then near the end of the week Dad reminded us once again that creatures should never be kept out of their natural environment. "He belongs back in the water. You've done all you can for him. He needs to swim and strengthen his muscles. If he feels like it, he'll take a little swim."

"But gee, he's so small," I protested.

"He can't get any food for himself," El argued.

"He'll *starve!*" We chorused.

But in the end, Furry was bundled up again in the canvas and carried down to the water's edge, where an extra gentle and reluctant push guided him into the quiet bay. He lay there quietly for a moment as though soaking up the sensation of being back in his own element. Then gracefully with a few easy movements his little body moved out into deeper water, the brown head just above the surface and getting smaller and smaller as Furry swam away. With one or two tentative dives behind him, the baby seal found new confidence and his longer dives took him out of sight and out of our lives, or so we thought.

All day long we looked and looked, torn between happiness for his quick recovery and sadness for our loss. Never were the bay waters searched so keenly by three pairs of eyes for a show of a brown head bobbing to the surface. Mother called us in for lunch, but appetites had sagged to a low ebb. After eating, Ray and El decided to row across to the fort pier to join the other youngsters in swimming. I stayed behind. All afternoon I sat on the beach ignoring the hot afternoon sun. The hours passed. Ray and El returned ahead of the fog which had begun to curl like a giant gray breaker over the crest of Point Loma. Sometimes the mist hung suspended for a while as though planning its attack on all things below. Other times it stole stealthily in along the channel gradually blotting out everything at a low level. I liked the fog, its windblown wisps rushing down the hill, its impenetrable barrier that slowed traffic to a frustrating crawl. At night ships sounded their bells to indicate anchorage positions and the raucous sounds of the fog signals disturbed even the hardiest sleepers. The diminishing light made it impossible to see any sign of Furry. My brothers helped me walk the beach for one last hunt for the seal, until the chill drove us inside.

The kitchen was warm and filled with the good smells of the dinner activity on the stove. Mom glanced at me as I came in. She was always worried about my catching cold. "Don't go outside again. Supper is almost ready."

None of us needed a second invitation to a tender pot roast bubbling in its rich brown gravy, mashed potatoes fluffed into snowy peaks, large slices of homegrown tomatoes, and fresh green beans, glistening with melted butter. In the pantry rested two apple pies with flaky brown crusts. Mother never baked an anemic pie in her life, and any pie with a pale crust was considered unfit to eat.

It was quiet at the table that evening. Dad was exhausted. It had been a long day for him, cleaning the lenses on the beacon lights and hauling up the heavy tanks to renew the fuel supply, and the day would be made even longer by the night watch he always had. With the fog already draped ominously over the brow of Point Loma, it meant little sleep for him, only an ever watchful eye. He must judge by the gradual disappearance of the lights around the bay when the time had come to start the fog bell.

The mechanism of the bell was a simple but beautiful piece of polished clockwork. Weights suspended beneath served to regulate the timing of the bell strikes. The weights descended slowly into a ten-foot-deep square pit, and were then brought back up by an hourly winding of the clockwork. On very rare occasions the mechanism came to an abrupt halt. Until repairs were made it was then necessary to hit the bell by hand, and to keep the proper timing of the strokes by the use of a stop watch, for it was the time between strokes that informed captains of the location and identification of the signal. This procedure could hardly be classified as fun as it meant sitting outside in the cold, and methodically swinging a heavy hammer at regular intervals, and then being subject to the deafening sounds of the bell.

As kids, we sometimes dared our unwary friends to stick their heads inside the bell while we gave a lusty bang on the outside. Once was enough! It was far more effective than placing your head inside a bucket and having someone swat it, for the ringing of the bell was almost completely deafening, leaving ears throbbing and ringing. For the rest of the day, anyone who lent himself to this form of medieval torture, roamed around with a very strange look. It's just a little less than a miracle that my brothers and I did not suffer some degree of permanent deafness. But on this day our thoughts had been of the young seal, and there had been no time for any peculiar forms of diversion.

Conversation was hushed. Dad finished his supper and went off to rest for a short while before taking the second watch from midnight to dawn. I ate too much gravy-laden pot roast and had little room for dessert. But according to a strange and ridiculous custom established by my brothers and myself, one could preserve rights to the dessert simply by taking a bite from our share. When my piece was handed to me, I took a small bite and put the rest away for later. This was a silly tradition carried to an extreme on the holidays, when portions of plum pudding and mince pie were cached away in secret places often to be forgotten. Dishes were sometimes uncovered with the food no longer in a edible state. This whole thing distressed

Mother very much, for food was always plentiful. Jams, jellies and cakes reposed daily on the pantry shelves, ready for the eating. Perhaps some modern psychologist could make something out of this sibling rivalry, but as far as we were concerned it was just an elaborate form of teasing. Fortunately for the family budget, our excursions into weird food habits occurred only once or twice a year, just enough to make our mother wonder what strange offspring had come to roost in her household.

After supper, I helped Mom with the dishes, but took time to glance out the window at the gloom. More fog had drifted in and was lowering to the bay. It was too dreary a night for a lost child of the sea to be wandering about alone. I wondered about Furry. When dishes were placed back on the shelves, I ventured out into the night, breathing deeply of the salt tang from the enveloping mist. It reached out and refreshed with every breath.

Through the gloom I could see the tide moving in, washing quietly over the rocks. Once in while there was the soft splash of a little fish jumping out of the water. Gradually the inexorable advance of the fog blotted out the surrounding area and muffled everything except the loud sounds of the fog bell at our station. Now and then the mournful wail of the fog signal at Point Loma Lighthouse stole through the night, and the lighter ringing sounds of ships' bells started nearby. This was before the time of radar or directional signals. Large vessels usually remained safely at anchor or stood off at the harbor entrance waiting for a clearing. Only the small fishing boats dared to thread their way through the narrow channel, with skippers blowing lustily on fishhorns to warn others of their progress and location.

Out on the pier I watched two birds resting quietly like decapitated creatures, with their heads tucked away in the snug shelter of their wings. Tiny fish left little phosphorescent streaks as they darted about near the surface of the water, perhaps trying to escape some larger predator. The kerosene lantern I carried gave out only a small glow of light, and I could see nothing along the beach. I thought to myself that wherever the seal was, he was in a spot well hidden from sight. The swiftly descending chill air finally chased me home to an early bedtime.

The next morning the fog quickly retreated to its ocean lair, fleeing before the onslaught of the warm sun. There was very little noise from downstairs. I heard only the quiet movements of Mom as she gathered up the remains of breakfast and washed the dishes. I dressed and went downstairs to fix my own breakfast. I placed a

slice of bread on a fork and toasted it golden brown over the coals
of the open stove. It was soon ready for a heaping of apricot jam.
A tall glass of fresh milk and a short conversation with Mom concluded a hasty repast.

My brothers had already left very early to try their luck at spearing fish. During the night halibut shuffled their way beneath a light
layer of sand in shallow water. Here they rested with only the shadows of their outlines visible, highlighted by the protruding eyes.
Before the morning wind disturbed the surface of the water, a quick
thrust of a spear could bring up a twenty-pound halibut, and a two-
inch halibut steak made a tasty dinner. Ray and El were energetic
souls and needed more than just wandering about the beach in search
of a truant seal, but I still couldn't give up the hunt for Furry.

As I left the house, they came back grinning, lugging a huge flat
fish. "Do you have to drag that thing along the sidewalk? Don't bring
it up on the porch!" Mom shouted, as she established her usual early
morning barricade around her immaculate home.

"Gee, we thought you'd want to see it. It's a whopper. Want
some for dinner?" El teased her.

"I'll enjoy looking at it more after it's cleaned. Now get it away
from here and stop dragging it along the sidewalk."

"Okay, Mom," Ray answered.

Dutifully, my brothers managed to hoist the dripping fish so that
it hung over El's right shoulder, slobbering down his clothes, and
slapping his backside as he walked off. Mom threw up her hands
in despair and retreated to the kitchen. Here she could take out her
frustration on a freshly mixed batch of bread dough.

"Save a piece for Furry when he comes back," I shouted.

"Ha, ha! We'll give you the whole fish if he shows up," El
laughed back.

I could hear Mom kneading the dough with loud thumps as I
hosed off the slimy walk. The boys left, leaving me to go after a sign
of Furry. The seaward shoreline disclosed no sign of the seal, only
gulls with full stomachs lazily riding the little waves. I continued
around the point, crossing the wave-tumbled rocks and past the little
sand spot below the bell tower. The tide was rushing out the narrow
channel entrance, making it impossible for any but the very strongest
oarsmen to pull their rowboats round the bend and into the wider,
less restless expanse of the bay. Some fishermen waited out the fast
ebbing tide, others walked the shore pulling the boats against the
tide. This was almost as difficult as rowing the boat. One man had
to heave on the lines as he stumbled over the smooth stones, while

the other fisherman used an oar to keep the boat out from the shore. There were many sudden dunkings in the water and flops on the beach from unexpected shifts of balance.

I retraced my steps over the shoreline carefully searching all the secluded spots. Disappointment crept over me as I moved along, still hoping for a glimpse of the little animal before lunch.

After a hearty noon meal I took up my vigil once again. It was a long afternoon for me as I sat on the beach outside the carpenter shop. Dad came out twice to shake his head and pat me on the back. His silence filled me with more despair, but I was determined to keep hoping.

Then late in the day, I spied an object moving just a speck above the surface of the bay. My heart beat faster as I stared. I couldn't be sure, but my hopes increased as the distance lessened between us. I remained very still. It was Furry! Could a wild creature remember gentle hands and kindness over so short a period of friendship? I moved closer to the edge of the water and hunched quietly down on the rocks. Furry slipped below the water, leaving only a slight ripple to mark his dive, then suddenly the surface was broken by a stirring of the area nearby. There was the lift of a brown head, alert and inquisitive, as though seeking a safe haven for rest. Brown eyes glinted in the sun and turned in my direction. I remained frozen to the spot, for I feared that with a careless move, all might be lost. For what seemed an interminable period, he circled and dived, swam back and forth, and dived again as if to test the assurance of his welcome. And slowly, there was the advance of friend toward friend as I moved into the water. We met in the shallow depths of the blue waters, the trustful gaze of a baby seal turned upward to me. For a moment indecision gripped me, then without another thought I leaned down and stroked the supple body so close. There was no nip of sharp teeth this time, just a pair of eyes staring unblinkingly at me as if to say, "you really are my friend."

He flopped out onto the beach and we both settled down for a bit of silent communication, secure in the knowledge that no harm could come of trusting one another. Furry still appeared thin. With a final admonition for him to stay there, I ran off to get a choice bit of halibut. Mom barely glanced in my direction, as in one breath and motion I asked for the fish, grabbed a sharp knife to whack off a good-sized chunk before she had time to protest. I ran back to the beach. This time there was no forced feeding, only a quick gulping of the boneless morsels. With the last bit of his dinner still in my hand, I coaxed Furry even higher up on the beach, where he curled up and settled down like a small pup ready for a nap. Dad had glanced out the shop window and came out to smile at me.

"Don't expect him to come back every day," Dad cautioned. "As soon as he feels better he'll leave for good."

"I don't care. He came back today." I knew my father was preparing me for a day of sadness.

But Furry didn't leave that day nor the next. He waxed fat and lazy, with frequent swims and sunnings on the beach, and with appetizing meals served regularly to his taste.

The seal pup rapidly became a lovable pet for us all. One day I asked Dad how we could train the little fellow to follow us around at our bidding. Dad's sense of humor sometimes proved the undoing of his trusting offspring. This time he suggested that a bucket full of sea water and a nice fresh fish might be fine training devices. But a large heavy galvanized bucket filled almost to the brim in one hand and a small fish in the other do not lend themselves to a balanced load, especially in the grip of an eight-year-old. Nevertheless his suggestion seemed very logical to me.

Down the boardwalk I started, carrying the lures, with Furry not far behind. The first steps were slow and awkward, but he flopped along faithfully right behind the bucket and dangling fish. But I couldn't move fast enough and somehow this lovable bundle of fur grew into a monster as he snapped at the fish. I'll never know why I became so frightened, but I did, and the training session became a mixture of overturned bucket, watersoaked trainer, and nuzzling seal. I sat unhappily in a puddle of salt water and tears. This brought Furry's extra curricular activities to an abrupt halt. That night at supper when my father blandly asked how the lessons were coming along, I proudly stated, "Oh, Furry's so smart, I don't think he needs any more lessons."

There was a silent answer in the twinkle from Dad's eyes, and again I was reminded that wild things should be allowed to pursue their instinctive ventures, free and clear of human direction. Thereafter, the little seal trailed behind us when it pleased him to do so and no further effort was made to impose our wishes on him.

19

And Say Goodbye to a Friend

As the days rolled by, Furry took his daily swims and forays after food, but always returned to sun on the beach and always welcomed our presence. We loved watching him frolic in the calm waters of the bay and marveled as he tested his new strength against the tidal flow. He still took a bite of fish from our hands, but really preferred getting his own meals. Most of all he still relished the rubdowns we gave him regularly to keep him free of the oil lingering in scattered areas on the beach. Now he willingly trailed us, but this was not encouraged, for sooner or later he would dive into the water and head away from us. For this great event, all his natural instincts had to remain uncluttered and unfettered by human relationships. He often flopped about near the house although land travel was slow and tedious, and when he meandered into the yard, the jealousy of our old tomcat and the overwhelming size of our gentle collie discouraged him from establishing any close relationship with the animals. His laborious path was still marked by faint oil smudges, especially along the white picket fence.

At the end of that first month, the seal, now much stronger, happily flexed his lithe muscles periodically continuing to test himself day after day by swimming vigorously back into the cove against the fast outgoing tides. Each venture took him farther and farther away from us, with lengthened absences, but at the end of these distant trips a tired seal still came back to flop upon the beach for a rest. None of this changed his attitude toward us. He maintained his quiet friendliness, enjoying a brushing of his now clean and velvety coat. I'm sure it was a concession on his part, but nevertheless a task we enjoyed to the fullest.

"He's ready to leave," Dad told us once again. "Any day now he'll be swimming out of here. You can see how big he is getting."

His words were strangely prophetic, for the next day and the next showed no sign of Furry. Loath to say farewell to our little friend, we hunted up and down the beach and sought out each favorite sunning spot, scouring every foot of the point over and over again. My brothers finally gave up. There were more important things to occupy their active minds and bodies, but I continued to follow the old faint smudges of oil here and there, but could find no clue as to Furry's whereabouts. An increasing sense of loss deadened my world. There did not seem to be any logic for the sudden disappearance, but was there logic in our interpretation as to how and when a young seal should follow his instincts?

"Something's happened to Furry. He's hurt or sick. I just know it," I spoke to my family at the dinner table in hopes of some support.

My brother El looked at me in his most philosophical manner and pronounced ponderously, "What it is, we'll never know." And with that, he apparently dismissed the seal from his mind, but knowing El I knew he was just as unhappy as the rest of us.

"I guess we'd better try to forget about it," Ray added. It had been the fourth day of a hopeless search.

After breakfast the following morning I combed every building area, every cranny and nook, even the recesses of the woodpile, under bushes in the garden and far beneath the wharf. I refused to give up. Nothing was left untouched, but my efforts were fruitless, and at last I climbed up to the bell tower to be alone in my misery. Here the ocean area could be scanned more easily. Mom had handed me the lighthouse binoculars with a cautioning word, but all I could see on the ocean's surface were clumps of loose kelp borne landward by the south wind. Nothing stirred along the beach area. I sat on the platform, with my elbows on my knees and my chin in my hands, still hoping to see something, anything, even slightly resembling a small brown head. But as the hours passed, so did hope.

"Hey, Norm, Norm, where are you? Mom wants you to come home for lunch," El yelled.

Through long practice, our voices were really exercised to carry, and when voices didn't, a loud old police whistle brought us home in a hurry. A voice could sometimes be shrugged off, but never the peremptory challenge of that whistle when Mom blew it lustily. The sound of its harsh shrilling tone broke into my reverie, and reluctantly I moved off the platform and down the steps, holding the binoculars tightly. We had always been instructed to look carefully when moving about on steps or ladders, and I was no less careful this time, but one step down was all I took. My eyes had spotted something unbelievable. There at the bottom of the deep weight pit of the bell tower was a familiar round blob in a very strange place.

"Furry? Furry?" It was more a questioning than a call. There was a slight ripple of movement in answer, or was it just my imagination playing tricks? A headlong flight down the steps and a quick dash over to the pit. There I saw our lost friend. He lay crumpled in a tight circle at the bottom of the narrow deep hole. "Stay there! I'll get you out." And I ran off to spread the good news. It was hardly likely that the seal would leave in my absence. The hole had become a shadowy prison into which he had fallen on one of his meanderings around the point.

Lunch was quickly shoved aside to stay warm as we all converged on the site of the bell tower, only to gaze in helplessness, knowing that none of us could descend into the small space, nor could the seal be dug out. The pit had been carefully lined with cement to keep loose rocks from tumbling against the weights or filling in the hole. One suggestion after the other was offered and discarded, and it looked as though Furry was doomed to a death by slow starvation. Dad had been very quiet while the rest of us rattled on with our wild ideas. When we had exhausted our imaginations and were left gawking in tearful silence, Dad gave a few quick, simple orders.

"Get a couple of those long bamboo poles you use for fishing. Get the biggest and the longest ones, and bring a batch of that old Manila rope outside the carpenter shop. Get the softest pieces you can find."

My brothers and I scrambled off to follow his directions. We knew then that all was going to be well. Dad always came up with a solution to our problems, and we were sure this one would be solved too. We rushed back, our arms laden with the rope and poles.

"You brought enough rope to make a towline for a battleship," Dad laughed as he took some of the material and settled himself comfortably, while the rest of us gathered around to watch him at work. It always fascinated me how he knew exactly what to do in any situation.

Within minutes he had secured long strands of rope to one end of each of four poles. "Well, now let's give it a try." Dad moved over to the side of the hole, handed three of the poles to us, keeping one for himself. "Now lower the poles down along the sides, but hang on to the loose rope end. Ray, you and El stay on that side, and Norm and I will work from over here. And lower those poles slowly so you don't jab him."

With painful slowness we edged the poles down into the pit until they just barely touched our little wanderer. "Ready? Now see if

View of Ballast Point from the channel. Victorian style dwellings and bell tower. Light attached to dwelling. *San Diego Historical Society-Ticor Collection.*

you can work the ropes underneath him.''

Furry wriggled a slight protest as we painstakingly tried to maneuver the homemade sling under him. The heavy bamboo poles were awkward to move about with so little leverage from above, and I could not handle my share. After Dad had his rope in place, he leaned over me and, grasping my hands on the bamboo, helped me to complete the job. I was so happy he had not taken it away from me, because I wanted to be a part of helping to save Furry. When we finally had the crude sling in place beneath the seal, we carefully, oh, so carefully, lifted Furry up and out into the light once again. He was so weak he did not struggle. As he came over the top, his muzzle lifted skyward to sniff the salt-laden air, and he stared at us accusingly as if to say, ''who pushed me?''

We slapped each other on the back and whooped as we jumped up and down. Dad grinned broadly and even Mom clapped her hands and hugged me. She was never given to great outward expression of emotion, but I knew she was very happy from the shining look on her face. There had not been such a joyous moment on Ballast Point in a long, long time. Loving lands carried him back to our house and there in the safe confines of the yard, he was placed in a large box, not to be imprisoned, but for care and rest. We had no way of knowing if he had been injured in the fall, although Dad reassured us that other than some minor bruises and lack of food and water he did not appear injured.

My brothers and I quickly went out to dig for clams. It was almost high tide and difficult to find them. El found two strays and went off to the little pier to catch some fish. Ray and I kept looking for the mollusks, but before we could locate any, El came running back with a little halibut in his hands. We all hurried back to the yard with the prize. The meat was soft and tender. Furry needed no lengthy coaxing. He was ravenous and gulped pieces of fish as fast as we could cut them off. Dad and Mom looked on in amusement.

''Not too much at once. You'll make him sick. Better get a bucket of salt water and pour over him. His coat is dry.''

Not one, but five buckets of cold refreshing briny liquid splashed over the little seal, and he enjoyed every drop, shaking and rippling his fur coat after each shower. His every action indicated no real harm done by his fall, just a very frightened, half-starved animal.

''Let him stay here for a day or two. After that you can take him down to the water. We'll know better then just how strong he is,'' Dad advised.

So the young seal rested, well fed and undisturbed, snug and warm in the box. He was fed and showered daily, and on the third morning began to move about in protest within the confinement of the box. We took him out and he flopped happily around the lawn. Dad and Mom came out to check on him, and laughed with us at the seal's quick recovery.

The following morning the sun shone bright and clear, free of any lingering fog, and just right for the launching of a small craft. Our family gathered outside for the great event. We all felt that this day would be the beginning of a new life for our friend of the sea. We carried the box with its precious cargo down to the water's edge and slowly turned it on its side, rolling Furry gently onto the smooth stones near the water. He looked at us questioningly, wonder deep in his eyes, as we all took turns giving him gentle farewell pats. Then he flopped awkwardly into the water—a little splash, a short swim, and finally after a few short dives, he moved out to join the fast-ebbing tide. We watched his head come occasionally to the surface for a fresh gulp of air, and then he disappeared from sight, headed for the ocean. We didn't know then, but this was the last we would ever see of Furry. With our loss of this lovable friend, we all hoped the new life would be all Furry could hope for.

20

That Wasn't Funny

E at or you'll get sick," Mom reminded us as she set a huge platter of pancakes on the table and filled our cups with steaming cocoa. "What are you up to today?" She always asked us even though the answer rarely changed. On these warm summer days, the cool waters of the cove beckoned to us.

"Oh, we'll fool around our pier for a little while and then go over to the fort wharf. The kids are all going swimming this morning. Can we have a couple of sandwiches to take along?" Ray asked.

Mom nodded. "I'll give you some brown sugar ones. They won't spoil. Are you going to take Norma?" She was always happy to have us out of the way for a little while. It gave her much needed uninterrupted time to do all her work around the house.

My brothers glanced at me with that "do we have to?" expression and El grinned. "Sure, there'll be some girls she can play with."

The hotcake stack flattened out to a last one. I wanted to eat more, but couldn't. El and Ray shared it.

We slipped into our bathing suits and as we dashed out the door, Mom handed El a sack. She held me back for a moment. "Here's something you can take."

I peeked inside. It was a bag of walnuts. "Thanks, Mom." It was always nice to have something extra to share with the others. I gave Mom a big hug.

By the time my short legs carried me to the pier, my brothers had already untied a boat and were beginning to row away.

"Wait for me," I yelled, but my brothers continued on their way leaving a frustrated sister on the pier. I climbed down into the little rowboat that Dad had designated for my use. It was too small to rent out, but just right for me. The oars were short and lightweight. With a good steady stroke the little boat would really skim across the water. I didn't catch up with El and Ray, but I wasn't far behind either. It was an easy pull over to the fort. The Army kids were down

on the float yelling for us to hurry up, and they greeted us with raucous "hellos." Most of this young Army brigade was full of normal
fun and mischief, but there was always that one individual who
somehow managed to create more than the usual friction that sometimes exists on military posts.

The major's son was just such a pest. He picked on little children,
and ran to his parents for support when the complaints rolled in.
We all disliked Henry, but he had a right to be on the swimming float
with us and there wasn't much we could do about it.

Everybody was having a grand time this lovely morning, doing
silly things. We jumped from high off the wharf into the water—the
greater the leap, the louder the cheers. Tiring of this we started "Follow the Leader," one of our favorite games, usually the main event
of the day, and often as arduous and daring as the Army obstacle
course. Around and around we went tirelessly, off the pier, into the
water, and out among the barnacled pilings, risking badly scratched
arms and legs. We did bellyflops and ran up and down the soft sand,
and finally took a rest. That day the final round eliminated all but
the most daring, a twelve-foot leap off the pier to the beach below.
Mixed moans and cheers greeted our leader's choice as heads peered
apprehensively over the railing. Courage evaporated rapidly.

"Hey, here I go." And over jumped Bill, like a true leader, knees
bent, ready to absorb the impact of the landing.

"That ain't fair. You've been practicing," one weak soul protested, searching for a way to retreat.

"What difference does that make? Come on down, scaredy cats!
Girls first!" Bill grinned at his cohorts who cheered lustily at this
announcement.

"You go first. You're the oldest," Betty suggested.

"Not me! Jane's older than me." Mary shoved Jane to the front.

There was considerable jockeying for last place, while the boys
jeered at our hesitation. So we started to retreat in the face of the
insults, still trying to preserve some semblance of dignity.

"Aw, there go the sissies. You can't play with us anymore," Bill
scoffed, and off trotted the triumphant group, flinging parting
taunts. They were equally relieved at having escaped the leap. On
the beach below, Bill glared in disgust at the abandonment of his
idea. "You can all go jump in the bay for all I care."

His great inspiration seemed doomed by lack of eager participants. We all knew there would be no end to the reminders of our
cowardice unless at least one of the female gathering stepped forth
as a sacrifice. The whole thing was typical of Bill. We thought he

was just plain nuts when he had the opportunity to be the leader. Whenever he was, some unlucky one usually ended up as a litter case. Still someone had to quiet the group.

I climbed part way up the railing to see what my brothers were doing all this time. I should have known better.

"Yea, yea, for Norm. There she goes," Jane enthused. I had no intention of going. Before I could get back, someone gave me a boost from behind and I found myself teetering at the top of the railing.

"Who's a sissy?" Mary encouraged. I was getting all kinds of vocal help; the air rang with plenty of cheers, but no offers to follow me. It was too late to turn back after all this publicity. With all those hands patting me on the shoulders and backside, I began to waver. Then someone gave me that inevitable push for which I was totally unprepared. I was still in the thinking stage when I plunged off into space. The short trip afforded no time to establish an easy landing. The beach came up abruptly and so did my right knee under my chin, snapping my jaws together. My teeth cut through my lower lip sending out little spurts of blood, and the gash drew "oohs and ahs" from my admirers. Even Bill acknowledged that the game had come to a fine conclusion. The cool salt water stemmed the flow of crimson, leaving only an aching and severely puffed lip. There would be questions to answer at home.

After all this excitement, we stretched out on the swimming float and munched at the snacks we traded with each other. My offering, the bag of walnuts, was saved for dessert. Into this peaceful gathering strutted Henry.

"Whatcha doing?" Henry wanted to know.

"We're lying down here and flying like birds. Whadya think we're doing?" Bill was disgusted.

Henry tried again, "How about a race, over to the quartermaster's wharf and back?" Swimming was the one thing he excelled in.

Stony silence from the rest of us. In exasperation, Henry began to stomp on the remaining sacks of food. I got up and grabbed my bag of walnuts, but made the mistake of turning my back on him. A sharp shove from behind and over the side I plunged, still clutching my bag of nuts. Instead of surfacing immediately, I found myself coming up under the float. Unfortunately it had no safety exit up through any section. It was just like an inverted box with the bottom cut out, and there I was—trapped. The quick immersion gave me no time to fill my lungs with precious air. With lungs bursting, I blindly scratched my way to the outer edge. My head finally broke through to the sunlight, and I saw frightened faces staring at me from

Mom and Dad taking a rest on the scraggly lawn he managed to maintain in spite of salt water intrusion.

above. Horribly scared and filled with anger, all I could see for the moment was Henry's gloating face, and hearing his, ''yah, yah, yah, you can't swim.''

I clambered back on the float, took a quick step toward the nasty boy, clenched my fist, and reached up and popped him in the nose as hard as I could. It made a nice crunching sound and I knew I had

had my revenge. Henry ran off howling to tell tales of his terrible mistreatment by the lighthouse keeper's daughter.

As Henry bellowed his way home, the others escorted me across the cove like a conquering Valkyrie, cheers ringing in my ears. There was less to cheer about at home. Dad thoroughly disliked unpleasant encounters with the military. I dreaded the ordeal of detailing the afternoon's events not out of fear of punishment, but because of adding just one more troublesome worry to the mind of an already overworked father. He just shook his head that evening when I told him. Nothing more was said. Everyone knew Henry. Now we just had to wait for the fireworks from his doting parents.

Three days later an impressive government letter arrived by mail. It issued a stern warning. In the event of any further misbehavior by the lighthouse children on military property, both keepers would be temporarily denied certain fort privileges, such as transportation, movies, and commissary admittance. Dad made it plain to us that from then on our behavior was to be exemplary.

The news made the rounds of the fort and although we had the sympathy of all, the major was a ranking officer. His complaint had to be acted on. He reckoned without the ingenious thinking of young children. Our loyal swimming group held an emergency session and planned a simple but non-violent retaliation. From here on Henry was to be ostracized. We would not talk to him, not even answer his insults. We would not play with him, rather we would retreat from his presence.

Henry couldn't wait to get down on the float the first day we were back swimming. He approached, smirking and acting like a bit of royalty. We just went on with our chatter, ignoring him completely. This infuriated him so much, he began to berate us with foul language. That still brought no reaction from us, so he resorted to pushing and slapping. That did it! We all crowded into the rowboats, and pulled away, laughing at Henry's chagrin. The rest of the day was peaceful. He had again retreated home to spout his complaints. The ensuing morning brought the expected reaction.

Down the wharf strode an irate father, Henry quick-stepping behind. Our planned strategy awaited the opening blast.

"You kids have been mean to Henry. He says you won't let him play with you. Now I want that corrected right now. Do you understand?"

"Yes, sir!" we replied in unison.

Bill stepped forward, "But Major, we were only trying to help Henry." Our leader was wise beyond his years.

"Help! Henry doesn't need any help," the major retorted.

"Oh, yes sir. Henry isn't as strong as some of us and sometimes when we play he gets hurt very easily. We just thought it would be better to play by himself. That way we wouldn't hurt him and we wouldn't get into any more trouble with you. He almost drowned Norma under the float, so she got a little sore. But that won't happen again, we promise, 'cause we'll stay away from him and not bother him any more." Bill was amazingly cool.

The major glared at us and his face reddened. Schooled in military tactics, he was totally lacking in the ability to counter-attack this bit of psychological warfare. Father and son beat a hasty retreat, Henry half-hopping and half-running to keep up, never once glancing back to see our celebration of triumph. When they were well out of earshot, we let out war whoops, gathered around Bill, and slapped him on the back. That day he had the pick of all our choice snacks. But one last problem still clouded the air. If Henry's mother entered the fray, we could expect a vociferous campaign that might well stir up the whole fort.

For three days serenity beamed down on us, but the atmosphere was still charged with tension. Henry's father was not one to give up easily and his words carried a heavy impact. But Henry was nowhere to be seen, his mother nowhere to be heard, and his father was observed just once going to the commanding officer's headquarters. The unexploded bomb still hung over us and we were really beginning to worry.

On the fourth day, down the ramp to the float came a reluctant and apprehensive Henry, a totally miserable ten-year-old boy. "Can I play with you again?" he pleaded. He wriggled uncomfortably as blank stares met his inadequate request. "I'm sorry I pushed you, Norma," he went on.

We went on talking to one another as though a boy named Henry never even existed.

Finally there was a last desperate effort. "I promise not to run home any more, no matter what. I promise, honest, if you'll just let me play too."

Bill called us all over to one end of the float for consultation while Henry awaited the decision. His utter capitulation stirred a bit of pity in our hearts, and we felt sorry he had to live with such parents. We decided to readmit him to the human race, but not without again stating his promise to cease being a complainer and tattletale.

Henry told us later about the three-day silence. The commanding officer had had enough, and in blunt terms had told the major it would be wise to cease the trivial complaining. Henry really tried to be one of the gang. He never quite succeeded, and there were times when he sorely tried our patience, but we remembered the two big handicaps he had at home. We were quick to forgive minor mistakes, and we no longer lived in fear of being denied fort privileges.

After months of hard labor hauling out cobblestones, our family at last has a start on a garden. Mom takes time in the morning to water the plants.

21

Water, Water, Go Away!

At extreme high tides, Ballast Point barely kept its head above water, so close was it to sea level that heavy storm waves frequently washed over parts of it.

In spite of this, my father and brothers spent long back-breaking hours clearing rocks from around our immediate dwelling in order to create a garden. Wheelbarrows full of cobblestones were hauled away to be emptied at the high part of the beach. After months of hard work, they finally brought in rich soil to fill in the excavated areas. This too, seemed to require endless time and effort. When at last the soil was in and strewn with aged horse manure from the nearby stable, we waited for the mixture to become a rich loam. Mother had appointed herself the chief gardener, for she knew exactly what she wanted in that garden, and her previous experience at Point Bonita qualified her for the job.

The day of planting came and Mother had assigned all of us a definite plot of ground, given us each a packet of seeds, and some detailed instructions. She delegated herself to planting tomato seeds. Dad had already stationed himself in the front yard with a big bag of grass seed. And literally, "come hell or high water," he was determined to have a front lawn, with a flower bed here and there. We made our rows, and carefully sowed the seed. A fine soft spray of the hose and the work was complete. Now all we had to do was wait for our crops to appear.

We had planted our garden in the warm days of August, hoping the sun would work wonders for us that late in the planting season, and that the evening fogs would be temperate. The high tides of August worried us, but this was not our winter season and sou'westers ordinarily did not occur at this time. Lovely weather blessed us and warmed the ground. But Dad reminded us that the passing ships still were a hazard to us. Nothing angered my father more than the unnecessary inundations of our grounds periodically by the Navy vessels or the speeding coastwise steamers, Harvard and Yale. The passengers loved to see their ships tearing out the channel leaving a high wake. Advertisements by ships' companies boasted that their vessels were the fastest on the coast for the trip between San Diego and San Francisco. These white liners ripped out past our little station, completely ignoring the height of the tide. At low tide the waves broke harmlessly on the shore, but when the water was high our cellar got flooded.

The Navy destroyers wreaked havoc too, but after a few letters from Dad, we had a spell of good luck from them. A bulwark was later erected and it gave us excellent protection from high seas.

Then a completely unexpected flood hit us during the rainy season of 1916. San Diego city officials had employed a rainmaker named Hatfield who contracted to work in an effort to bring more moisture to our dry area. He built elevated platforms in our back country, from which he sent up billows of smoke filled with a chemical. He was one of the first cloud seeders. He did his job well and was so successful that soon torrential rains pounded San Diego and the surrounding areas. After days of heavy downpour, the ground became saturated and the dams filled to overfilling. Most of the San Diegans just grumbled a bit at the inconvenience of wet weather, but others cast worried looks at our dams which had never been tested by such pressure before. Excess water rushed down the spillways, but even they were being overtaxed, and there seemed to be no end of the cloudbursts from the sky.

Mission Valley was aflood from bank to bank. The bridge at Old Town had gone out. But other trouble this night in January 1916 was in the making. The spillways at the Lower Otay Dam could not handle all the water coming at them, and the thin rock core of the dam broke loose, sending a flood of water rushing down the valley and into San Diego harbor. A ferry landing lookout spotted a section of torn bridge as it floated by the Coronado ferry landing. The great torrent swept away everything in its path—animals, homes, crops— and deposited them in the bay. Here this sudden avalanche made the harbor water fresh for nearly one-quarter of a mile. Mangled bodies of cattle were washed ashore as far down the bay as La Playa. The sudden rise of the bay water, enough to flood the areas around our house, puzzled us. In the morning as we observed sections of broken homes and dead farm animals drifting past the point, we began to realize that something awful had happened. We saw no people, just the animals which were beyond our aid. Except for a few frightened chickens roosting on lengths of broken wood, the rest of the livestock had perished in the first few minutes.

Our own basin-shaped ground was covered with water, and in order to leave the house the first few days, we used a small rowboat to paddle out to the coal shed for fuel, or to the carpenter shop to do some tinkering. Our house, which was built up four feet above ground, suffered no damage, except for the butter barrel floating around in the cellar in a little extra brine. We had learned from past experience and all cellar food stuffs were sealed in watertight containers, which left us only the inconvenience of waiting for the water to subside. Day by day the ground began to dry out leaving little smelly pools here and there.

My brothers and I scoured the entire beach later, picking up odd bits of debris and avoiding the unpleasant objects. We had before us a small panorama of one of life's tragedies, part of a chicken coop, railroads ties, a dead creature, a rooftop. For days we wandered about seeking the unusual, but the excitement wore off for El and Ray. They had gathered nearly five hundred standard railroad ties and piled them in a neat array. Twenty cents for the fair ones and thirty cents for the good ones would bring a good amount of cash. My brothers went back to the fun of swimming and fishing and left me to beachcomb.

A few days later I was idly poking among the rocks on the beach. The fun was rapidly dissipating for me, too. Then the slow wriggle of a tiny tail around a rock caught my eye. It certainly didn't look like part of an established resident of our region, so I grabbed it and pulled. Out came a foot-long beautiful thing, with faint tracings of a dark diamond along its back, and there attached to one end was a cute little button. This was a prize and demanded immediate recognition from the rest of the family. Dad would be the first to offer congratulations, I was sure. He was outside by the wood-chopping block, splitting some kindling for the stove.

"Bet you can't guess what I found! Nobody else has got one."

My father stopped and rested while he answered. "A bird, no? How about a starfish? Hm, well I give up."

Triumphantly I swung my find up before his startled eyes. His bemused expression turned to a look of horror. I had never seen his dark tanned face go so pale in all my young life. Before I could blink my eyes, my lovely treasure ended up on the chopping block, and in a second had become a series of disjointed segments as Dad swung his axe. Then he grabbed me and unceremoniously I received a complete physical exam, along with repeated questioning as to whether or not I had been bitten. At last reassured, he sat down, wiped his brow and spoke. "Sorry I had to do that, but I think you ought to

Years after the event, Charles Hatfield scans newspaper reports of his cloud-seeding results. *San Diego Historical Society-Ticor Collection.*

know that even a baby rattlesnake is not something you pick up by the tail or any other way.'' And with that he gave a fatherly pat on my backside, and some more information about dangerous reptiles. I didn't sleep very well that night.

The city of San Diego recovered from that flood, but Hatfield never received any pay for his outstanding results. The city fathers thought he had overdone it a bit.

Assistant keeper shows my brothers how to start one of the torpedoes they have retrieved from the firing range.

22

Bounty Hunters

N avy drill exercises off Point Loma gave my brothers an opportunity to earn some extra money. Combined with noisy gunnery practice, the destroyers launched non-explosive dummy-head torpedoes as well. Early guidance systems were very unreliable and many of the torpedoes strayed far off course. After completion of the drills, small boats were launched to recover the weapons, but they often returned to the ships without all the torpedoes.

After each practice, Ray and El rowed back and forth across the outer channel for days, especially in the tangled kelp near the end of the long breakwater. Here they hoped to find that the tides had brought them good fortune. Too often aching backs and sunburnt noses were the only rewards.

One bitter windy day in November, the Navy ordered another drill. Large swells were running off Point Loma chasing small craft to shelter on the leeward side. Seagulls flew in great circles as though testing their wings against the buffeting winds before setting out for the Coronado Islands. There were other signs of the impending storm. A restless ocean tore kelp from its roots on the ocean floor and swept clumps ashore along the beach. Clouds scudded across a darkening sky.

We watched the Navy vessels steam out early in the morning. They had been preceded by the slower tugs towing the large floating targets. Crews of the tugboats hated this duty. It was hazardous. Gunnery crews in 1918 lacked the sophisticated aiming devices now in use, and shells periodically fell near the tugs and on one occasion a tug was hit. Happily there were no casualties.

The booming of the guns echoed against the hills of Point Loma. But as the morning wore on, the seas heightened and the tugs had great difficulty controlling the positions of the targets. Tow lines snapped leaving the targets to blow ashore on the Coronado Strand.

It was time to call a halt to the drill. Before long we spotted the ships heading back rolling from port to starboard in the heavy seas. They came charging up the channel with a "bone in their teeth," leaving a high wide wake behind them. A low tide saved us from another garden flooding. It was going to be a nasty night before this storm passed through.

Before I arose the next morning Ray and El had already rounded Ballast Point headed for the open sea in their little skiff. They strained their backs against the rough waters. Lingering swells were still breaking over the end of the jetty, but that's where the boys pointed the boat. They hoped to find a vagrant torpedo in that area. Late into the morning they scoured the channel and treacherous areas near the rocky jetty. Sometimes they edged dangerously close. With still no luck by noon, they rested their oars and ate lunch, allowing the boat to drift in the swells, using the oars occasionally to keep from hitting the breakwater.

If they were to have any success it would have to be in the next two hours before the ebbing tide. Pulling a torpedo in slack tide is a major task, but in rough seas and against the current it was nigh impossible. They continued eating, all the while surveying the nearby waters. Wind gusts swung the boat around on choppy waves. The boys did not want to get caught out in the tail end of the storm.

Ray slowly put down a half-eaten sandwich, and pointed toward a spot near the jetty. "Say, El, I think we've got one."

"Where?"

"Over there, in that big mess of kelp, see?"

"Yeah, but it just looks like loose kelp to me."

"Well, let's take a look anyway," Ray persisted.

"All right."

They bundled up the rest of their lunch and rowed over to the area.

"A little more on your right oar," El directed.

"Do you see anything?"

"Not enough to tell. It's low in the water, whatever it is. Take it easy. It's close to the rocks," El warned.

They pulled the skiff closer and, steadying it, carefully peered over the side. There rolling sluggishly in the seaweed lay their bounty, a stray torpedo.

"We're in luck," Ray whooped.

"Yeah," El yelled and slapped his brother on the back.

Skipping further conversation they cleared away the tangle of weed, and then while El steadied the skiff, Ray looped a rope around the missile a few times. He carefully snugged it down in a series of half-hitches. The more the torpedo pulled away the tighter the hitches grew. When the tying was complete, Ray gave the tow a shove away from the boat and hurried to help El at the oars. The wind had picked up again and it would require some skillful maneuvering and hard rowing to get this dead weight home.

They both pulled hard to move away from the rocks. Out in midstream, the slackening flood tide offered them assistance, but it still was hard to work against the angle of the stiff south wind. It put the boat almost against a crosswind and made the tow swing from side to side. The boys worked the boat onto a different course that placed them before a following sea, but this was equally bad. A following sea is one which comes from behind. Surfers start out on a following sea and allow the waves to bring them to shore. but a boat is in a dangerous position if it is not kept right on course. If it turns sideways to an oncoming wave, the boat could capsize. My brothers had the ability to handle their craft by itself, but with this heavy tow it was quite different. They were well aware of the danger involved, but hated to see their bounty money slip away when it was so close. So they rode the heavy swells, dodging the wild rushes of the torpedo as it charged down on them from behind. A single smash from it could have battered the rowboat to pieces and perhaps overturned it. A twelve-foot skiff is no match for a Navy torpedo. The boys were lucky.

An hour and a half of strenuous rowing at last brought my brothers to the pier with their prize. The thirty dollars reward for the return of the weapon to the U.S. Navy was going to be used in a joint venture as part payment for a very old motorcycle. Ray and El secured the torpedo to prevent it from banging against the wharf. "Let's see if it will run anymore," Ray ventured.

"Let's give it a try," El agreed.

Sometimes the weapons ran out their complete supply of fuel before coming to a stop. Others came to a halt when the propulsion system took a notion to shut off before reaching the target.

Ray squatted down on the torpedo and triggered the mechanism by hand. The propeller turned over and churned the water.

"You kids stop fooling with that." Dad poked his head out of the launch and made his order a firm one.

"Gee, Dad, we aren't hurting anything." El was a bit chagrined.

"I know that. Now call the Navy Station and tell them to come and get it. I want to bring the launch alongside the pier in a couple of days."

Ray climbed back up on the pier and my brothers pulled the torpedo around to the side and refastened it. Then they ran off home to inform the Navy. Strangely, the Navy always seemed to take its time about reclaiming such things, even at the cheap price of thirty dollars. Two weeks later a Navy whaleboat chugged down the bay and arrived at our pier. My brothers had been on the lookout for them day after day, and were on hand to meet the crew.

"Hear you have something for us to pick up," the bo'sun remarked.

"Yep, it's right around the side. We'll untie if for you," El offered.

The boys loosened the lines and brought the weapon around to the front of the pier. It didn't take long for the crew to take charge and be on their way up the bay. Before they left they handed over a receipt and assured the boys that sometime in the future they would be getting their bounty money in the mail. From past experience the boys knew that the future could be a good while away. El and Ray started along the boardwalk to the house watching the launch go up the channel.

"Hey, look. They've stopped. I wonder what's up?" El questioned.

"They're probably tightening the ropes. Why should we care. It's not our worry anymore. Come on, let's get home. Mom was going to bake a cake this morning and I'm hungry," Ray answered.

They gave only a passing glance at the sailors leaning over the side of the boat, hard at work on something.

Two days later a noisy telephone bombardment began. An irate Navy officer called and demanded to know who had tampered with the torpedo. Dad's mustache bristled and he fired back a full broadside of angry protestations and banged up the phone. He said nothing to us and I forgot all about the matter. Not Ray or El, they began to wonder if the thirty dollars was still on course.

Four days later I stopped at the Army post office to pick up our mail. A long official envelope addressed to Dad rested in our letter box. I ran all the way home with it, wanting to be the first to hear the news. My father was outside the carpenter shop cleaning paint brushes. He gave a quick warm smile as I handed him the message. But he just glanced at it, let out a disgusted "humph" and returned to his task. I knew better than to disturb him any more.

At the supper table we all ate quietly, knowing that Dad would choose his own good time to tell us the contents of the letter. The last cup of coffee had been poured and the last piece of cake sliced.

And then, with great deliberation he pulled out the crumpled letter.

It was an informal invitation to lunch with the captain of the U.S.S. Dayen. Included in the letter was the reward for the return of the torpedo. Dad handed the check to his happy sons.

My brothers read and reread the check while noisily planning their purchase of the motorcycle. Mom's curiosity broke into the clamor.

"Are you going?" she wanted to know.

"Sure, I have to find out what this is all about," Dad grinned.

"Seems kinda funny though." Ray had some doubts.

"Yeah, we got the check. What else is there?" El wondered.

"Better wear your good uniform, Hermann. I'll press it for you." Mom loved to see him dressed in his very best.

"Oh, I'll think about it." Dad was nonchalant.

We all helped to compose the reply, to avoid the mistakes in syntax that our father struggled with. In times of stress or excitement his Teutonic background often rose to the surface, and we couldn't have him embarrassed by minor errors in grammar. Four busy minds contributed flashes of humor.

"Why don't you tell him to go shoot another torpedo," El suggested.

"Yeah, and tell him to bring the ship alongside our pier and we'll all join him for lunch," Ray chimed in.

"Sounds like a trap to me. They'll probably feed you some old Navy beans and toss you over the side," I had to have my say.

"Want us to shine the buttons on your uniform?" El was serious.

"Leave your father alone," Mom scolded us, but she was laughing too.

On the next Tuesday, Dad, mustache trimmed, uniform pressed, buttons brilliant in the bright sunshine, rolled with his seaman's gait down to the little pier. The rest of us formed a grand entourage of proud family members. We cheered lustily as he took off in little "Useless" as dignified as any captain on the seven seas. We hoped he would enjoy the afternoon.

We took turns keeping watch for signs of the little launch on its return trip. Four o'clock came and wisps of the evening fog began to drift over Point Loma, presaging a cold, blind night. "Gee, Dad had better get back. He's got the first watch," El reminded us.

"Oh, we can start the fog bell. Norm, you go ask Mom what's for supper. I'm hungry." At the moment Ray was more worried about his stomach than anything else.

Happy to relieve tired muscles, I dashed home. Mom looked

anxious as she met me at the door. "Have you seen anything of your father? It's getting late and I'm a bit worried."

"Nope, and Ray wants to know what's for supper."

"Baked beans, and let me know when you catch sight of 'Useless'."

"I will, Mom. Baked beans! Oh boy!"

"Baked beans a la Engel," a labor of love, simple ingredients, plus hours of tender loving care. Beans simmered in water until partially cooked, firm, but with skins beginning to curl. Then drained and placed in a crockery bean pot, immersed in a mixture of sweetened tomato juice mixed with some of the drained bean water. A touch of salt and pepper to give a bit of character, and topped off with generous slices of good bacon.

The secret is in the baking as well as in the ingredients—low, low heat and constant attention to prevent burning or going dry. The result after eight hours—some magnificently browned beans rich in savory juice. For Mother, this meant a two day job, one for the initial boiling and baking, the second day to finish off the baking. Our stomachs and salivary glands suffered over this long interval, subjected as they were to so many hours of heavenly fragrance. Later, when the bean pot was set on the table and the first spoonful of beans made their appearance, Mom received the appreciation she truly deserved. The beans disappeared down to the last bit of nectar. Bread pushers scoured the plates spotless. No one ever baked beans like Mom.

I rejoined my brothers on their watch. The thickening fog cast gloom everywhere. "Say, that looks like the 'Useless' now." El pointed up the bay.

"Norm, go get the glasses," Ray ordered.

Mom frowned as the door slammed behind me. "Now what do you want?"

"Ray and El want the glasses. They think Dad's coming now."

"Be careful. Don't drop them," and the inevitable reminder, "remember, they're Lighthouse property." This was just like saying the binoculars belonged to the president of the United States and should have attendant care.

I handed the binoculars over to Ray and he peered through them. "Hey, it's Dad all right. Let's go meet him. Here Norm, you take the glasses back." I was always running errands for my brothers.

"Ah, he won't be here for another half hour. Let's get something to eat." It was El's happy thought this time. They beat me to the door, and to the freshly baked bread on the table.

"Leave that bread alone! You'll spoil your supper. Can't you wait 'til your father gets home?" Mom knew it was a hopeless battle.

"Nope!" we all said, and grabbed slices, covered them with slabs of butter and mounds of lumpy brown sugar, and ran out the door back to the pier. Mom really didn't mind. She was happy we had such good appetites. These snacks were a routine, planned and executed with precision every evening.

It took us only a minute to get back on the pier, and just in time to help Dad tie up the launch. We heard him shut off the engine, and were impatient as he carefully checked everything.

"What happened? Did they court-martial you?" El began the teasing all over again.

"Did you get a medal?" Ray joined in.

"You just wait. I'll tell you all about it at the supper table when your mother can hear it too."

"Hermann, is everything all right?" Mom opened the door to us.

"Just fine," he answered. "It's my watch and I want to check on the light and the fog bell. I'll be right back." And he left quickly toward the light tower.

"Supper in half an hour," she reminded him.

The fog had settled like a thick blanket of mist over the bay, and the bell began to toll its doleful sound. We gathered around the kitchen table close to the warmth of the cheerful wood stove, and talked about the day's events while we waited for Dad. In a few minutes he returned, washed his hands at the sink, and sat down at the table.

We were all hungry and before long the level of the beans in the pot lowered rapidly as the spoon dipped deeper. Milk, bread and butter disappeared almost as fast.

Dad polished off his plate, pushed back his chair and sighed, "Freda, that was *good*!"

Mom beamed her pleasure.

"Well, it was some day," Dad started his story. "Yesiree, some day. That young skipper was all right."

And then we all listened to the rest. Dad arrived at the ship on time. It was anchored in midstream. He was met at the gangway by a pair of alert sailors.

"The captain is waiting for you, sir."

Dad paused to make sure the launch was secure then stepped up the gangway. The shrill of a bo'sun's whistle suddenly split the air, and Dad looked in astonishment.

"Welcome aboard, sir. I'll show you to the captain's cabin."

This was getting a little ridiculous. The elaborate greeting was too much for a hardworking lighthouse keeper. The seaman knocked at the door.

"Captain Engel is here, sir."

"Come in, Captain. Glad you could make it."

There stood the skipper, very young for this command.

"Sit down, Captain." He motioned to the seaman. "Tell the steward we'll have lunch now." The door closed and the clean-cut officer turned to my father. He was chagrined as he plunged into an immediate apology.

"I'm sorry about the mix-up. I've learned quite a few things the last two months."

"Your first command, it is?" Dad tripped on his syntax again.

"Yes sir, never expected it so soon."

"Well you must deserve it or you wouldn't have the ship. Tell me, what did happen to that torpedo?" Dad had already guessed the answer.

The lieutenant looked uneasy for a moment and then laughed when he saw the twinkle in Dad's eyes. "Well, the whaleboat crew removed the alcohol from the torpedo. They drank it later, but they really banged up a few parts and damaged the thing quite a bit. Luckily, an oldtimer on another ship put me wise to what had happened. I'm glad you didn't make a complaint at headquarters," he said gratefully.

"No reason for doing that. It's over and done with," Dad assured him.

The lunch and afternoon passed in lively conversation. The skipper was genuinely interested in the tales Dad told of his days aboard the old wooden sailing vessels. Time passed too swiftly for both. At four o'clock Dad put down his coffee cup, thanked his host and set off homeward in "Useless." He was a happy man.

23

The Young Entrepreneurs

N ow at last, with the thirty dollars reward money firmly in their grasp, plus a bit more meager savings, my brothers planned to go ahead with their purchase of an old motorcycle they had been eyeing so long. It was a two-wheel scrap heap and the ridiculously low price should have been adequate warning. My parents knew of their hopes to get the bike. Dad told them of the dangers and shortcomings of such an acquisition. But Ray and El knew they could spend the money as they wished for they had earned it, and decided to do the buying the next day.

"Wonder where those boys are." Dad looked at Mom across the breakfast table early the next morning.

"They went over to the fort, Hermann," she answered. "They said they had to get something." Mom was busy at the stove and her mind was not on the conversation.

"Funny, they didn't say much about it. They could have picked up some groceries for you at the commissary." Dad was upset. It wasn't like my brothers to leave without first asking Mom if she needed anything. He glanced over at me for a hint of information, but as usual my brothers had kept me in the dark, too. I had a good idea what they were up to. They had talked a great deal in my presence. I wanted a ride on that motorcycle and knew that if I said one little word, the ride would never be offered. Dad looked skeptical when I shrugged my shoulders, but made no comment. He would have enough to say when the boys came home.

At eleven o'clock Ray and El loomed into sight far down the sandy spit on the wagon-rutted road, dragging, pushing and hauling a battered old contrivance. Now and then they lowered it to the road to rest themselves. Dad came out of the carpenter shop and joined me in staring at the sight.

"Looks like your brothers," he remarked sternly. "Yep, it is. What are they bringing home this time?" he questioned me.

"I think it's a motorcycle, Dad."

He watched in stunned silence. "Motorcycle! *Gott in Himmel*! What are those kids up to now?"

In one of his rare moments of exasperation he lapsed into idiomatic German. But then he broke into a hearty laugh, and leaned on the gate at my side to await the grand arrival. There had never been any doubt in my Dad's mind that the value of quality buying was again about to descend upon these embryo mechanics. Dripping with sweat and covered with dust and grease, the boys lowered their rusty machine to the ground before their father's critical gaze.

Ray announced unnecessarily, "We bought a motorcycle."

"It's real good. Just needs cleaning up," El added with a fifteen-year-old's typical assurance. They both awaited their parent's comment.

"Well, it does look like you might have a little work to do on it. Who sold it to you?"

"Oh, one of the fellows at the fort. He's being sent overseas, so we had a chance to buy it." El was puzzled at the lack of protest.

"Hm, well, don't use any of the shop tools when you work on it. You have enough old ones that will do the job. Leave the bike there for the time being. Your mother has lunch ready." Dad did not appear too disturbed. He might just have been thinking that his sons could well be out of puberty before they ever got that thing running.

Mom's horrified reaction was, "you'll kill yourselves!"

All through the meal Dad's eyes sparkled with amusement, as he tried to calm Mother. El and Ray gulped their food, thinking only of that first exciting ride, and dashed out to begin work on their new possession. I followed them later to make a closer inspection of the latest folly. To my eyes the wreck seemed beyond repair. It was certainly going to be a challenge to their indomitable spirits.

By evening, parts were scattered all over. Some lay immersed in a bucket of kerosene, others set aside to be sanded and painted. Only two worn tires and a bent frame gave any clues as to what the whole endeavor was about. I watched quietly as they worked feverishly the first hour or two, then the pace slackened as the machine was nearly disassembled. Still they worked through the dinner hour, no small miracle in itself. Mom kept their plates warm in the oven, hoping her sons would come to their senses before too late at night. Two weary boys crept into bed that night.

As the days wore on, it became evident that reassembling the bike might be delayed for quite a while. I was given the task of wire brushing and scraping the kerosene-soaked parts. It was painstakingly explained to me that not everyone was qualified to do this job. I had never read *Tom Sawyer*, so didn't realize that these two junior "con" artists were pulling a "Tom-Sawyer-painting-the-fence" trick, and had handed me the dirtiest job. It made little difference how carefully I handled the parts, pieces of metal gave way with rust, and by the time I had finished there were more than twice the number of pieces that had originally gone into the bucket.

Their greasy hands dripping with oil, El and Ray squatted in the middle of the debacle, and surveyed the remains. "We're gonna need some new parts." El whacked the proverbial nail right on the head with this remark.

"Say, do you think we should have bought this thing?" Ray was beginning to have some doubts.

"Oh, sure, a few new parts here and there, and we'll have it running in no time."

"Where are we gonna get the money?" Ray wanted to know.

"Look, we can caddy on the golf course. We've always picked up good tips there," El reminded him.

Tramp, tramp, after school and on Saturdays and Sundays, my brothers made the rounds of the golf courses earning a bit here and there. Enriched by such small earnings, they carried an old torn catalog for reference and scavenged used parts from junk yards. Within two months the bike began to take on a rebirth, with only a gear here or a bolt there needed to have the motorcycle in motion again. Although the motor had yet to utter its first snort, the slow but sure assembly filled my mother with dread and foreboding.

It did not make her any happier to see her husband give the boys a helping hand occasionally. We all had had the usual children's diseases. Mom accepted those as part of childhood, but she feared broken bones. And after many months, the day she had hoped would never come arrived. The family gathered to see the first trial run. The cycle stood shiny and bright, tires blackened, and everything that could stand a coat of paint had been painted a glorious red. I gazed in awe. Now that it was spotlessly clean, the bike appeared twice as large and powerful as when the boys had first dragged it home. Perhaps too powerful for a couple of inexperienced teenagers. but they were big and strong for their ages.

Ray jumped astride the machine, while El fiddled with the throttle. This was the simplest of bikes, started with a push or roll down a hill. Ray dismounted and my brothers wheeled their prize out to a level area.

"You get on and I'll push. Be sure you have the throttle turned so it'll get enough gas. And remember it starts in gear so you'd better be ready to go." El gave some quick instructions.

El heaved and shoved, but the weight was too much for him. He looked hopefully at Dad. Dad glanced at Mom and decided he had participated enough in the impending catastrophe. El tried again and moved the motorcycle a few feet, but it just emitted a few soft "whooshes."

"It's no use. You'll have to get off and help," he panted.

"All right." Ray got off and moved to one side, holding on to the handlebars. "You shove from the back. Ready?"

"Yeah, but remember this thing is in gear. You better hop on pretty fast when it starts."

"I know, I know! Now, come on. One, two, three and *push*!"

The bike rolled along slowly, then into a pretty good clip. Ray worked the throttle vigorously, and yelled at his younger brother. Bang! Bang! Amid a Vesuvian eruption of black smoke and choking shudders, the monster came to life jerking forward a few feet, before giving out a few consumptive coughs and lapsing into silence.

"It runs. It runs," Ray exulted.

"Not yet. It just barely started. I bet it needs more gas. Turn up the gas more this time." El thought he had the solution.

"Are you sure you know how to handle that thing?" For the first time Dad had his reservations.

"Sure thing, we've been riding bikes long enough." Ray was confident.

They pushed the motorcycle out to a small clear area and headed it toward the fort. Before them lay an almost limitless flight path to the Army buildings, straight but extremely hazardous because of the weather-washed ruts and dips and rocks thrown up by storm waves. In the other directions lay the dwellings, the pier, and the chicken yard.

"Let's give it another push." Ray couldn't wait. "One, two, three, *go*!"

With a great belch of smoke, a squealing spin of the back tire, the dragon leaped forward, pulling Ray off balance, but he hung on heroically and finally clambered aboard, headed for the rocky road to oblivion. His hand was glued to the throttle in a fixed position and he no longer had control of the speed. We all marveled at how he managed to keep his seat on the bouncing bike. The tremendous noise contributed to a sensation of speed that did not exist. El ran along close to Ray and yelled, "Cut the gas. It's in gear."

"I can't. It's stuck!" Ray made the mistake of turning his head to answer, and in so doing, steered his mount on to a different course.

"Look out! Turn it! Turn it! You're headed for the chicken yard!" El yelled.

Too late! Ray and the bike disappeared into a flock of squawking chickens and came to rest on the latest scrapings from the floor of the chicken coop. El and Dad ran to the wreck. Standing beside me, Mom at last opened her eyes and we walked over to the disaster.

"Is he hurt, Hermann?"

Dad was still leaning over Ray giving him a careful inspection. "No, I don't think so. Come on, son, see if you can get up." He pulled the bike away from my brother and helped him up.

"I'm okay, I think."

"Boy! You stink!" I said. My desire to have a ride on that contraption had quickly dissipated in the mess of feathers and manure.

"That's enough of that," Dad scolded. "You go back to the house with your mother. We'll take care of things here."

"Yes, come on, Norm." Mom was glad to get away from there. "You can take some clean clothes out to the wash house for them."

I went along reluctantly. It wasn't often I had a chance to laugh at my brothers, after all the daily teasing they handed me.

Ray limped painfully homeward, nursing a bruised leg, skinned nose, and hurt pride. Dad and El dragged the cycle out of the chicken yard and laid it to one side, stirring up more feathers and protests.

"Leave the bike here. You can bring it back to the shop tomorrow," Dad said.

The two of them followed Ray home. El went to the outside bathroom and helped him get out of his soiled clothes. Dad came in with strong disinfecting lighthouse soap, scrubbed him down from head to toes, rinsed him off and then splashed him generously with bay rum. "There now, I guess you can go in the house," Dad observed.

El, relieved that his brother had come through the ordeal intact, flapped his arms, crowed like a rooster, and ran into the house. Ray put on the clean clothes and followed. He found Mom waiting for him at the door. She wanted to make sure he qualified for the human race again and could enter her immaculate kitchen.

"Are you clean? Are you sure you got all *that stuff* off? Let's have a look." A detailed inspection ensued. "Now let's see the bottom of your shoes." This area was always suspect. "All right, you can come in but you still smell strong of something.''

"Just a little of Dad's bay rum, Mom.''

"Just a little, whew. I guess it will wear off. I don't know how you and that terrible thing managed to come out in one piece.'' She gave a wry laugh. "Dinner's ready. Come in and eat.''

Over a supper of hearty soup good-natured banter flew around, brought to a climax by El waving a white chicken feather aloft. When the laughter wore itself out, Dad took on a serious tone. "Better take a good look at the damage tomorrow, and decide whether you want to do any more work on it. You can't do anything in the dark tonight anyway, and I don't think the chickens will run off with it.''

That set us off in laughter again. We knew by his tone that he was not happy with the thought that the boys might try to ride again, but he would let them make up their own minds.

Ray made his way to bed early that night. I sneaked out quietly with a kerosene lantern in my hand to the chicken yard. There it lay, partially covered with debris and exhibiting a few minor scratches. But it still smelled and was a mess, and would be even messier in the clean up. I decided to stay out of my brothers' sight the next day. As I pulled the blankets over myself that night, I wondered if they would ever be successful riders. The murmur of voices from my brothers' room kept on until I heard Dad call to them, "you boys be quiet and go to sleep.'' The sounds dropped off to soft whispers and then finally silence.

Next morning, the tranquility of our breakfast was shattered by this startling announcement.

"We're gonna sell it.''

Dad gave of sigh of relief, Mom smiled and I was speechless.

"Well, you know you could make a few dollars on the bike if you fixed it up and put it back in good running condition. If you're not in too big a hurry, I'll help you a little,'' Dad offered. He didn't know all about motorcycles, but he understood engines and what made them run. Ray and El grabbed at his offer.

So an even more painstaking thoroughness went into the second overhaul. First, a good wash and cleaning. Dad tinkered around a bit on the engine, although he couldn't solve the matter of the gear. Another bright red paint job went on, this time with contrasting blue stripes. It was complete with a shiny leather seat that had been rubbed and rubbed with saddle soap. This time the finished cycle was truly a thing of beauty. How and where to present it for sale remained a problem. There might be a possible buyer at the fort. The boys were reluctant to push it all the way over there, and were

still a little shy of another attempt at riding. The situation forced
my brothers into some serious thinking, and they came up with an
elaborate sign.

FOR SALE

Good motorcycle, runs good, new
paint and good tires. Ready to go.
See El or Ray Engel at Ballast Point.

They tacked the sign up in the bowling alley just before payday.
Three khaki-clad hopefuls, eager to try anything to relieve the dol-
drums of Army life, banged on our door early the next day. When
the soldiers arrived the bike was already out for their perusal. El
and Ray stood back while one soldier made a slow check, with no
comment. He broke the agonizing silence with, "I'd like to try it out."
    "Sure, go ahead," El replied.
    The soldier stood astride the cycle with the casual stance of the
experienced rider. "Oh, gosh, we'll never sell the darn thing,"
thought Ray, as the man turned the throttle expertly. The other two
men gave the bike a hard push, the motor sprang to life, and the
rider took off for a bumpy jaunt across to the fort. If this obstacle
course could be passed, the sale might be made. The rider became
enveloped in swirls of dust as he picked up the pace. The absence
of a muffler helped us to follow its progress. The distant roar suddenly ceased and my brothers envisioned all their hard labor going
down the drain. But the man had just slowed for a turn, and back
he came at a faster pace, dodging rocks and holes and finally coming
to a snorting stop.
    "It needs a little tuning up. How about forty bucks?"
    El and Ray didn't waste any time in argument, they just held
out their hands for the cash. The soldiers dug into their pockets and
came up with the required amount, and while the one man rode off
on the bike, the other two hustled after him. My brothers congratu-
lated each other, Dad went back to work in the carpenter shop, and
Mom breathed a great sigh of relief.
    Word drifted down from the fort the next week about the further
adventures of the trusty bike. One of the fellows had gone off to
town for a little fun. About two o'clock in the morning, he started
home in control of neither his wits nor the motorcycle. The evening
had been filled with good company and bottled spirits, and by the
time he neared the fort he was weaving happily from one side of

the road to the other and singing at the top of his voice. He entered the encampment with the motor roaring, shattering the calm of the early morning hours. There was no stopping him even when the guard shouted, "Halt!" and brandished his rifle. The inebriated soul rode cheerfully onward, down to the flat area where men were sleeping in their tents. He plowed through, uprooting tent stakes, dragging tents and tangled ropes behind him until the bike slid to a stop.

Fortunately, no one was injured, but the rider was somewhat limited in his activities by an assigned stay in the guardhouse. The old red motorcycle endured to carry others on joyful trips to and from San Diego, but none quite like this first happy-go-lucky fellow.

24

Fish and Chips

O ur beaches on the channel and bayside dropped off abruptly into deep waters that sheltered scores of fine eating fish. They ranged from small perch to forty-pound halibut. Calico bass and the ugly sculpin lurked in the depths and these were the fish we considered choice eating. Sculpin, with their poisonous fins, could give any fisherman a miserable time, and many of these fish were thrown back quickly to avoid any further contact with them. But their flesh is flaky and sweet. I fished for them in a very easy way, using a set line.

Early in the morning, I baited a long strong line with cut bait, using as many hooks as possible, sometimes up to ten, all to be weighted down with a good-sized sinker. The line was then taken out off shore by boat and dropped in the water and stretched in to the shore. This end of the line I tied to our fence to secure it. Later in the day all that was needed was to pull in all the hooked fish discarding the ones you did not want. Fileted, dipped in beaten egg, rolled in cracker crumbs and fried quickly, what a wonderful meal fresh from the sea.

Along the shores at low tide, we dug for softshell clams. It took a bit of hard digging to get through the rocks on the beach, but the effort was worth the toil. We knew better than to eat the mollusks the first day. Instead they were placed in a gunny sack and hung in the water by the little pier overnight. During the period, the obliging little shellfish rinsed themselves free of all sand. At supper we all gathered around the table, each with a soup plate, fork and spoon.In the center of the table sat a huge pot of steamed clams, and to one side a large platter to catch the empty shells. No need to dip this tasty seafood in butter. They had a sweetness all their own that could not be enhanced by any added sauces. When we tired of eating, the broth from the steaming pepped us up again for another onslaught on the delicious clams.

Another toothsome denizen of the deep was trapped and brought home by Dad from his trips to the buoys out at sea and the beacons in the harbor. This was the delicately flavored Pacific lobster. They roam far and wide, in shallow waters or deep, in rocky crevices or along sandy bottoms. Some traps were set out in the deep ocean waters off Point Loma, near the bell and whistler buoys. Others were tied to the beacons in the bay. Dad constructed the traps out of rough wooden slats in his spare time. Old smelly fish heads were wired securely to the inside of the traps to attract the lobsters, but the aroma lured not only lobsters but crabs, eels, starfish, and minute fish. Hauling the loaded traps up from the great ocean depths meant back-breaking labor, but Dad was forever trying to earn that extra bit of money to make life easier for his family. For most of the years that Dad sold the lobsters to the wholesale market he received twenty-five cents a pound. On a good haul he could bring home twenty to thirty pounds. These lobsters would be kept in floating crates at the wharf until Dad had enough to make it worthwhile to take them to market about once a week.

The beacons in the bay harbored these shellfish too. The best catch was made at No. 3 beacon near a mud flat which has since been filled with dredged material to make Shelter Island. A fish cannery was operating in La Playa near this area, and so it is easy to understand why the lobster catch was so good at that particular beacon. The tides carried the fish scraps by the beacon on every turn of the tide and lobsters climbed happily into the traps without a second thought. Unless some early riser poached there first, Dad always found a bounty of crustaceans.

From the village called La Playa, came the Portuguese. We could expect them on any Sunday with a low tide in the afternoon. They came eagerly to gather octopi that could be found in rocky holes near the water's edge. If your eyes were sharp, you would spot the little mound of rocks interlaced with the broken fragments of clam shells, the mark of the abode of the devilfish. The clam shells were the remains of the many meals the octopus had enjoyed. He was always neat enough to clear his table and carry the shells outside.

Hasty digging sometimes brought up a squirming rascal, but too often it quickly found its way back into a tiny crack away from his home, and the hunter was thwarted. My brothers and I found an easy method of coaxing them from their lairs. A quantity of lime which was used to whitewash the sheds was placed in a pail along with water, and stirred. This mixture was then poured slowly down the hole where we suspected an octopus lived. This soon brought forth an indignant sputtering creature seeking relief from the fiery liquid. Only a quick grasp kept the octopus from sliding back into the water. Sometimes it released a black inky substance to cover its retreat, just Mother Nature's way of providing a little self-defense. We saved all the octopi for the friendly Portuguese, who enjoyed eating them. I never had any desire to sample any, and we just used them for fish bait because the meat was so tough.

In return we were often presented a bottle of fine homemade wine. It was wonderfully refreshing chilled with ice and, laced with lemon juice and sugar, made a good hot drink. Whenever we had the sniffles Mom would fix us a glassful and we would be asleep and resting as soon as our heads touched the pillow. We liked having these people visit the point. They were always so courteous and friendly.

Beyond Ballast Point on the rocky shores of Point Loma, abalones clung stubbornly to the underside of rocks out past the low tide line. The abalone is primarily a huge muscle with just a small portion of its body devoted to organs. With this strong muscle, it forms a vacuum hold on the rock. It can best be pried off with a flat bar like an old tire iron. So strong is the suction that divers try not to let their hands slip between the abalone and the rock until the vacuum is broken and the shell pried loose. If they are careless the mollusk will clamp down firmly in a secure grip. For a long time we were able to wade out, turn over the rocks at low tide, and find these excellent shellfish. We gathered so many abalones in the early days that at times we did not use them all. There were no freezers then so we used an old method of preserving the meat. We set the excess on the fence to dry. From a beautiful light texture the meat turned to a metallic brown, no longer fit for the frying pan. But in place of gum or candy it made excellent chewing. Mom was horrified at the sight of the ugly chunks drying in the sun along the fence, but my brothers and I enjoyed chewing on a piece. It was the toughest meat to bite into and a small piece lasted for hours. It was cheaper than gum, there was always a ready supply, it satisfied our hunger for a spell, and it was an excellent gum massage. We all grew up with good teeth.

If you have never eaten abalone, you are in for a real treat. But be sure you find someone who is skilled in the correct preparation and cooking of it. As the abalone is removed from its shell, it constricts becoming as tough as shoe leather. Old timers spend laborious minutes pounding the thinly sliced steaks until tender. The modern method is to use a meat tenderizer. I still prefer the old way as a means of insuring the best flavor. Properly sauteed, it is a mouth-watering morsel.

There are always frightening tales that accompany discussion of old-time abalone hunting. We had a favorite one that varied in the telling from one time to the next with more scary embellishments. We told of a Chinese fisherman who was scouring the inside of a cave on the ocean side of Point Loma, trying to get a sackful before he traveled to market. Turning over a large rock he located a choice mollusk, but without thinking, reached to pull the shell free with his bare hand. The abalone muscle was relaxed at the moment, but the minute it felt the man's touch it clamped down on the fisherman's hand. And thus the Chinese became a helpless prisoner in the face of the rising tide moving into the cave. There was no escape from the flood of water. Finding himself trapped and no help in sight, the desperate man sawed off his hand in order to free himself, managed to climb out of the cave, but unfortunately bled to death before going any farther. I've always thought the story held little truth, but I first heard it when I was just eight, and it horrified me so that it has remained with me all these years.

Before the bay became so cluttered with ship traffic, the one- and two-man albacore boats rested inside our cove. Others took refuge in the lee side of Point Loma. At night the little gatherings of boats looked like a floating city of lights. The men would go out daily to make their catches of albacore, first icing down the previous day's catch.

From them we obtained fresh albacore, and Mom thought it would be a great idea to preserve some for the future. We baked the fish first, then skinned and boned it, cut it into chunks to fit into the jars. For a tight seal we had to steam the jars for hours. The first fishy smell didn't seem so bad but by the time we had finished the job the whole house reeked of the odor, even the clothes in our closets. There was no escape from it anywhere in our dwelling. Mom said, "Never again!"

But we ate it all with relish, except for one jar, to remind us of the folly of home fish canning. We finally threw that one jar away after more than thirty years. The seal was still tight, but none of us was very enthusiastic about trying the fish.

The albacore boats often kept their fish for a day or two, going out to get a full catch to take to market, and being men of the sea, often ate some of the fish. They dumped the fish heads and entrails overboard as they cleaned the fish, attracting scavengers and large sharks. The sharks that lurked around the boats were large to us, some six to eight feet long. Dad had told us of once seeing man-eaters when he was working on one of the beacons, but these in our little cove were not. We had no fear of them as we swam around our pier, but they still fascinated us. Even the small ones could be nasty on a fishing line. When pulled in they rotated their bodies, snarling hooks and lines, all the while gnashing their teeth. We never ate them, and if we could untangle the mess they made soon enough, we released them.

My brothers were fascinated by the thrashing about of the larger sharks as they fought over the fish scraps thrown overboard. Some of the bolder ones occasionally swam near our pier, and El and Ray decided to try for one. They baited a huge hook with some old bacon and tied the hook to the end of a sturdy clothesline. The boys rowed out about fifty feet with the baited end and dropped it in the water. The other end they tied securely to the rail on the wharf. We knew if we caught one of the big sharks we could not hold it by ourselves. Before long, one of the voracious predators cruised by the bacon, sizing up his next possible meal. A triangular fin cut the surface of the water smoothly, leaving a small rippling wake to mark its path. The shark circled and moved closer to the bait.

As any fisherman can tell you, there is always that feeling of anticipation when you toss out the line. You just never know what will take the bait. You wait for a little nibble or a strenuous tug. And as we watched the water for a sign of further activity, there was a sudden violent swirl and quick jerk at the clothesline. The hungry fish had struck viciously, and its greed had imbedded the hook deep in the jaw. Whipping back and forth, the shark strained at the line, yanking and pulling, making every effort to free itself. The rail on the pier bent under the force of the struggle and I yelled at my brothers, "Cut the line. He'll break the rail and we'll all get heck from Dad."

But my brothers were transfixed by the battle going on, and were determined to bring in the monster. The boys pulled, the shark pulled, on and on went the struggle, until with one last desperate try the shark made its final stand, and then completely exhausted, it floated belly up and the boys hauled in their prize. It certainly wasn't a man-eater, but we could see that our feet easily fit inside its jaw. We began to have some qualms about swimming in that vicinity.

One of our strangest catches was a huge black sea bass that meandered by our little pier. El was puttering in one of the rowboats,

bailing and scrubbing off old dried fish scales and coiling the anchor
lines. Ray, broom in hand, busied himself cleaning up the pier, when
he heard El let out a yell. "Hey, look at that crazy fish!"

Ray rushed over to the side where El pointed. Sure enough, there
near the surface and swimming very slowly in the direction of the
pier, was a large black sea bass. It seemed unaware that it was
headed on a collision course with the wharf. This fish is normally
found in ocean waters and was certainly alien to our little cove. El
scrambled up the ladder and stood by his brother as they stared at
this strange sight.

"Hey, let's get it." Ray grabbed for the nearest weapon, a long-
handled boathook. Just as the bass swam along by the wharf, Ray
gave it a terrific whack on the head with the boathook and that was
all that was needed. The stunned fish gave up without another wiggle
of its tail. El went back down into the rowboat, cinched a line around
the bass, and went back upon the dock to help Ray haul it up by
block and tackle. Dad judged it to weigh about two hundred and fifty
pounds. The how and why of its appearance in the bay could not
be explained. We just accepted it as another one of the sea mysteries
that touched our shore.

We all loved to fish. Even Mom would drop a line in sometimes.
We used to have great fun watching her excitement whenever she
had a bite, and had the joy of pulling in a good pan fish.

When Grandpa and Grandma visited us, it was time to go eel fishing. Families of big morays lived in the rocks right next to our pier.
At low tide we could see them, heads sticking out from the holes,
jaws agape, with sharp needle-teeth making the eels appear even
more ferocious. We never worried about swimming around them for
they never bothered us. They usually retreated when we started
splashing in the water. Then when all was quiet again out would
come those nasty looking heads, beady watchful eyes staring about.
Periodically we would try to catch one of them. They didn't take
the bait too readily, but once having taken it, they gave us a terrific
fight. Some of them were very large, up to four feet in length, and
very, very strong. Our sport soon resolved itself into a tug-of-war,
for the eel simply wound himself around some rocks and held on,
while we pulled and pulled, hoping to catch the eel in a careless
moment. Sometimes luck favored us, but more often the eel was the
victor and all we pulled in was a tangled mess of hooks, line and
sinker, enough to keep us busy for an afternoon. When we were
lucky to snag one of the big ones and haul it in, we put it in the wheel-
barrow to take home for parental approval. After Mom's, "take that

nasty thing out of here,'' we bestowed it upon some grateful fisherman who took it home to be smoked. And when our grandparents visited, we caugtht eels for Grandpa. He wanted them boiled in vinegar with onions. Ugh! We never touched them.

We never fished for stingray, but they certainly made themselves obnoxious by gobbling our bait before the lazy halibut got to it. If we caught a ray, we cut off its tail above the stinger and rendered the ray harmless to waders along the beach. Sometimes Ray and El speared large rattail rays, ones with big bony heads. One was so strong that it towed their rowboat around before giving up. The skulls of bat rays were so different that some fishermen cleaned them and then bleached the skulls in the sun. We hated these fish. They presented no real danger to us, but they appeared so frightening with their large bulky heads and long whip-like tails. Fortunately, we were never stung by one. People who waded along the beaches were occasionally stung by one of the small stingrays, but without any fatalities.

All in all, the sea life that inhabited our surroundings was friendly and a real boon to us. My brothers and I were never harmed in anyway by anything. Skinned knees and skinned elbows, nothing more.

Our relatives enjoy the sight of the steamer *Harvard* moving by the point at a rare slow speed.

25

Pelicans and Picnickers

G ulls soared gracefully overhead, their flight reflected in the
quiet waters below. It was Sunday, the air was warm, and picnickers and fishermen began to gather for a restful day on the beach.
Fishing poles and lines quickly spread like a network along the shore.
Anglers stood alert to snatch up a jerking pole.

Dad greeted the oldtimers who had staked out the choice areas,
and asked the others not to denude the beach by taking small flat
stones to use as skimmers. Through years of gentle erosion, some
of the stones had become flattened and thin, and a good strong toss
would send them skipping across the water, literally bouncing along.
The challenge was to see how many times you could make the stone
skip before it disappeared below the surface of the water. But Dad
feared that the continual throwing of the rocks into deeper water
would at last create a shallow landing area for boats near the pier.
He diligently made the rounds politely asking visitors to desist. His
point was well made.

Many years ago, the sailing ships that came to the California ports
for rawhides sometimes had to head home with partially filled holds.
They then stopped at Ballast Point and placed hundreds of cobblestones aboard to act as ballast on the way back to the East Coast.
When these vessels returned to the Atlantic ports, they emptied the
cargo holds and tossed the ballast into the water. Ship after ship followed the procedure and before long the water by the wharves
became too shallow for vessels of deep draft. It was then decided
to place the stones on the wharves so they could be hauled away.
Winter rains created a mire of mud as heavy loaded wagons moved
the cargoes from wharf to warehouse, and the Ballast Point rocks
came into use. They offered a firm but bumpy surface. I visited Boston years ago and wondered which of the cobblestones I walked on
might have been from Ballast Point. Where the asphalt had worn
thin some were still visible. Well, as I said, Dad had a point.

By mid-morning the happy fishermen were pulling in excellent catches of bass, halibut, all good tasting fish for baking or frying. Many threw the sculpin back because of their poisonous fins. The sculpin is one of the tastiest fish in the sea, but only knowledgeable fishermen will take a chance on handling them. The slightest puncture from one of the spines can cause intense pain. I fished for them regularly, but used extreme caution, all except for one time. A sou'wester had just swept through two days before and I knew it was a good time to snag a few sculpin. They would be hunting for food in their favorite spot, just at the inside bend of the point, and at the turn of the tide. I had a hand line with two baited hooks, a gunny sack, and a pair of old shears, so I rowed out and threw over the rock anchor. If it got caught below, I had merely to cut the line. There was little loss except for some old Manila rope. The fishing line sank quickly to the bottom and I settled down for a wait. Sculpin are usually slow biters. A slight tug might mean they were just beginning to nose the bait. Too quick a pull on the line might yank it away from them, so I waited until the line grew taut with the weight of the fish on it. They were large ones, huge of head and small of body, but what filets they would make. I nipped off their spines and put the fish into the sack. Sculpin bit as fast as the line went down, and I was busy baiting the hooks, hauling in the fish, cutting off the fins, and putting the fish into the sack. It soon bulged with fish enough for family and friends, and it was time to stop. I pulled up the anchor and reached down for the oars, and hit the side of the bag with my right hand. My shears had missed some of the spines and my hand jammed into them as I grabbed for an oar. From the fishing spot to the little pier was only a distance of two hundred feet, but before I could get the skiff underway, my hand had swollen so badly I had difficulty in gripping the oar. Intense pain shot up my right arm. There was no one on the beach I could yell to for help, so I just started trying to row home as fast as I could, alternately blubbering in my misery, and hollering for someone to come to my rescue.

Sculpin had left their mark on me before. But at those times there had always been someone close by to render immediate first aid. I needed to reach home as soon as possible, where the wound could be treated. It seemed hours before I finally got the skiff to the pier, climbed up the ladder, and tied the boat before I ran home crying hard every inch of the way. A few bangs on the door brought Mom. She knew I had been fishing, and one look at the puffed hand I held up told her the story. Out came the reliable bottle of hydrogen peroxide bubbling and frothing as it entered the puncture. Next came the basin of hot water for good soaking. Between sobs and sniffles, I at last came to the realization that death was not imminent. But the misery is just like being seasick. First, your think you're going to die, next, you wish you would, and last, you're past caring about anything.

While my family sat down to a delicious dinner of sculpin that evening, I groaned myself to bed for a painful night. Mom and Dad stepped in to comfort me from time to time. El and Ray had a few comments to make about being stung by the "rattlesnake" of the sea, but they were duly sympathetic. They had suffered the same pain. Strangely enough, by the next morning little pain remained and the swelling had subsided. All that was left of my experience was a slightly tender hand and minor puffiness. More than once the bottle of peroxide came out to some unfortunate angler who didn't hear the cry of "rattlesnake" when he pulled in a sculpin.

Sunday fishermen continued to enjoy good luck. Birds took advantage of the smorgasbord spread before them. They swooped down to snatch bits of bait or scraps from fish cleaning. Their appetites were insatiable and they could be a nuisance with their constant searching for food. However, we considered them to be the best sanitary engineers along the beaches. Early Monday mornings the feathered crew would be out in full force. All along the length of the shore they cleaned up on leftover bait, pieces of fish, and scraps of lunch. Their job done, the tides washed the areas free of refuse.

It was fun to watch the many kinds of birds at our location. Each had a different way of life and intriguing habits. The killdeer pretended to have a broken wing, and dragged it along the sand hoping to lure any intruder away from the nest. The sandpiper made funny little bobbing motions as it hunted food. The snipe stubbornly kept poking his long bill into the sand, searching for a tidbit. But one bird rated the lowest on our popularity chart, the *pelican*! To us the pelicans were ugly, ungainly creatures. Known sometimes to have a disagreeable disposition and a strong bill to match, we avoided them as much as possible. Besides, they always managed to spoil our fishing activities by diving after our bait. Sea birds are inflicted with lice, and we felt that the pelicans possessed more than their share.

One old fellow became the mascot of the fishermen. He grew lazy, gave up diving for fish, and begged from the people near him. Old "Pelican Pete" was smart. He often stood on the pier, wings spread majestically in the warm sun. Most everyone thought Pete was showing off, but we knew he was hoping some of the vermin would drop off and cease to annoy him. The pier was his favorite hangout, where he could view the passing scene. First-time visitors were fascinated by his size and lack of fear. A person could approach within five or six feet before the bird took off with a great flapping of wings. Pete tolerated people only because they were a source of easy food.

The activity on the shores slowed to a halt. Tidal waters slackened and fish took a siesta. Anglers lay stretched out, straw hats shading their faces. Fishing lines hung limply from the poles. Time for rest.

Suddenly an old car, rattling and bumping its way across the dirt road to the spit, entered this peaceful world. It came to a jarring stop in a swirl of dust and disgorged its contents. Out squirmed five small children, bent on out-yelling each other. They ran screaming and pushing up and down the beach. That wonderful silence was shattered, and fishermen sat up to protest.

"Where did all those kids come from? Where's their mother and father?"

"If you kids don't shut up, we'll throw you all in the water."

The protests made little impact on any of the wild-eyed youngsters. They continued to raise havoc until they all collapsed from exhaustion. Pelican Pete viewed all this commotion with a jaundiced eye and was ready to take off from his usual perch on the pier. He watched as the family congregated beside the car to discuss the best possible place to eat lunch. The mother quietly suggested, "Let's go down to the beach. It's nice and warm there."

One of the children whined, "That's no fun. Look! There's a wharf and it's empty except for that big bird."

"Yeah, and we won't get sand in our sandwiches." The group stomped over to the pier carrying their picnic baskets. Pete delayed no longer. These were not the two-legged, slow strolling creatures he had come to know. He resented the abrupt noisy intrusion on his privacy, and he flew off to a safe distance to float lazily on the water, and wait further developments. Down the wharf they came, screaming once again, and parents yelling for them to be quiet. The mother spread a bright red tablecloth on a clean dry spot, and arranged the food on it.

"Mom! Pop! What's that funny thing down there?" The oldest boy pointed over the side. Crawling about in the shallow water below was a small lobster.

"Say, that's a lobster. Sure looks different from the ones back East. It hasn't any big claw, but I'll bet it's good to eat. We'll try to catch it," the father said. He ran with them to the beach below, took off his shoes, and waded in to snatch up the hapless young lobster. "I got it! I got it!"

"Come back here and eat or everything will be spoiled," called the mother. She placed a small towel over the food as far as it would spread and moved along the wharf to watch the rest of her family.

"Maybe you can get another, Pop," the children urged.

The search continued but the scuffling around frightened the remaining lobsters into retreating to deep water. Pete viewed all the activity with great interest and seeing that his resting place on the pier had been deserted, he returned there, landing next to the picnic lunch. He pecked a bit, but found little that appealed to his taste. Too lazy to move unnecessarily, Pete just relaxed in the middle of it all and spread his wings once more.

The family below the pier at last realized there were no more lobsters to be had, and remembered that lunch was waiting. Pete, half asleep, woke up in time to flap safely away, and the father began to reach for the potato salad.

"Oh, that——dirty bird!!" he blustered angrily and pointed to the bowls of food.

"What's the matter?" the mother worried.

"Well, just look at the stuff. Look close. Look at the tablecloth, too. See?"

"Just a little sand or dust. That's all," one of the boys explained.

"Dust, my eye. It's lice! It's that dirty bird. I should have known. I saw him flapping his wings around here."

"But Poppa, how can it be the bird? Look, he's out in the water taking a bath," came from the smallest child.

"This is a mess. Everybody pack up, we're leaving right now," the father ordered.

It didn't take the family long to toss the lunch over the side, shake the tablecloth and close the picnic baskets. The children were still asking questions and crying as their parents hustled them into the car. The car rattled away and the point returned to a sanctuary of peace and quiet.

Pelican Pete opened his big bill in a smile. Perhaps he was thinking, "it's the little things in life that count."

Gunnery targets stored along the beach. Note rugged access to Ballast Point. *San Diego Historical Society-Ticor Collection.*

26

A Distant Conflict Draws Near

The population of Fort Rosecrans exploded during World War I. The original barracks overflowed with men, and tents sprawled over the dusty parade grounds. More barracks shot up under hurried construction. Most of the buildings are still in use today.

Atop Point Loma and just after you enter the military reservation on the way to the Cabrillo National Monument is another group of old buildings once called the "upper cantonment." These now house Navy materials and work.

Somewhere between this area and the fort below sprung up a small section known as the "middle cantonment." This was a place of mystery to us. While the "upper cantonment" and the fort swarmed with soldiers, this in-between section seemed set apart and we never ventured there. There are no buildings left to mark its place.

Overcrowding and boredom brought on the attendant difficulties. Fights were frequent and deserters tried now and then to make off with our rowboats, and the little town of San Diego was overrun with the military. Although the scene of the war was far removed from us, we felt its impact clearly and forcefully from the activities near us.

My brothers were in their teens and got caught up in the daily excitement. I was still too young to understand much of what was going on. I knew that Dad's Teutonic accent embarrassed him now and then, that frankfurters and wienies later became known as "hot dogs," and that lovable little dachshunds were no longer in favor and some were even destroyed by owners.

We couldn't play as freely as before, no more racing hospital gurneys up and down the once empty wards. Blistered feet filled these spaces first, and later when the "Spanish Flu" hit the fort, beds and cots strained the facilities to overflowing. With so little knowledge of how to fight the deadly virus and the lack of modern medication, the fast-moving disease took the lives of many young men. It was a fearful time for all. At night the bodies of the dead servicemen were carted quietly away. I don't know how much of this particular activity appeared in official records. We just knew it was happening and no one said much about it. For a long time, people went around wearing gauze nose masks trying to ward off the "flu." The whole episode reminded me of the plagues of the Middle Ages.

Our whole family escaped the ravages of that disease, but to be different, I came down with pneumonia. My brothers continued to be active, and I suspect that they moved so fast all the time that no bug could catch up with them. With the pneumonia along came a case of miserable pleurisy. My fever shot up alarmingly and Dad sent for the overworked fort medical officer. Stern instructions were given to counteract the fever. On the hour, every hour, day and night, I was to be given an ice-cold sponge bath. For the following forty-eight hours, Mom and Dad were by my side, pulling off the warm blankets, sponging me down with ice water, and then tucking me back under the covers. The sharp pains of the pleurisy blotted out all other discomfort. Even the cold cloths were almost welcome. The fever finally subsided and things began to return to normal. My mother lived to be ninety-eight and all those years we were together, she never failed to remind me almost daily, "take a sweater or you'll catch cold."

The war years treated Ray and El much better. They struck a bonanza in the newspaper business. Fort dwellers were hungry for any little shred of information coming from the war zone, and the news publishers took advantage of this. Bundles of newspapers arrived at the fort one after another. Any small item brought forth another "Extra." After doing the daily rounds of their regular customers, my brothers stuffed their carrier bags full, slung them over their shoulders, and made the long haul from the fort below up to the upper cantonment, always coming back with empty bags and jingling pockets, repeating the hike as more news and papers came forth.

They made money fast and spent it just as quickly. Ray was becoming aware of the opposite sex. El had decided to quit school after a short time in high school. Dad had simply said, "go to school or go to work." So El found a job as an auto mechanic helper, doing the easy grease jobs, but that didn't last long. In a few months he was back to the sea working on one of the Catalina boats as a seaman.

Drilling of the recruits went on at a reduced pace. Soldiers were shipped out and new men took their places. The fort gradually moved back into its regular routine, but the routine was unexpectedly broken by orders given to revive the old ten-inch gun batteries that faced across the outer channel from the lower section of the fort. It had been a very long time since they had been fired and we wondered what brought on this sudden announcement. Before the practice firing, warning notices were distributed around the area so small children, housewives, and boatmen had a chance to be prepared: small children to stuff cotton in their ears, housewives to remove good china from their shelves, boatmen to get out of the firing range, and dogs to remain inside, preferably under beds and near loved ones.

Like the torpedo runs, gun practice was never really highly successful. The guns had very limited mobility and range. They had been placed to fire directly across the outer channel, but shells flew high and low, occasionally striking the towed targets, but too often landing close to the tugs. Firing was soon discontinued and the children of the fort were once more free to use the darkened tunnels of the gun emplacements as a playground for tag or hide and seek.

Back from the fort, up the road from the bakery, and tucked in between two steep hills sat a mortar battery. Walt Disney may have obtained one of his cartoon ideas from these little cannons had he ever seen them. They were small, squat, and bulbous in shape, supposedly able to project a missile high up over the brow of Point Loma to plop down on an enemy vessel in the ocean. After a few firings the mortars became strangely silent and stayed that way. Gun practice must have been a great deal less than successful. If ever there was blind shooting, that had to be it. It was always a mystery to me as to how these guns were aimed. There was even some quiet talk that the powder charges were not strong enough to send the projectiles over the hill. Whatever the reason for the silence of this battery, we gave no further thought to it.

The recreation building offered the soldiers some release from boredom. A few pool tables on the lower floor were always in use. On the upper floor entranced spectators sat on uncomfortable folding chairs to watch silent movies. An inexpert pianist made up with dramatic thumpings of the keys for what he lacked in technique as the changing scenes unrolled on the screen. Movies, fortunately, were scheduled separately for the soldiers and for families. For one thing, space was limited and the raucous comments of the men might not have met with familial approval. Then on Sundays, the chairs were reversed and Sunday school was held, but with less appreciation and interest on the part of the children.

Recruits had few free hours, but they still tried to fill them with
more pleasurable activity than "hup, two, three, four." Tired men
lolled along the beaches. Some gathered in the crowded two-lane
bowling alley, and others just chose to rest their weary bones on hard
cots.

On rare occasions rabbit drives took place on North Island. I don't
know where the orders originated or even if there were official ones,
but numbers of soldiers were ferried across the bay to the flight field.
Here they lined up at the southern end of the field and moved in
a steady line toward the north, driving great hordes of frightened
animals before them and out onto the mud flats. I never wanted to
hear about these drives, but I could not escape the word that some
rabbits were clubbed to death while others were driven into the bay
to drown. Perhaps these drives took place because the rabbits and
the burrows they dug became a nuisance and danger to the early
planes that used the dirt runway. No matter the reason for it all,
I hated knowing about it.

These were days of worry for Dad. He had enough on his mind
taking care of the station and lights, but as at Point Bonita, he realized that among the military there would be a few undesirables.
Security around the point was difficult to maintain and night prowl-
ers were reported to the commanding officer of the fort. Dad did
not want his family disturbed or harmed, but with the exception of
a missing rowboat now and then, we were left alone. Deserters
usually headed over the hills and away from their encampments.

We were always free to roam anywhere, including the fort, as
long as we were home before dark. The stable there held a number
of nondescript mules and horses. On a rare day we kids could sometimes wheedle a good-natured stablehand into letting us have a ride.
So when the animals were not in use, we'd hop aboard and head
for the hills above. A narrow steep road led out the back of the fort
up to the crest of Point Loma. From there we made our way along
the top, and thence down to Point Loma lighthouse where we took
time to wander along the beach while the animals rested. The first
steep climb took some of the initial spirit out of our mounts and they
were glad to quietly munch on grass for a bit. It made a full happy
day for us all, especially if we carried a few good sandwiches along.

At other times we found as much joy in hiking over the hills.
In springtime, colorful wild flowers brightened the area, the brush
was green, the sky clear and the ocean a deep blue, with the air crisp
and fresh from the sea. On the ocean side we'd turn our way to the
northwest and follow the old rough path that led us pass the "old

well," actually a deep pit dug by early Mormon trailblazers. If memory serves me right, it was down on a flattened area near the ocean, and below what is now a Navy Electronics work area.

The story is that the Mormons were hunting for coal, but ran into salt water and had to abandon their digging. For years the hole was left uncovered, partially hidden by brush. On our meanderings we used to creep up to the sides of the pit on our bellies and toss rocks down waiting interminably for the sounds of the rocks hitting something. The hole was deep and scary. Later we heard that a mule had strayed by and fallen in, and the area was sealed over to prevent any further accidents. We were lucky youngsters!

At the end of World War I the fort soon became a quiet, almost deserted area. Just enough men were kept to maintain the facilities in good order. We were very glad that peace had come, and we could get back to our quiet life.

JOURNAL of Light Station at ....Beacon ....Lights

MONTH. 19/6	DAY.	STATE WORK PERFORMED BY KEEPERS REGARDING UPKEEP OF STATION, AND RECORD OF IMPORTANT EVENTS. BAD WEATHER, ETC.
		Repairs copper-taking over for which 8 A.M. to 12 M. wind S.E. to N.W. wind rain cloudy
		Inspected quarters good Light S.E. cloudy
		Strong S.E. squalls rain
		rest of yard N.W. wind clear
		adjust light but found adjusting screw broke light N.E.
		" Light N.W. to S.W. overcast
		" " cloudy
		inspected to putting away journal " " rain. clear
		to sea " N.W. wind
		" a very high hill " " "
		" " " "
		horse out to sea " N.W. to S.W. rain overcast

Log entry: ''Horse out to sea.'' This refers to the burial of the champion Clydesdale.
Daily Journal, U.S. Lighthouse Service.

27

And Then Some More Pets

During World War I thousands of soldiers were quartered in and around Fort Rosecrans for drilling and awaiting assignment overseas. The quiet little town of San Diego offered meager recreation to the soldiers stationed nearby. In their spare time some of them lounged along the beach, or idly threw rocks at the gulls gliding overhead. Infrequently a bird would fly into the path of a rock and flop into the water with a broken wing. Unable to fly or swim, it would sadly drag its injured wing along the beach trying desperately to reach a bit of food before it was snatched away by other birds.

They possessed voracious appetites, and when a gull suffered a broken wing, there was little difficulty in trapping the starving bird.

Mother Nature healed the minor abrasions, but a broken wing required drastic action. Setting broken bones was beyond our capabilities, so it was off to the woodchopping block where a swift downward stroke of the hatchet severed the useless part. We wrapped the end carefully before releasing the gull and were proud to record an absolute zero mortality rate. This was probably due to our providing food during a brief convalescent period.

After each of these crude operations, the gulls no longer experienced difficulty in moving about on land or water. They could paddle as well as ever and ran speedily along the beaches scavenging for food. Sometimes we fed them for so long a period of time that they would strut up and down in our front yard, raucously insisting upon immediate room service until Mom firmly indicated we should move the recovery room to another spot. We never tired of watching the seagulls.

The great influx of recruits necessitated building of more barracks. Draft horses and mules hauled the heavy loads. A stable had been built at Ballast Point prior to 1900 to house many of the workhorses that were used in the earlier building of Fort Rosecrans. This same stable was repaired and another batch of horses was stabled there during our time. They were beautiful Clydesdales and a joy to watch. We spent all our spare time watching the huge draft animals, so majestic in size and gentle in manner, but it was a long time before we had the courage to stand close and pat their sleek sides. We could never reach their backs and their heads still seemed a bit formidable in close proximity.

The workmen were quick to notice our interest and took advantage of it. With a few rides on the backs of these giants, and assurances that they were quite harmless, we found ourselves in charge of the horses on Sundays. Our job was simple—feed and water, and an extra quarter for stall cleaning. Stall cleaning required stamina, might and main, and an insensitive nose, for the Clydesdales did nothing on a small scale. Feeding and cleaning presented no great problems, but watering did. Watering troughs were at the fort, easily accessible to the horses on Monday through Saturday. Troughs had never been built at the point.

By the time we undertook this task, the horses had quickly learned the Sunday routine. They knew their way along the spit and back and had acquired a pattern of behavior they enjoyed a great deal. The first Sunday on the job, my brothers and I each grabbed a halter and led the animals to the beach, where we dropped our hold on the lines. Like young colts, they splashed in the shallow water, romped ponderously along a bit of beach, and rolled on the warm beach sand. For a moment I thought things were getting a little out of hand. Quiet descended as quickly as the playful interlude had begun. There stood the ten behemoths ready to be led along the way. I picked up the halter rope once again, and started out all in good order. The horses drank their fill and like good steeds made their way back to the stable without any further playfulness. Watching them calmly munching their oats, it was hard to believe what had transpired on the beach.

The next two Sundays passed without any unusual incident, but by the fourth Sunday the routine began to pall on my brothers, and they stuck their heads together for some significant planning. I was excluded from the formative ideas, but by the time the next weekend neared I had a hazy notion it would be another one of their self-destructing operations.

No more leading horses to water! We would ride 'em! Ray chose the one that seemed to be the leader. El lifted me aboard a wide-back Clydesdale that left me with my legs sticking out at right angles. I felt like I was sitting on a big barrel. It never occurred to me to keep both legs on one side. An eight-year-old is not often given to deep reasoning.

El clambered aboard his horse and after a few plodding steps my brothers gave their "Clydes" a few kicks in the ribs and we were off in a clop-clop of rump-bobbing trots, hoping all the rest would follow in good order. The sun sparkled on the ocean and the animals were ready for their dip in the refreshing salt water. Ray and El slid off their backs in time, but it was a long way down for me and I flopped off onto the damp sand happy to avoid the heavy hooves. After the snorting and splashing ceased, down on their backs the horses went rolling and kicking, sending sand flying. They finally stood quietly rippling their backs in pleasure and shaking the remains of the sand from their bodies. Aboard once again, the next scheduled stop was at the troughs. I bounced painfully, determined not to complain about the rigors of keeping up with my brothers. The usual peace and quiet of a Sunday morning was broken only by the soft snorts of the Clydesdales at the troughs or an occasional barking of a dog.

"Are you ready?" Ray yelled at me.

"Ready for what?" I wanted to know how far into the noose I was poking my head.

"Just come along and you'll see," El answered.

So soon there we were, Ray and El astride the leaders and I, as always, bringing up the rear, with horses pointed in the wrong direction. I shut my mouth and followed. My brothers had a way of exploding a simple idea into a massive and often uncontrollable activity. After an initial milling about, the horses were finally headed up the road to the fort. Clop, clop—past the enlisted men's barracks, and then the hospital with an occasional early riser cheering us on, past the officers' quarters on what we called the front road. By this time the Clydesdales sensed something different, but went along good-naturedly. Irate heads poked out of windows here and there with angry shouts, most of which could be interpreted as "what the hell's going on out there?"

Stimulated by the reception, my brothers decided to return by the back road, and at the end of the long line of buildings, turned the horses about and headed home. We rounded the last dwelling and entered the road which was really nothing but a narrow alley, large enough to allow small wagons to pass. Maneuvering ten huge Clydesdales through this area proved a little too much for us and the horses, and there was immediate turmoil. Trashcans were banged and dumped over, and there were a few kicks aimed at the cans.

As we exited from the officers' section a small group of soldiers cheered us on, and we waved back proudly as we passed. For just a few minutes on that one day, the boring routine had been shattered for the soldiers and for us.

But a telephone call from the commanding officer and a few firm words from our Dad put an end to any future straying from the watering routine.

You can't live so close to nature and not be aware of and even involved in the daily flow of life and death. From the tiniest hermit crab to the great gray whales, the pattern of existence unfolded before us. For us there were more happy than sad times, but some of the sorrowful events have never been erased from my mind.

One day a magnificent Clydesdale arrived in a makeshift trailer. His arrival puzzled us for it was apparent this was no ordinary draft horse. Great in size, with a glossy warm brown coat, the only thing lacking was pride in bearing. His eyes held little brightness and his head hung low. We could only wonder at these contradictions, and hope that he would be added to the other ten so we could soon pet and ride him.

Our hopes were quickly smashed. The champion horse had been struck with a kidney ailment. It was difficult for him to walk steadily. While his front legs held to a straight course, the hindquarters wobbled and the back legs splayed out almost felling the animal. The best of care and medication proved useless. Within two weeks the distraught owner stood by crying as efforts were made to support the grand body in a sling. For a week the champion remained supported almost solely without aid from his legs as the disease progressively worsened. We had the hope of the young, but the sad look in the big brown eyes relayed the inevitable tragic end. Early one morning in the following week the tired animal drew his last painful breath and lay slumped in the sling, the gallant fight mercifully ended. Our breaking hearts tried to find some comfort in the carefully prepared funeral befitting a champion. He was gently lowered from the sling and placed aboard a small barge which was towed out to sea. Here the barge was set afire and the Clydesdale entered Valhalla in a blaze of glory. As the barge burned slowly to the water's edge we said our silent goodbyes. The owner wept as the flame was at last extinguished. That was a time of deep sorrow for me. Even though the area has changed a bit over the sixty-five years since then, I am sure I could still go out and stand on the exact spot where the supports were erected, so indelibly is the tragedy etched in my memory.

Two months later El and Ray returned from a small carnival at Ocean Beach with a scrawny lop-eared burro. They had seen this long-eared bag of bones beaten, ridden, and harassed to a point of dropping in its tracks. There seemed to be no other logical solution to this problem than for my brothers to pool the money they had made caddying and purchase the creature. It was the end of the carnival season, the owner was tired of the whole business, and he gladly handed over the animal for a few dollars.

It was always "Be Kind to Animals" week at our home, to birds, sea lions, squirrels, dogs, and other wonders of nature. No two young teen-age boys could be happier with their prize.

Maggie, as we later named her, followed them quietly enough, too exhausted to question her change of fortune, but there was a suspicious glint in her eyes that indicated a bit of unquenched spirit that was yet to make an appearance. They put her in an empty stall in the stable, filled the oat bucket, pulled down some fresh hay, brought in a bucket of cool water, and stood back to evaluate their purchase. Maggie inspected her new quarters briefly before turning to the fresh food. Her gaunt ribs told some of the story of past abuse, but hungry as she was, Maggie ate like a lady, chewing slowly and quietly as though to relish every bit. The workhorses gave only casual looks in her direction and went on with their feeding.

For days we tried to gain Maggie's confidence and to erase memories of her past harsh treatment, but it took a long, long time to smooth out many of the scars. After her ribs finally disappeared with the constant feeding and rest, Maggie no longer flattened her ears in distrust, and in a few weeks would even let us astride her back without a fuss. But that was as far as the action went. No amount of coaxing, giddy-yapping or tugging at the halter, nor even the temptation of a handful of oats could get her to budge once we were on her back. No wonder the previous owner had handed over the bill of sale so quickly. And it was as if Maggie knew that we would not beat her. She had a newly acquired "bed of roses," and fully intended to lie in it. If ever there was an immovable object, it was Maggie. In her own quiet way she had discovered that she was now the possession of some soft-hearted individuals who would never injure her.

El and Ray began to revise the value of their purchase and started looking around for another lover of forlorn creatures, in hopes of making a profitable sale. And then El walked into the barn one day fresh from his paper route, carrying our paper. He banged it on the rail next to Maggie and that's when the fun started. The burro jumped and whirled in her tracks and glared at us. There hadn't been so much movement from her since she had been safely tucked away in her stall.

"Hey, that gives me an idea. Norm, you put the halter on her." I pulled the crude harness over Maggie's head. She eyed me warily.

"Okay, it's on. Now what?"

"Lead her out." Maggie followed meekly enough as she had always done, keeping a watchful eye on my brother and the newspaper clutched in his hand. "Now you hold her head while I get on." And he climbed aboard.

"Well, she's still standing there. I don't see anything different."

"Maybe not, but you never know." And with that, El slapped Maggie smartly on the rump with the folded paper.

Wow! All the energy Maggie had been storing up in the past days exploded in a sudden furious burst of speed in to a rip-snorting gallop.

"Hey, look at her go," I yelled and ran to keep up with them. I should have saved my breath. They were already halfway down the beach, so I stopped and watched in awe, this long-eared Pegasus, and El whooping and hollering in glee. The newspaper blew to the winds, and then just as suddenly as it all began, it stopped. Maggie, no longer feeling the slap and noise of the paper, came to an abrupt halt, planting her hooves firmly in the deep sand. Her rump hunched up and she lowered her head. My brother flew off and all but buried his head in the soft sand.

El got up rubbing his eyes. "Darn you, what didja wanna do that for?" Her answer was a little flip of her tail and she trotted sedately back to the stable.

Thereafter, the paper routine became a standard operation. A sharp slap against our hand was enough to produce the desired reaction. It soon became a happy game for all of us. Maggie knew we would never hurt her, and she entered into the fun too. But when she ran out of that first burst of speed, that unscheduled stop always dislodged us. The halt never occurred at the same place or same distance, primarily because it was impossible to guide Maggie once she got up a "head of steam." Each ride became a great adventure, where she would head for the beach or along the narrow dirt road, or perhaps over to the chicken yard. I'm sure Maggie also enjoyed these daily outings.

The little burro lived quite happily with us, and we loved our unusual pet. Mom was the only one who had some misgivings. The burro lured us away from our chores, did nothing in return for its keep, and worst of all publicly humiliated my mother. Maggie roamed freely, never straying too far from the security of the stable, but she did fall into some of the same habits as the rest of our gathering. Our collie Rover met us daily as we returned from school or from a trip by boat to the city. Soon dog and burro formed a strange friendship, and Maggie often followed Rover on his meanderings. One such was trudging along the beach, through the fort, down to the wharf to meet us as we came off the boat from a trip. In the morning we had to sneak off to school to prevent our pets from following us. But in the afternoon we could be sure of seeing them somewhere on the road or wharf to await our homecoming.

If Mom spent a day in San Diego shopping and returned on the same boat as we did, she tried hard not to notice our unusual greeting committee. She must have been very embarrassed in front of all the other passengers, but she only said, "you children run on home." And we did—Rover, Maggie, three hungry youngsters and anything else that had joined our little parade, leaving Mom behind to restore the dignity of the United States Lighthouse Service.

My brothers' legs finally grew too long for Maggie, the excitement of the rides had evaporated, and they decided to sell her. My objections fell on deaf ears. Our little friend, now sleek and tractable, happily found a new home where she was loved and lived long to give pleasure to more children.

The menagerie reached its peak when a little wild goat from San Clemente Island joined the group. Small and wild, what the kid lacked in size it made up for in the speed of its unexpected charges. The assistant keeper's child presented an especially enticing target. The child was only three and just the size the goat thought it could handle with safety. Life for the infant became a series of butts from the rear, with no real harm done. But it is disconcerting to be bowled over from time to time, and howls of frustration and anger split the air. I think there was a bit of bully in the little animal. It never tackled anything larger than itself. In the interest of keeping peace at the station the goat was given away.

Our environment blessed us with the many creatures to love and care for, and to bring their measure of happiness to us.

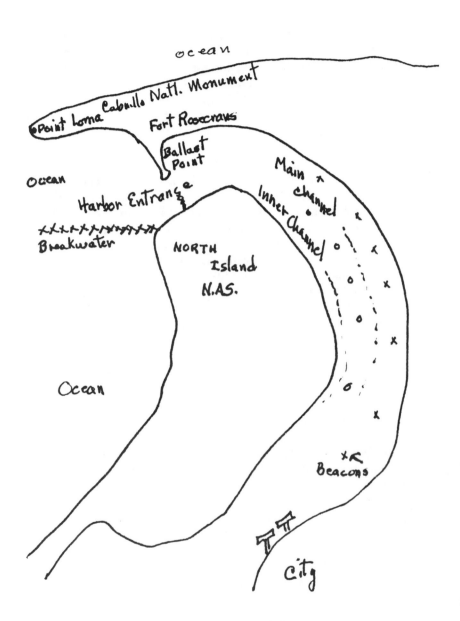

Map of San Diego Harbor

28

Fortune Hunters

None of us ever wanted to miss being at the supper table. Stories of our day's activities were usually routine, but when Dad started one of his yarns, we all perked up our ears and put down our forks. How we loved his sea tales about his life aboard old sailing vessels—rounding the Cape, seeing the St. Elmo's fire on the masts, being one of the U.S. Navy's first divers, and somewhere in all this managing to find work on a rubber plantation in Brazil. Mom loved the stories too, except once when with eyes a-sparkle, Dad began to describe a tango he enjoyed with one of the Latin senoritas in a Brazilian bar. We never heard the end of that.

One winter evening the subject turned to whales. We had seen them many times passing Point Loma on their yearly migration to the warm waters of Mexico to breed or calve. Now and then a stray even wandered past our station and into the harbor for a cursory inspection. Bleached whalebones rested against our carpenter shop, huge white vertebrae. Ballast Point had once been a whaling station. We heard Dad tell of the great whalers, whale oil, blubber, and whale bone. We learned that Mom's corset stays came from such great mammals. It seemed funny to us that Mom was being held in shape by some whalebone.

But when the subject of ambergris arose, my brothers began to pay close attention especially when Dad mentioned its great value as a base for fine perfumes. Dad had a hard time trying to explain how such foul smelling substance could be used in the manufacture of fragrance. The dictionary defines it as "a waxy substance found floating in tropical seas, and as a morbid secretion in the sperm whale from which it is believed to come." We knew from the dictionary and from Dad that it was smelly and repulsive to touch. But the fact that it came from a whale was really all the boys heard. No matter that the sperm whale received the credit or that this secretion was usually found in tropical waters. To them a whale was a whale. Yes, Dad had once seen a small amount brought in to a port many years ago, a stinking, decomposed blob, but worth a sailor's fortune. My brothers from that night on held a sharp lookout for this gray substance. Ray did more so than El, and became the victim of our jokes, but he resolutely kept his eyes peeled whenever he was on the beach.

One sunny morning in July, my brothers took off for North Island to tramp for crawfish on the mud flats. Crawfish were excellent bait for the calico bass we caught at the point. The procedure was similar to playing mud pies with your feet. First you tramped a circle about five or six feet in diameter, moving closer and closer to the center in the black ooze. The constant disturbance aroused the crawfish and they emerged protesting to the surface, waving their little claws and trying to determine what was clogging their passageways. The boys snatched them up quickly, placed them in a bucket to which they added handfuls of mud flat grass. When their buckets were full, the boys started back to the skiff. Here the long sandy beach was filled with debris from a high tide and brisk westerly wind. It was a beachcombers delight, but so cluttered in areas they had to climb carefully over broken logs, battered boxes and clumps of slippery kelp. Somewhere in all this, a spectacular discovery might be made, perhaps a broken fishing pole, a single oar, a water-soaked life preserver, or a length of good Manila rope.

Ray and El ranged back and forth, back and forth, turning over the kelp, peering into boxes, and opening Navy paint cans. It was on one of these rounds that Ray spied his long-sought treasure, a huge hunk of ambergris, a large irregular evil-smelling mass, a moldy mess, gray, waxy and utterly repulsive.

"Gosh, it smells awful. Are you sure it's the right thing?" El was more than doubtful. He wanted no part of this highly offensive discovery and moved around to the windward side to escape most of the strong odor.

"You betcha, it's just like Dad said. Gee, a big piece like that oughta be worth a lot. Let's get it home and weigh it," Ray urged.

By now the "ambergris fever" had struck El as well, so with little concern for their clothes the two boys pushed, heaved, and finally worked the lump down to the water's edge and into an empty crate for easier handling. El went back up the beach to bring back the boat, leaving Ray to guard the new-found wealth. The sound of the oars snapped Ray back to reality and he waded out to help bring the boat ashore, stern first.

"Help me lift one side up first, then we'll get the other," Ray ordered.

El hopped out to give a hand. This meant getting their noses close to the awful "ambergris" once again. It was so bad that even a skunk would have backed off in a hasty retreat. At last the precious cargo rested safely on the floorboards of the skiff, and my brothers headed homeward, taking turns rowing against the incoming tide. They wanted to reach home as soon as possible to spread the good news. When at last, the boat nudged the pier, El climbed up the ladder, tied up, and lowered ropes to Ray to haul up their find. The blob slithered back and forth in the crate, dripping a greasy substance as they pulled it up to the pier. The little rowboat was going to need a good cleaning but that could wait.

"It sure is messy. What are we gonna do with it now?" El was anxious to get this venture over with.

"Go get that old tub we keep for live bait and we'll put this stuff inside," Ray ordered.

"Yeah, we can't take it any closer to the house, the way it stinks," answered El and he went to the little shed at the end of the pier and returned with a big galvanized tub.

"It sure does smell, but golly, just think what Mom and Pop will say when they find out," Ray agreed.

They turned the crate over sliding the mass into the tub, and lugged it to the shed, shoved it in, and closed the door. The two hurried home and into the house, waves of the strong odor announcing their arrival. The kitchen immediately became a battleground of mixed aromas, which was finally brought to an end by a stern command from Mom.

"You boys go to the outside washhouse, take off those filthy clothes, and don't come back here until you're clean!" she ordered.

"But, Mom—"

"No buts, out, *out! out!!*"

The great news was shouted back at her. "We're all rich. We found a big batch of ambergris," Ray yelled happily as he ran backward.

"Yea, that stuff that comes from sick whales," El joined in. They wanted their mother to be suitably impressed with their grand achievement.

"*Out! Out!* And wash with soap. I'll send Norma out with clean clothes." Mom pushed them along gingerly.

For the first time in a long while, the boys found that they had to scrub a little more energetically than usual to get clean, but some of the odor lingered on. Dad came out of the carpenter shop and took the fresh clothes from me. He knocked on the door.

"What did you kids get into today, anyway? Never got a whiff of anything like this before." He handed in the clean underwear, shirts and pants, and took the dirty ones from the boys. "Whew, this is awful. Don't expect your mother to wash these. I'll get you some yellow laundry soap and you can take care of it yourself. I'll put them to soak in a bucket of water." Dad left shaking his head.

"Wait, Dad. Gosh, you won't believe it. Guess what we found."

"Ambergris!" The boys shouted at once.

Ray went on, "A great big hunk of it, too. Come on, we'll show you. It's locked in the shed at the wharf. Come on!"

They all hurried down the boardwalk to the shed. El unlocked it and opened the door. Dad unsuspectingly poked his head in and just as quickly withdrew it.

"Where did you pick *that* up?" he gasped.

"Over on the beach at North Island. It must have been washed ashore," Ray answered.

"Oh, uh, uh, you've certainly got something there. I think you'd better find out as soon as you can, before the weather gets much warmer. That shed won't hold together too long under the strain." The twinkle in Dad's eyes belied the serious tone of his voice, and Ray and El should have been warned. "We'll take another look at it in the morning," he suggested. The boys closed the door and followed Dad home.

Mom met them at the door. With a sniff and a quick glance, she permitted them to enter, wash their hands and go to the supper table. "What on earth did you two get into?" Mom quizzed as she turned back to her task at the stove.

"You'd never guess, Freda. The boys think they've found some ambergris, you know, that's the stuff used to make the most expensive perfume."

"Yeah Mom, a great big hunk," El hastened to add.

"Say, Dad where shall we take it?" Ray inquired in a business-like manner.

"Oh, to be sure, it should be checked by a chemist, but that costs too much. Why don't you take some to the drugstore, and have it checked there? I bet they can tell you for sure what you have found. Just let it be for the rest of the day, and you can take a piece to town tomorrow morning." Dad didn't look up from his plate as he spoke. The boys ignored the tone in their father's voice; they were too excited. Nothing could cloud their bright blue sky of dreams. Wise indeed, our dad. Better to let us dream, struggle a little, hope even more, be disillusioned now and then, and then battle back through childhood setbacks. Dad's sense of humor sometimes got in the way of better judgment, and so it was this time. No one was ever really hurt by it. It was with mixed feelings that he watched my brothers set off for San Diego early the next morning, a carefully wrapped package accompanying them.

"Hermann, are you sure they should be going?" Mother sensed the indecision on his part.

"Yes, I guess so. They really won't be satisfied until they find out for themselves."

"What do you think it is, then?" Mom asked.

"Well, let's just wait until they come home. I can make a guess, but I may be wrong," Dad suddenly chuckled as though he had a little private joke. "I don't think even a whale would want to be found dead near that piece of 'ambergris.' "

"Oh, Hermann, you shouldn't have let them go."

"Maybe not, but it'll be good for them to do it on their own. I sure want to see their faces when they get home," he chuckled again.

I remained a puzzled and quiet non-participant in the whole affair. I wasn't quite sure what was really going on. The early afternoon tug pulled in at the fort pier. I was hoping my brothers would come home on the early boat. Soon, two small figures appeared at the end of the spit, trudging slowly homeward. They should have been rushing home to share the good fortune. Something had certainly gone awry. Maybe no one wanted to buy ambergris anymore, I thought. I ran back to the carpenter shop. "They're coming. They're coming."

With a serious look on his face, Dad watched as his sons neared the shop. Their faces were long enough to rest on their shoe tops, and without a word they passed by us straight into the house. Dad hestitated for a moment, then put down his tools and followed. I tagged along behind still trying to figure it all out. I could tell that something interesting was about to happen by the loud voices coming from the kitchen.

Mom met us at the door, "Hermann, you ought to be ashamed of yourself! You should have told them!"

"I wasn't sure myself." But he didn't say it with much conviction. "Anyway, it was fun for them while it lasted."

"Yeah, Pop, you should have told us." Ray was indignant.

"That fellow in the drugstore almost died laughing," El added. "He wanted to know if we wanted a couple of slices of bread to go with our 'ambergris.' "

"Gee, aren't they going to buy it?" I was still far behind in this whole episode.

"Buy it! It's nothing but a hunk of old cheese, just old stinking cheese," Ray said disgustedly.

Dad explained that it must have originally been a large round of cheese, too ripe for eating aboard ship. Covered with mold, filled with fermenting gases, battered, decomposed, and eroded, it at last came to rest on the beach, just as the boys had found it. After Dad had finished, things quieted down for a little while, but then the thought of that moldy cheese squatting in the shed and awaiting shipment to a perfume factory was too much for us all. The whole affair had become ludicrous, and we all dissolved into a heap of unrestrained laughter. We held our aching sides and gasped for breath, only to be set off again if we dared glance at one another. Ray contributed his full share of laughter as he at last relinquished his hope of obtaining a fortune with the "ambergris."

In a short while things had calmed down and the word "cheese" could be safely mentioned once more. Dad gave his bit of advice to bring the matter to a conclusion.

"Okay, now you boys take that cheese and dump it somewhere in deep water. Better put on some old netting around it and add some weight. It's so rotten and full of gas, it might just float back on our beach."

Mom dug out the old clean work overalls for the boys and when they had changed their clothes they walked down to the pier, pushing and shoving at each other. They hesitated before opening the shed door. The heat of the day was beating down. It certainly could not have improved the quality of their treasure.

"You open the door," Ray urged.

"Nope, it's all yours. You do it." El backed away.

Slowly and cautiously Ray turned the handle of the door. The first wave of foul air rushed into his face. He gasped and slammed the door. Backing off hastily with his face turning slightly green, Ray turned to gulp in deep breaths of fresh air.

"Gosh! That's *awful*! How are we going to get it out of there?" El began to feel sorry for Ray who sat limply on the edge of the pier. "Let's figure out how we're gonna do it." He joined his brother, and they pondered their plight.

For the rest of the afternoon, there were no further intrusions into the shed, but the boys had strict orders to remove the cheese by nightfall. That evening they armed themselves by tying wet rags around their faces before entering the shed.

"All right, this time when we get ready to open the door, let's take a deep breath first. That way it won't smell so bad to us," Ray suggested. They approached with great care, yanked the door open quickly, and pulled out the leaking tub. It left a trail that had to be cleaned up later.

"Leave it here and I'll get some rope." El had a new idea. He tied the rope to the handles of the tub, and the boys found it easy to move it off the side of the pier, down over the rocks, where it could be lifted into the boat. Here they enclosed the cheese in some old net, added a few good-sized rocks for weight, and rowed out to midstream where they dumped the mess overboard. It sank slowly sending back bubbles of gas to mark its path downward.

"Well, there it goes," El remarked unnecessarily.

"Yup, and that's the last time I'll look for ambergris," Ray added with conviction as he thought of the cleaning jobs ahead—the shed, the pier, the boat and clothes to wash. These tasks were to remind him for a long, long time of the tribulations of trying to acquire wealth in a hasty manner.

Dad on one of his many rescue missions, trying to keep the plane afloat until help arrives. *Harry T. Bishop photo, Union-Tribune Publishing Co.*

29

Unscheduled Dunkings

During the turbulent years of World War I, North Island, the U.S. Army pilot training base across the channel from us, buzzed with activity. As the war progressed the training complement included fifty-one students, nine instructors, and thirty-two planes. They kept our air alive with the flight training. We were fascinated by the unpredictable behavior of the winged craft, especially in the hands of a beginner. Enthusiastic officers were anxious to make that solo flight that would qualify them as pilots.

Two-winged, single-engined De Havilands lumbered down the crude airstrip, doing everything but flapping their wings trying like awkward birds to gain the air. Sometimes lack of adequate speed forced them to nose into the ground. Unskilled landings ended in "pancaking" the craft, causing it to squat down suddenly, jolting the pilot, and crushing the undercarriage. In most cases the injuries were few and slight.

These planes never flew very high. They labored off the ground and into the air where they flew slowly above the field. The take-off pattern was into a prevailing westerly wind. Pilots had to bank either north or south after leaving the field, for the abrupt rise of Point Loma was too much to ask of the engines. Planes routinely turned south toward the channel and away from the inhabited areas. This brought them close by our lighthouse station. We followed their training activities daily, marvelling at the courage and skill of anyone being able to hold these fragile bits of metal, cloth and glued wood in the air. Dad kept a special lookout as he made the rounds of the beacons and trips to the ocean buoys, and in his way became the unofficial air-sea rescue service of the area. There was no established service ready to pick up fliers downed in the water. If a pilot flopped into the bay, he was usually on his own, with little hope of immediate rescue from an official organized group, and could only look for a passing craft, perhaps a fishing boat or Dad's launch.

Late one September morning my father and brother Ray were heading back from the front range beacon in the lighthouse launch. They kept close watch on a plane that had just taken off and seemed to be having difficulty in gaining sufficient altitude. The plane's nose rose abruptly and the plane hung in the air, and then dipped into the dreaded stall. There was not enough altitude for the pilot to straighten out the flight of his craft, and it plunged into the bay. Dad and Ray barely escaped being hit. As quickly as possible they maneuvered the launch to the spot of the crash, hoping to aid the fallen flier. But the angle of crash had been too great and the plane was quickly pulled under the waters of the strong tide as the pilot struggled helplessly to free himself. Dad held back Ray who wanted so desperately to jump in and do something. But to Dad's experienced eye, the increasing depth of the lost craft forestalled all hope of giving any aid, and the plane sank out of sight. Nothing else could be done except to put down a marker in the area. For days Navy divers searched the tragic scene, but the current had dragged plane and flier out into unknown depths without chance of recovery.

Other aircraft hit the bay but with happier landings. One such must have been the source of embarrassment to two crack fliers. A Navy vessel was to arrive, carrying the Secretary of the Navy. For days planes flew a series of simple acrobatic stunts in preparation for his arrival.

Weeks later upon the entrance of the ship into San Diego harbor, the two fliers were sent aloft to demonstrate their daring exploits. They did a few easy wing-overs and figure eights, climbed as high as these early craft could go, and came down in cautious dives. The whooping and gestures from the sailors aboard ship indicated that there was not much to be said about the exhibition. Goaded into further action, one pilot started a few turns not listed in the training manual. Not to be outdone, the other pilot fell in with the idea, and there began a little dogfight. From regular observation over the practice days, we almost all knew what these planes were capable of doing, and there was a definite limit to their capabilities. Only five minutes of military stunting had elapsed before one pilot dared to try the impossible. Over the ship he zoomed, almost clipping one of the masts, and then pulled up his craft into a steep climb, too precipitous for the ungainly plane with such limited power. The reluctant craft fell over on one wing, responding sluggishly to the controls, but the pilot managed to pull it into a gentle glide and came down to land flat upon the quiet bay.

We had been watching from the shore, and Dad who was ever ready for an emergency had the "Useless" tied at the pier, stationed there for just such an event. It took only a few minutes to get the little boat headed out to the downed craft. It was still afloat with the fliers clinging to it, apparently unhurt. The Navy transport continued to steam up the bay, offering no assistance. By now the fliers had stripped to their underwear, getting ready for a swim if necessary, while goggle-eyed sailors watched them from aboard the passing ship.

Dad eased the launch alongside the plane, took the two fliers aboard and tied a line to the plane, hoping to keep it afloat until other help arrived. An Army launch got to them soon, but the combined efforts of the two boats were not enough to keep the plane afloat. Ray stood by to cut the line if Dad should give the word. The plane continued to sink lower in the water, but the tug Koko arrived from the quarantine station just in time to take over the job and successfully salvage the craft. The "Useless," relieved of her charge, carried a happy crew of fliers back to Ballast Point. From there they were picked up by a speedboat from North Island.

Planes created great diversion for us just by being in the air overhead, and our hearts went out to those intrepid pilots who dared so much to prove the value of flight, and Dad continued his rescue missions.

Years later when the Navy became involved in the flight program, a real mystery presented itself to Dad. There were many types of channel markers in our harbor—beacons, nun buoys, can buoys, bell and light buoys and spar buoys. Spar buoys were placed in the narrow channel areas to mark the strength and direction of the tidal flow. One was just opposite our station in the bay entrance and the other was situated inside the bay near the north side of North Island. These buoys were simply long smooth logs with chain attached to one end and then anchored in the water. Being buoyant, the free end stuck up out of the water like a huge matchstick, swinging back and forth with the flood and ebb of the tide. Sometimes they were almost swept under by an extremely heavy tide, but ordinarily a good fifteen feet of log remained above the water. The rare times when a buoy disappeared beneath the surface, a ship traveling at a good speed could easily snap off the marker with its propeller. There was never any adequate explanation that could be sent to the superintendent of lighthouses when this occurred. There was just a simple request for a replacement as soon as practicable. A section of the spar buoy near our station came up missing every now and then, but the one inside the harbor suffered few mishaps. Here ships moved at slow speed, the tidal force was minimal, and this buoy suffered only an occasional gouge, never being lopped off.

Dad was working on the No. 10 beacon one morning doing some

scraping and painting. Now and then he stopped to watch the sea-planes take off nearby. This was a fine place to survey the inner harbor and he checked the area and other beacons close by. All seemed to be in good order, but something was missing in his count. And then he noticed that the usually well-behaved spar buoy had lost most of its upper portion. It still showed high enough out of the water so that it could not have been cut off by a passing ship. Mysti-fied, Dad examined the damaged spar. It had been snapped off fairly cleanly above the high tide line. This was a completely new develop-ment and Dad returned home, racking his brain for an answer. The next day he returned to finish the job of cleaning and refueling the beacon light. There again, it confronted him—the decapitated marker. And as he tried to solve this baffling mystery, he noticed seaplanes taking off across the water, sometimes passing near the remains of the buoy as they taxied across the water, or coming down nearby in their practice landings. The possible answer seemed too ridiculous to be worth considering, but it was the only one in sight at the moment and Dad decided to give it a try when he returned home.

Back at the station, he phoned North Island to inquire. Yes, a plane had been checked for slight wing damage, but the pilot had not been able to offer an explanation. A detailed examination of the wing area and a careful comparison with the diameter of the broken buoy strengthened Dad's theory. The plane must have been traveling at a fairly good speed and snapped off the spar with its wing. The slight damage to the aircraft still was mystifying, but stranger things have happened in the field of aviation.

Flight had always fascinated me, whether it be by bird or man. In later years when I reached the ripe old age of sixteen Ray took me to a flying field near Santa Ana. Here a friend of his was giving lessons in a "Flying Jenny." The ship was an old friend to us, like one of the many that used to fly from North Island in World War I days. Barnstorming groups sprang up after the war years with dar-ing wing-walking, auto-to-plane pickups, racing, and stunting. Amer-icans were caught up in this new fever and flight lessons were offered to an eager public for three to five dollars an hour. Somehow Ray had managed to convey to the pilot that I had some cash, had flown before, and even had had one or two lessons.

It didn't take long for the pilot to steer me to his plane and help me climb in. It was like sitting in an old wooden chair and not very comfortable. The only gear in my cockpit was a set of rudder pedals and the stick, certainly nothing very complicated. It looked like a bit of coaster gear. We taxied up the field with hacking coughs from the engine. We turned to line up for the take off. The old craft sputtered down the crude runway not missing a single bump on the way. After what seemed hours, the old plane finally became airborne. Wind whipped in my face and whistled through the wire struts that held the wings in place. Now I knew how a bird felt, free and high above the earth, or at least I thought a thousand feet was high. We gained even more altitude and headed for some low-hanging clouds. In and out we went, the motor struggling to keep going in the thinner air. After a few minutes of this pure enjoyment, the pilot turned around to me and said, "Take the stick."

I couldn't hear him clearly, but his sign language was easy to interpret. I grabbed the stick gingerly and watched his outthrust arms to guide my efforts. It was certainly a simple procedure. If his left hand lowered, I moved the stick to the left. If he moved both arms forward, I pushed the stick forward. No flying lesson could be any easier, and I went up and down, back and forth. After a little while, he turned and grinned, then put his arms back into the cockpit, signalling that the stick was totally in my control. Well, I still wasn't quite sure what I was doing. Up there in the air it was sometimes hard for me to tell left from right, but we stayed in the air. I thought I was doing pretty well as I tried to stay on an even keel and keep in a straight line of flight.

He turned back to me again and shouted, "Those were the best figure-eights I've had a student do in a long time. Now how about a few stunts?"

That was fine with me, but I thought it was about time he learned that I was just an amateur and not the semi-experienced flier he thought. As I finished shouting the truth to him, he stared unbelievingly at first, then a look of pure horror came over him and his face paled. Without any further word, he turned the plane around and guided it back to the field. Not a word from the pilot as he helped me from the "Jenny." Instead, he headed for my brother, and there was no doubt from the gestures that Ray was hearing a few choice words from a frightened pilot. I walked over to our old Ford and waited for the tirade to cease. Ray finally came over and climbed into the car, a look of chagrin on his face.

"Guess you won't have a chance to fly with him again. He was sore because I told him you had flown before."

I didn't say anything. I was just happy to have flown like a bird, a somewhat noisy one, but flown anyway for the first time in my life.

A lot of splashing and confusion at this first scheduled channel swim between North Island and Ballast Point.

30

The Big Splash

The years of the twenties might have been the "flapper" days, but as far as we were concerned, they were certainly the "flipper" days when we were to be invaded by swimmers kicking and splashing their way across the channel. During those times channel swimming was the rage around the world, and our little narrow entrance was set for a contest sponsored by a local newspaper.

In the weeks preceding the first scheduled contest, September 3, 1922, a few tested the waters in the crossing between Ballast Point and North Island. Others looked at the short distance, and declared the project as too easy to waste time on. The one-fourth mile swim simply didn't seem to present any problem. They were to learn different.

Dad had no idea what was in store for the little spot he so loved. His twelve-hour day and six-hour night watch left him little time to serve on an advisory committee and he was ignored most of the time. The total planning fell into the hands of the inexperienced. Nothing could have been more poorly administered.

The day of the first big event arrived and so did unchecked hordes of people. Cars lumbered across the dirt road of the narrow spit, kicking up dust and filling up every bit of space as they tried to find a place to park. Spectators trampled through our garden, cluttered the beaches, and strained the supports of the wharf. They threw rocks about thoughtlessly, demanded rowboats that were not available, and scattered their litter all over the place. Dad could see all his hard work of maintaining an immaculate station crumbling before his eyes. He never imagined that people could behave this way. He was furious.

The officials had planned to begin the race at slack tide, that is, between the tidal changes. It would make a smooth start, and if the swimmers were really good, they could cross to the other side before a changing tide ran at full force. But the great numbers of people and boats milling about and the unlimited number of participants caused massive confusion and delay.

Upper: The crowds all but buried Ballast Point.
Lower: Too bad Dad didn't charge for parking.

Swimmers lined up with difficulty, jostling one another for what they considered to be the best positions. By the time the event got underway, the tide had already changed and was beginning to head up the channel. Swimmers misjudged the strength of the incoming tide and soon found themselves farther up the bay and completely out of line with the finish point. Contestants and accompanying boats were scattered all over.

It was difficult for a landlubber to judge the power of the current. Appearing so peaceful in movement, it had a strong steady pull. Inept rowers could not compete with it either. Oars waved aimlessly and many swimmers were left without their guiding boats to plot courses. Some of the contestants were picked up and never finished their swim, while others struggled on slowly trying to reach the sandy shore. Then interest in channel swimming waned as rapidly as it had come upon the scene and in a few years the event here was finally discontinued.

Dad never forgot that first contest. Mom didn't either.

Near the carpenter shop stood a small building, about six by eight feet. Its only contents were a wash stand, a toilet, soap, and towels. We often washed up here after swimming or fishing to save Mom extra work inside the house. A few rules governed the use of the shed. It was to be kept absolutely clean, no dirt or sand, no fish scales. Water must be mopped from the floor, and towels were to be placed in a neat array on the rack.

On the day that this mob inundated our area for the first swim, our big-hearted father opened up the washroom to all. All day a long line made its way in and out of the place. Although most people were thoughtful and appreciative, it didn't take long for a handful to ruin the area. Dad stood by and tried to estimate how much work it would take to repair the damages. A neat little washroom had been turned into a refuse heap. Sand and grit were ground into the shiny linoleum. Soiled paper was strewn around the floor. Walls were smeared with lipstick, and water was splashed carelessly everywhere. That did it! Thereafter, only a trusted few ever gained admittance to the little shed.

My brothers and I lent Dad a helping hand in cleaning and painting. We were glad we could help him. He worked so very hard every day and this was just another added burden.

The big swim left its mark on my brothers and me. We decided to be channel swimmers too and try our luck at the crossing. Ray and El had no trouble at all. They knew exactly how to judge the tide, its direction, and its strength. I wished they had entered one of the channel races. They might not have won, but at least they would have known where they were headed and the quickest way to get there.

I tried the crossing too, but I should have known better than to ask my teasing brothers for help. Their generous offers of help should have made me suspicious, but I had this strange mental weakness of forever trusting them. They agreed to row the boat and to pick me up if I became tired. Day after day I swam farther and farther around the little cove to build my endurance.

Then one fine warm day I began my channel swim, with El and Ray nearby in the little skiff. The water was pleasant and the tide just right. I was soon halfway across the stretch and things were going very smoothly, with my brothers yelling encouragement. Then something slithered along my leg and I panicked. The boys spotted my trouble, and I heard cries of "Shark! Shark! Look out! There's a big shark!"

I paddled frantically toward the boat crying for help, wanting to be picked up, but for some strange reason they seemed to be having trouble handling the oars. The boat drifted farther and farther away from me. Fear overwhelmed me as the slithering contact returned. I really knew what that strange feeling was, just some drifting kelp, but by that time I was exhausted and ready to end my efforts. And besides I had become a blubbering idiot from a mixture of anger and fear. My brothers hooted with laughter, but they also knew when to end a good thing. The boat was soon back in control and the rescue performed. Yes, I should have known all along, even before the whole thing started that it wasn't going to be a smooth swim. My brothers loved me, but they also loved to tease me.

One good thing happened from all the channel swims we had at the point. A truly nice individual stopped by Ballast Point. She arrived unobtrusively, requested help graciously, got along famously with Dad, and swam across the channel without great fanfare, and with good speed. We enjoyed having her at our station. Lottie Schoemmel, a noted European long distance swimmer, left us with pleasant memories.

31

Battle Stations

There was a loud pounding on our back door, "Hey, hey, anybody up?" The voice from our porch demanded attention.

We opened the back door to find a wild-eyed assistant keeper trying to catch his breath.

"Where's your old tomcat? Bring him over to my place. I've got a big rat in the living room," he gasped.

"You don't need our cat for that. Whack it over the head yourself." Dad turned to go back to an early rest before his midnight watch. He was irritated at being disturbed unnecessarily.

We wondered why the assistant was making such a fuss over a rat. Inside our home we had little mice that had somehow managed to get between the ceiling of our pantry and the floor of the bathroom above. Sometimes when we could hear them scurrying about, Mom thumped the end of her broom handle against the ceiling and they scampered away to a discreet silence. We finally lured them into the open where there were trapped. But so much ado about a single rat seemed silly to us.

"But we need help. It's a rat, a big one, a big water rat," he pleaded.

We all knew that such creatures existed, but I had never seen one. They lived in the holds of ships or along the dark places under piers. When ships were in port tied to wharves, the mooring lines held rat guards, huge round shields that prevented the rats from creeping along the lines. The immaculate dwellings and workshops and our clean surroundings did not invite such nasty beasts. This one must have swum ashore from one of the passing ships. It was a doubtful Engel family that followed the agitated assistant. Ray carried our hefty "Ol' Tom" in his arms. We thought he would be a match for any intruder. Perhaps it wasn't a water rat at all. Our station had always been free from such vermin. With our big cat and large collie on the alert, it was doubtful a water rat would stay around for long.

The keeper led us into the living room where his sturdy wife stood brandishing a broom. "There it is! Ugh!" She pointed in revulsion. Faintly outlined by the dim light of the kerosene lamp, crouched a dark form. It sat motionless, eyes glittering. The rat was huge and ugly with a coat of coarse mottled gray and black hair. None of us ventured any closer.

"How did it get in?" El wanted to know.

"I think he climbed up that vine and over to the open window. He was running along the top of the piano when I came in," the assistant explained. "I tried chasing it out but it just backed into that corner."

We all stared at it. Mom pulled me by my arms. "This is no place for us. Let's go outside and wait."

Ray put down "Ol' Tom" who had been squirming to get free. He gave the cat a push into the line of batttle. But Tom was no dummy. Our trusty champion had already fully gauged the situation and sensing that he was outweighed and outarmed, suddenly decided he was a peace-loving feline. He quickly reversed directions and scrambled out of the danger zone, banged the screen door open, and disappeared.

The water rat took advantage of the confusion and crept even farther into the dark corner. Here with his back propped against the wall, he reared back on his haunches, and drew himself up to his full height. He appeared to have suddenly doubled in size. There he stood baring his filthy fangs and daring us to approach.

For a short time, we stood eye to eye with our antagonist, each reluctant to make the first move. Everyone knew the rat was not bluffing. The glare from his red eyes brooked no interference. Mom's tugging and pulling became more urgent, but we held back reluctant to miss any of the activity.

Dad moved over to us, "Freda, you take the children and wait outside. We just have to figure something out and I don't want you in here if the rat makes a charge at us." He was fearful that we might be bitten and suffer a horrible disease from those filthy fangs.

We backed off slowly, relinquishing the field of battle to more seasoned warriors—Dad, the assistant keeper and his wife. Mom worried about Dad so we all lingered just outside the door on the porch. For a long time there was only the mumble of voices, silence and then some more unintelligible remarks, but no other stirring of activity. Suddenly the voices rose in an argumentative crescendo, loud and defiant. Higher in tones than the men, and befitting her ample size the voice of the keeper's wife commanded the situation.

Crash! Bang! Thump! Thump! Furniture toppled against the wall. The broom swats resounded even outside. El and Ray dashed over to the living room windows, jumping up and down, trying to get a look, but the shrubs screened their view. Then El clambered up on Ray's shoulders, but that unsteady venture ended in a flop on the lawn before El had a chance to get a good look.

Bang! Bang! Staccato voice commands and then an abrupt silence. We waited, wondering and worrying.

The door finally opened, framing the keeper's wife like a triumphant Brunhild, a blood-stained broom in one hand, and held by the tail in the other, a limp, battered rat. We watched admiringly as our heroine strode by us and down to the beach. Here she heaved first the rat and then the broom into the bay, and marched back to the house. We all stared at her with the greatest respect.

"Men! Heap big brave souls," she joked. Her eyes twinkled as she went by us into her home.

On the way home, Dad was laughing so hard he couldn't say a word, and we had to wait until we had all gathered around the kitchen table. It seems that all the more conservative forms of strategy proposed by the two men had been dismissed. Our heroine decided to disregard any immediate dangers of her plan, and started her attack with a surprise frontal charge; around and around the two maneuvered, while the men stood by gaping. Neither of them wanted to get in the path of a vicious rat or a determined Amazon. The rat was not outnumbered. He was whipped even before the broom ever landed on him. Two or three well placed hefty swats and he was counted out; and she gave him a few more blows to assure her victory. Singlehanded, she had accomplished in less than a minute what the men might still be arguing about. Anyway, it was a long time before the two men heard the last of their part in this event. We were thankful it never occurred again.

View of our little cove and its occupants—the junk, pilot boat, and the launch, "Useless." *San Diego Historical Society-Ticor Collection.*

32

Olaf and the Chinaman

Within our quiet cove, many fishermen took time to rest from their arduous task of fishing. Albacore boats lay at anchor, swinging around slowly on their mooring lines. Wisps of smoke arose from tiny stoves. The men spent most of their days aboard the little craft, and pleasures and comforts were few. Shore trips were made only to buy provisions or to fill an occasional bucket of fresh water from our tap. In return, Dad often found a fresh albacore awaiting him on the dock. My brothers and I enjoyed knowing these hardy souls. Nothing they did seemed easy, but they would have been lost in a life ashore.

After a day or two at sea, the men spent time cleaning fish for themselves, mending lines, scraping, patching, and painting around the boats. In a moment of luxury, time was set aside for sunning on deck. Most of the boats were small and operated by one man. But these men were never truly alone on the sea. Their code made every man a brother. It was never unusual to see one boat break off in the middle of a profitable day's fishing to tow in a disabled friend.

Sometimes on warm evenings the fishermen gathered on one boat with their demijohns of wine, loaves of sourdough bread and fish, or if they had snagged a crab or two, some good fish stew. Their hearty laughter revealed men free of major troubles, free men who loved their hard life.

Two men became permanent residents of our cove—Olaf and the Chinaman. Olaf was a small wiry man, possessed of unusual strength and endurance. His home was a battered old Monterey boat, hardly seaworthy even in the best weather, but for a few years he maintained a daily schedule out to the ocean to catch a few fish for his daily fare and some for the wholesale market. But as time went on he did less and less of that especially after he salvaged a small flat barge that had foundered on our beach after a storm. He patched up the unclaimed wreck, spending weeks caulking the open seams and adding new planking, until bit by bit it was floatable. Olaf moved out of his boat into a shack he built atop the barge and so had the first houseboat in our cove, crude as it was. From then on he spent his time beachcombing, picking up all the scrap wood he came across and in the months that followed the barge sank lower in the water under the additional weight.

His fishing companions were puzzled by his strange behavior, but they continued to supply him with food. Olaf still came ashore for his supply of fresh water, but my father was the only one with whom he would converse.

As children we never ventured near him. He looked like a diminutive Viking with his bushy red hair, scraggly beard and glaring eyes. Whenever we went spearing along the sandy shore close to the barge, he would stand with his arms folded, legs astride, and stare at us. Although no more than five-foot-six, Olaf had the mien of a towering warrior of old. Rumor had it that he once possessed a fortune but lost it in a gold-mining venture and soured on the world. Romantics suggested he became a hermit as a result of an unhappy love affair, but no one really knew.

Olaf remained as long as we lived at Ballast Point, but we heard later that his barge had erupted into a fire, and the fort residents complained about the unsightliness of his accumulated junk and tried to have him removed. But Olaf just pulled anchor and found a spot a little farther away from the shore dwellers.

But when dredging started to make a home for nuclear submarines, the Navy towed Olaf, boat and barge, farther up the bay to a commercial anchorage. He lived there undisturbed for years, but when the basin began to fill with a great number of boats, complaints again rolled in about the potential fire hazard, and the collection aboard the boat and barge was sold for junk. Soon after that the worm-eaten Monterey sank and Olaf lived out his days on the barge. I still have two clear pictures of Olaf in my mind. Every morning, rain or shine, clad only in a pair of old Army pants cut off at the knees, he took his morning shower by tossing a bucket over the side; then no matter how cold it was he emptied that bucket of water over his head. On the winter days when he did this daily routine, I felt he was a true Viking. And I can still see him striding along the streets of La Playa, a torn straw hat on his head, those same raggedy pants, barefoot, and always, very, very clean. I wish I could have known the secret of Olaf.

His back bent forward over the long oars as he pushed the heavy skiff against the outgoing tide. Our Chinaman, as we affectionately called him, was returning to his junk from the far haul out to the ocean for lobsters. He spoke no English so we never learned his name. Whenever we met ashore we never spoke and communicated primarily by gesturing. His was a gentle nature and his tanned leathery face was always creased in a shy smile. No one ever came to visit him on the junk, and he lived a very solitary existence. He was one of the workers left over from the building of the railroad.

Contractors brought Chinese immigrants to San Diego in the early days to do railroad work. With the completion of the line, the workers scattered, trying to find other employment. Some settled in the city and others migrated to the fields to do agricultural work. Then in the late 1800's some Chinese built good-sized junks out of redwood, and began a fishing fleet of ten to twelve junks near the harbor entrance. They fished for albacore, gathered abalone along the shores of Point Loma, and sold their catches in the local markets. But by the time our family arrived at Ballast Point, just one lonely junk occupied by a solitary elderly Chinese rested in our waters. What about his family and friends?

My mother chose to include him in her worries and she often sent me out with some of her baked goods. The short row from the pier to the junk gave me time to wonder where he had come from, why he was here, and how old he was. Later I learned that San Diego had quite a Chinese history.

On those trips with Mom's gift of food, I never was quite sure if I should whistle, "Yoo Hoo," or just bang on the side of the junk. I certainly couldn't yell, "Hey, Chinaman," even though the word was never used disrespectfully. It just seemed a rude way to address a friend, so I rapped against the hull as a signal. In a minute he would appear from below, smiling and bobbing his head up and down in little bows to indicate his pleasure at my visit.

If the food was not to his liking, it was never evident, and in the next day or two, Dad would come into the kitchen carrying a choice piece of carefully cleaned fish. For years our friendship with this kind man remained a quiet solid bond. Sometimes when I saw him working on a sail on deck, I'd row out to go aboard and watch him. What wonderful wordless communication we enjoyed with gestures, head shaking, and smiles. At times he'd laugh quietly while we shared a bit of simple fun.

His age was indeterminate. It seemed that centuries of living were encased in the tiny body. We only knew that he was old—very, very old. Yet morning after morning he put to sea in his skiff to hoist his lobster traps, using the tidal flow to ease his way in and out of the harbor. There were times when rowing the huge boat seemed too difficult for him. For many years his junk stayed anchored nearby, with once in a while a small sail hoisted, but the craft never sailed anywhere. Perhaps it just made him feel good to do that.

On very rare occasions the Chinese found it necessary to beach his craft in order to scrape and paint its bottom or to make repairs. That's when everyone in the cove came to his aid. Dad, the other fishermen, my brothers and I, and even Olaf helped this gentle soul. With towlines attached to our rowboats and to the junk, we pulled the junk over to the beach on a high tide. As the tide ebbed the craft rolled over to one side and we were able to scrape off the moss and barnacles, and then caulk the seams where needed. That night the Chinaman slept on the beach covered with a bit of canvas. At the right tide we pushed the boat over to its other side and repeated the work along with a fresh coat of paint. As usual, my brothers and I were handed the old worn brushes. We had to rub rather than stroke the brushes, but the paint went on from bow to stern and the home of the Chinese was once again secure. We tried to get the painting done and immediately refloat the junk, but sometimes we had to wait for the return of the high tide.

This was a day of horrors for Mom. She knew we would literally throw ourselves into the work. It was fun for us and the fun was reflected in the amount of the paint we personally absorbed. Mom didn't care much about the clothes we wore. They were the ones set aside for such activities. They would be washed and put away for another time. But red lead paint has a way of staining, clinging to the skin through kerosene, gasoline, turpentine, and scrubbing with soap and water. For days after, we walked around with skin scrubbed almost raw and ugly red stains here and there on our faces, arms and legs. But what satisfaction we had from seeing the junk safely afloat again, and knowing that our friend could sleep restfully.

His life followed such a simple routine that it was easy to anticipate his activities each day. Tied to the stern of the boat was his heavy skiff. When it was not there, we knew he had gone out to his traps, or come ashore for water. When it was there, we looked to find him on deck doing little chores. There came a quiet morning when the rowboat was still swinging on its line at the stern, and we couldn't see any sign of movement aboard the craft. We had never known the Chinese to be ill. Dad went over and returned with the sad report that the old man had died. The authorities were informed, and the San Diego Chinese community took care of matters. Within a week, the junk disappeared during nighttime. Its leaving left a big void. I had lost a dear friend.

Ready for inspection! Dad in his uniform.

33

Thar They Blow

Year after year Dad's station was awarded the efficiency banner, a small blue pennant with a golden "E" emblazoned on it. Following a superintendent's visit, a formal letter always arrived stating that the station had the privilege of displaying the "E" for another year. Dad never had to return the pennant to the main office for his station was maintained in excellent working condition. But he rarely flew the award. He knew he was doing a good job and saw no point in advertising the fact.

Inspections were a nuisance, but any person living or employed on government property knows he is subject to inspection at any time. A common bond of comradeship existed among the keepers on the Pacific Coast. They always tried very hard to convey to each other word about the possible arrival of an inspector. If he were coming by the lighthouse tender, a warning letter might reach us in time; if by some other means, then we could be in for a surprise since we had no telephone in our early years at the point.

The arrival of the official never fazed Dad for he maintained every square inch in top order. Mom, an excellent housekeeper, could have had an inspection at any time. Our rooms, including the closets, were kept spotless, and the floors were highly waxed. Before we went down to breakfast, my brothers and I made our beds and hung extra clothes in the closet in neat order. Dust was non-existent. As immaculate as our home was, the mere mention of an inspection frightened and upset Mother so that none of us could ever reassure her that things would go well. But the exception to the rule descended upon us, and during one official visit events got a little out of control. In a way it all resulted from our love of homemade root beer. During the hot summer months Mom and Dad bottled great amounts of it. I've never tasted better. After bottling, the root beer was placed in the cellar to keep cool. Sometimes we lost a bottle or two when the caps flew off unexpectedly. We could hear the "pop" in our kitchen.

But Dad thought this soft drink lacked a certain sturdy quality. So one day off he went to town with a gleam in his eye and and a thirst in his throat. He returned with a large paper sack bulging with malt, hops, yeast, bottle caps, and everything else needed to brew real beer. Mom's face was a picture of despair when Dad unloaded his purchases. Prohibition was in effect then, and it was also against lighthouse regulations to have liquor on the station except for medicinal purposes. My mother was already visualizing Dad being drummed out of the Service in disgrace. She could see the efficiency pennant being torn to shreds, and the lighthouse emblem being ripped from his cap. Dad's sense of adventure had not yet been quenched by hard work in the Service and he was determined to carry out this project. Opposition was voted down by one vote, Dad's, and the brewing began. The initial stages did not take long. Fermentation started the pungent mixture bubbling in the large crock by the stove. What an aroma! It permeated every crack and cranny in the house and Dad walked around sniffing the air appreciatively while the rest of us held our noses.

The ingredients finally worked themselves into a quiet state and our father announced it was time for the bottling. Dad had bought a new bottle capper that was supposed to insure a tight seal. It was really much better than the one we used for the root beer, and he expected no trouble from it. A certain amount of ingenuity and skill were still required for its proper use. We all tried our hands at the job. Tight caps went on some bottles, but others became misfits and popped open. We finally performed the rites of stowing the wonderful brew carefully in a cool, dark corner of the cellar to age. Dad had never made beer before, but he had followed directions carefully. The grand opening took place on a warm Sunday. Dinner was on the table. By our father's place stood a tall brown bottle, and at its side, the opener. We watched as he took up the bottle, gently worked the opener on the cap. Out came a soft "pffft," and Dad poured a beautiful amber liquid into his glass, a happy froth edging the top. With a hearty swallow he drank his first taste of Engel brew, and smiled. As the weeks passed, a glass of cold beer now and then just seemed to be the thing for our hardworking dad, and even Mom voiced fewer fears, and before long another batch was set to work.

A few days later, the lighthouse tender rounded Point Loma and anchored in our cove. That struck dread into Mom's heart for sometimes the superintendent chose to travel to the stations by ship. But rough seas had changed his mind. He had left the ship and no one knew where he intended to go next. The next day word came

through that the official was due at our station on the following
morning. He was arriving by train and Dad was to pick him up. And
there sat the crock filled with incriminating liquid! Mom and Dad
shooed us all off to bed early. We could hear loud conversation, banging and clattering, opening and shutting of the back door, and finally
the footsteps of our parents coming up to bed. We could still hear
muffled voices as we dropped off to sleep.

Mom bounced us all out of bed early the next morning, reminding
us to clean up our rooms. I saw that worried look on her face before
she rushed downstairs to prepare a big breakfast. In between bites
of French toast, I noticed that the crock had disappeared from its
place by the stove. Mom told us that she and Dad had spent much
of the night siphoning and bottling the brew, and stowing it in the
cellar. Burnt toast had erased most of the tell-tale odor. Later we
learned that Mom had urged Dad to toss the beer, crock and all, into
the bay. That was too much of a sacrifice for Dad. When breakfast
was over, Mom handed us hefty lunch bags and asked us to stay out
of the way until the inspector left. We left knowing that our father
would do well, but we still worried about Mom.

Dad always gave his equipment the best of care, but some things
would normally wear out. These tools and materials were then listed
as needing to be condemned and set aside for final inspection. The
procedure involved a great deal of paperwork with such questions
as: lengthy description of the article, when received, reason for con-
demning, and detailed reasons for need of replacement, and on and
on and on. The Lighthouse Service even designated a prescribed period of time for the life of a paint brush, regardless of the use it
received. Dad wore out many brushes in order to keep his station
bright and shiny. Having acquired a working knowledge of the
involved budget details of the Service, we often asked Dad for any
old worn brushes to use in painting the rowboats. With brushes worn
to the nub, we energetically scrubbed on the paint. He always
admonished us to clean the brushes and return them to the condemned pile. Once in while at the completion of our job, we let a
completely useless brush slip into the water, thus saving endless
reams of reporting. Now all he had to do was to list one brush missing
and request a new one. I doubt if Dad ever knew of the little conspir-
acy we had going for him.

This morning he took the station launch up the bay to pick up
the superintendent. They would check the condition of all the bay
beacons and buoys on the way back. It was nearly eleven o'clock
before we saw them leave the rear range beacon and head for the

point. We watched from our vantage spot on the beach. When the boat was docked the two men climbed the ladder and walked off to the light tower. They were up and down in ten minutes and went to our dwelling. Normally the inspector had nothing but praise for our station, but it always made me furious to have him go poking into our closets and drawers. We were never able to have a "junk" drawer into which we could toss our favorite things.

It was nearing noon and by now Mom would be near a state of exhaustion and hoping that the official would leave. Time dragged on for us too. We were anxious to get home to hear the good news, but the day wore on with no sign of his leaving. We thought the worst. Then at two o'clock two figures emerged and strolled down to the pier, engaged in animated conversation, and soon both men were in the launch and on their way to San Diego.

As soon as the boat disappeared up the bay my brothers and I ran home for we were famished for news and food. There would be plenty left from the midday meal. No one ever starved at Mother's table. By now it was evident the inspector had remained for a bite to eat. This was a rare thing. Although my Dad always extended an invitation, this was the first superintendent to accept. We resented Mom having to be "inspected," and then offering to feed the intruder.

We dashed up the steps of the back door and into the kitchen hoping to see her happy smile. She was not in the kitchen nor anywhere else downstairs, and I yelled, "Mom, Mom, where are you?" and still no answer. I ran upstairs to try the bedroom. There she lay quietly crying to herself. "What's the matter, Mom? Are you sick?" But she continued sobbing and gave out some indistinguishable words that sounded like, "Ask——comes home."

Downstairs I heard my brothers yelling for Mom too, so I hurried down quickly to quiet them. We all sat around the table asking each other what could have happened? It certainly must have been a major tragedy. But tragedy or not the noises in our empty stomachs needed to be stilled, so while Ray sliced off generous pieces of still-warm pot roast on the stove, El cut bread. I brought in a jug of milk from the outside cooler, and we munched in silence.

After finishing our snacks with oversize portions of chocolate cake, El said, "I'm going to go out and wait for Dad," and he rinsed off his plate. Ray did the same and the two boys left.

There was nothing for me to do, so I tiptoed upstairs to peek in at Mom. I was surprised to find her sound asleep. Whatever had bothered her had certainly worn her out, and I left her to rest. My

brothers found little to do sitting out in front of the house, except
to toss some rocks into the water. As the sun dropped behind Point
Loma, they caught a faint glimmer of the lights of the lighthouse
boat. El came running, "Dad's coming. Come on, let's go meet him."

We jostled each other along the narrow boardwalk, trying to be
the first down to the pier. Understandably I came in last. We wanted
an explanation and waited impatiently for our father to pull up in
the launch. We wanted to ask a lot of questions, but knew better
than to bother him until he had the boat securely tied, the engine
shut down, and a thorough check made before he stepped on to the
wharf. When he started climbing up the ladder, he received a full
blast of questions all at once.

"What happened?"

"What did the inspector do to Mom?"

"Didn't you pass inspection?"

"Now, just hold it for a while," Dad slowed us down, "I'll tell
you all about it as soon as I get home and have a cup of hot coffee."

Long-legged Ray ran ahead in order to move the coffee pot over
to the hot side of the stove. There couldn't be any delay in hearing
this story. We went inside quietly trying not to awaken our mother.
Dad settled himself in his chair. El poured coffee. Our dad looked
very weary. He took a deep swallow of the hot liquid and sighed,
"Where's your mother?"

"She's upstairs sleeping. She's been crying."

"I don't wonder. Well, let her rest. You kids be quiet for a while.
The inspection was quite a strain on your mother. We've never had
a day like this!"

We searched his face for some clue, only to find a calm expression, and a sly twinkle in his brown eyes. We sensed that this was
going to be good! We listened carefully as he recited the happenings
of the day.

Everything had gone just fine, up to a point. The bay lights, station light, fog bell and outer buoys were checked and found in good
working order. Tools in the carpenter shop shone with fresh oiling.
The coal in the coal shed had been shoveled into a compact pile, and
the floor swept free of coal dust. Freshly hosed dwellings gleamed
brightly under the sun. The yard we had so laboriously brought alive
with green vegetables and a newly cut lawn had received ample
praise. Then what had gone wrong?

"Yep, I'm sure glad you kids weren't around when it happened."
He gave out a chuckle. "One of you would have given it away. Yep,
you sure would. We passed everything just fine, and your mother

was real pleased. And then when we were coming downstairs—"
he broke into another chuckle. "Sure was funny, but it scared the
daylights out of your mother."

"Come on, Dad, don't take so long," El urged.

"Well," he went on as he leaned back in his chair, "we were
finished upstairs, and coming down to take a look at the lower rooms
when some of the caps began to pop off that beer we put up last
night. We all heard them. Your mother looked like she was going
to faint, but I just told the superintendent we had made some fresh
root beer and wouldn't he like to have a glass? He said he certainly
would, but I think he really had a suspicion of what was going on.
Those darn caps kept popping off. Every time one did, your mother
acted like she was shot. Anyway lunch got underway and by the
time we were halfway through the barrage had ceased. Lucky we
had some root beer in the cellar."

"Didn't the inspector say *anything*?" Ray asked.

"Nope, he just said it was the best root beer he had ever tasted
and thanked Mom for an excellent lunch." Dad gestured to me,
"Norm, run up and see how your mother is."

I scurried upstairs, had a quick look at the quiet figure, and took
a fast trip down the bannister on the way down. "She's still
sleeping."

"Good, resting will be the best thing for her. You know how nervous she gets. Now let's all go see what happened to the bottles."

Dad lighted the kerosene hand lantern and we all trooped outside, down the steps, and waited as Dad pried off the little cover
that led to the cellar. Down below we could hear him bumping into
overturned bottles and muttering to himself, and then he came out
holding two closed bottles. There was a big grin on his face. Not all
had been lost.

"Golly, Dad, did all the rest pop? They must have made an awful
racket," I wondered.

"Well, your mother certainly thought so." Dad held the two good
bottles gingerly. "Here take these and put them down carefully,
They may be all right. But watch out, those caps may fly anytime."

Ray grabbed the bottles firmly and laid them to one side away
from us. Then he and El joined Dad in the cellar giving the beer-
flooded area a good cleaning. I could smell the stuff clear outside
and wondered why the superintendent hadn't. After all the empty
bottles had been removed Dad gave that part of the cellar one last
hosing. In spite of his steady temperament, we knew this had been
a day of trial and tribulation for him and Mom. We returned to the

kitchen just in time to hear Mom stepping softly down the stairs. Still wan and teary-eyed, she emerged from the hallway, shaking a finger at her contrite spouse.

"Hermann, I told you that beer hadn't worked long enough. You should have thrown it all out. It was still fermenting."

"I guess you're right," Dad teased. "Next time, I'll let you be the bottling judge."

"Next time! Next time!" Mom spluttered in horror. She stared at him, and then sat down to laugh with the rest of us. In disposition, Mom was the complete opposite of Dad. She was usually the last one to see the humor of the situation. Life to her was the serious job of taking the best possible care of her family, and that meant all the worries, imaginary and real. So when she occasionally let go with a hearty laugh, it was enjoyed by all of us.

Weeks later when all had sufficiently recovered from this episode, Dad worked up another batch of beer and properly aged it before the bottling. There were no more crises.

The lumber schooner and its grateful skipper pass by our point on the way into San Diego. Assistant keeper on the lookout.

34

High and Dry

Entering or leaving San Diego Harbor in clear weather was not difficult, but in the fog skillful navigation was needed through the narrow passageway at Ballast Point. Our fog bell rang out its clear mellow tone, warning mariners away from the shore. Nights of dense fog restricted the waterway traffic. Many ships remained safely moored in the harbor, while those awaiting entrance chose to anchor outside the bar until the morning clearing. But some of the coastal lumber schooners had skippers who knew our harbor well and guided their ships in and out in all kinds of weather.

I had tucked myself into bed one wet and misty October night. There was nothing better than being snugged down under a blanket with a good book to read. The little kerosene lamp on the night stand gave off its faint glow. After a bit my eyes grew heavy and I pulled up the covers and settled down to a good night's sleep, still hearing the faint sound of a ship's bell and the raucous blast of a hand horn from a nearby fishing boat. These fishermen could navigate with their eyes closed and were never the cause of any worry to us.

I dropped the book on the floor and took a last glance at the curtains puffed out slightly with the damp breeze ushering in the sweet salt air off the bay. The beautiful sound of our fog bell lulled me to sleep.

My rest was short-lived. It was abruptly interrupted by a heavy crunching and grinding just outside my west window. I roused myself from sleep and peered into the foggy darkness. Shouts rang through the air, and I could hear Dad rushing downstairs. I didn't know what to think. All the action seemed too close for comfort. In a few minutes when my eyes had adjusted to the outside light, I made out the dim hulk of a ship. There, outlined sketchily in the fog, towered the huge shape of a lumber schooner. Its bow was staring directly into my bedroom window. That really woke me up. I pulled on my robe and slippers and scurried to the stairway only to be met and crowded out by my brothers. Mom was not far behind. Dad was already outside surveying the situation and when we reached him he was laughing heartily. There before us, definitely beached at a low tide, sat a large vessel.

"What goes on here?" yelled Dad at the disconcerted lookout. Before he could receive an answer, an officer appeared at the bow and identified himself as the captain.

"Where are we?" His voice was almost incoherent.

"Right now you're resting on the bay side of Ballast Point. Welcome aboard." Dad hadn't forgotten Navy courtesy.

"Welcome be hanged. What I want to know is how can we get off this place and back into the channel? Who are you anyway?" It was becoming more difficult to understand the skipper. He glared over the side of his ship as though holding us all personally responsible for his predicament. He sounded as though he were close to a state of apoplexy. "S' fine business," he muttered loudly enough for us to hear and staggered back to the bridge.

"Just be patient," Dad hollered after him. "We've got a high tide in a few hours. You've just got your bow on the beach. The rest of the beach drops off into deep water. You should get off with the tide without any trouble."

"Le's hope so," the captain answered back over his shoulder as he reached the bridge. "I told those fools not to get liquored up across the border."

From his speech, it was apparent that the rest of the crew were not the only ones who had imbibed. It was the time of Prohibition and the Mexican town of Tijuana was a mecca for thirsty souls in search of pleasure and drink. From what we learned later, no one on that ship could have negotiated the channel in broad daylight, let alone on a foggy night.

Suddenly the skipper returned to the bow and leaned over the rail to talk to Dad and was alarmed at learning he had landed on lighthouse property. "You don't have to report this, do you?"

"Don't see why I should. There's been no damage done to the station." Dad had no wish to make trouble for these hardworking seamen. "And you ought to be able to back off before dawn."

The captain waved his thanks and started shouting commands to his woozy crew. There were more loud voices and the sound of a winch being started. We wondered what this was all about. This was no time for the ship to start backing off. Worn gears squealed and groaned under heavy strain. Without warning a boom swung over the side and a large sling of fine Oregon lumber crashed on the beach.

"Look out below!" came the tardy warning, but we had already backed away from danger.

"If you can use it, there's another load coming," the skipper bellowed, and another batch landed on the beach. "Hope you can use it."

"Gee, Dad what are you going to do with all that wood?" I was curious.

"I don't know, but it will come in handy sometime," he answered.

It was too dark to make a careful inspection of our windfall, but we could see it was beautiful wood, No. 1 Oregon pine, two-by-fours, and one-by-twelves. It smelled of both forest and sea. We stayed a bit longer listening to the diminishing activity aboard the ship. Dad checked to make sure the wood was high enough up on the beach so it would not float off with the incoming tide, and then we all retreated to our warm kitchen where Mom had the cocoa hot and bubbling for us. By the time we had downed a cup or two, the chill had vanished and we went back to bed, except for Dad. He wanted to be sure the ship would be headed in the right direction when it left.

I sat on the edge of my bed and looked at the ship, planning to stay awake and watch it back off. But it was too cold near the window, and even though I drew a blanket around me, it was still not comfortable. I finally gave up, hopped into bed, slipped beneath the covers and was asleep in a minute. In the morning when I awoke and looked out the window, the ship had gone.

No official report was ever made of the event. No letter disclosed the navigational aberrations of that particular lumber schooner, and for years after, a grateful skipper pulled the ship's whistle in greeting whenever he passed our station. Years later, when Dad retired, the then well-seasoned lumber formed a major portion in the framing of our new home. It was good to be in our new home and still have a part of the old life with us.

The only other vessels trying to take a short cut across the spit were two Navy destroyers. Again the fog was the culprit; only this occurred late on a lazy autumn afternoon. El was out with the pilot who was bringing in a foreign ship that afternoon. We weren't worried about them. It was the kind of day that made beachcombing a pleasure. The ocean was quiet. Even the birds settled down from their constant gliding and diving. As time wore on the fog curled over Point Loma, thick and heavy, and crept in from the ocean along our channel. It draped itself over everything, but there was still a little light where the sun stubbornly tried to break through.

Off in the distance I heard the first blast of the incoming steamer and then the toot of the pilot boat. In a few minutes the ship moved slowly into sight, and following in its wake, the pilot boat. I heaved a sigh of relief to see that El was all right. Dad had come up beside me, quietly and unexpectedly. He was always glad to see his son safely home.

"Well, don't you think you'd better go in and get a sweater? It's getting damp out here," Dad urged. I turned to go and caught sight of El coming out of the cabin and pointing to the stern.

"Dad, what's he pointing at?"

"I don't know. The pilot boat is going along all right. I don't see anything wrong there. Must be something farther back."

We tried very hard to see what my brother was concerned about, but it was too misty. Then two gray shadows emerged from the fog, Navy destroyers, and to our amazement headed straight for the sandy beach. The rest of the squadron trailed the pilot boat and moved safely up the channel. Why the two vessels had decided to veer off to the port in this manner we never found out, but they came on steadily without any sign of diminished speed. Dad waved at them futilely. We backed up as the ships kept advancing, until they quietly settled themselves on the sandy bottom in the nearby shallow water. There the two ships sat in embarrassed silence on an almost even keel. We wondered if they had dug in too deep to be able to back off. Dad was satisfied that no harm was done, so he couldn't resist a word or two to the three young sailors that peered over the bow.

"Hey, would you like to have some rollers so you can go over land?" Dad joked.

His remark evoked no response. Dad had had enough trouble with the Navy ships as they sped out our channel, leaving large waves to flood our gardens, so it gave him a little satisfaction to address a few caustic words to the ships in person.

With such powerful engines, the destroyers backed off slowly, their propellers churning up great quantities of seaweed and sand until the vessels were in deep water again. Here they straightened up on the proper course, and the last we saw of them, they were groping their way into the harbor. There was no notice of the incident in the newspaper, and Dad wondered what kind of report was made by the commander of the squadron.

35

Time to Leave

The childhood years slipped by, but we never grew too old to participate in the fun activities: fishing, rowing, swimming, and watching the ships as they entered and left San Diego.

In the early 1920's, Ray married and moved to Imperial Valley. El became a seaman on board one of the ships that ran between the mainland and Catalina Island. I started high school.

In the years that followed, Ray became an engineer at the Douglas Aircraft Plant in Long Beach. El, with just his eighth grade education, worked his way through the intricacies of calculus, logarithms, and other mathematical fields to advance in the maritime world, gaining his master's license, a license that permitted him to command any size vessel anywhere in the world, but he chose to remain in Southern California. He served in the Navy during World War II and upon his discharge returned to pilot work, advancing to the rank of senior pilot at Long Beach Harbor.

I finished high school and went on to San Diego State Normal School for a teaching credential, and spent most of my working years in the San Diego city school system, interrupted by a four-year stint in the Navy during World War II.

During those first teaching years, fellow teachers and their families came to visit at the point. Mom served her fabulous dinners and Dad regaled us all with his early sailing adventures. He even established a non-smoking section, taking himself off at the end of the meal to sit halfway up the stairs to enjoy a good cigar. From this vantage point he could still take part in the conversation. Nobody thought it was strange, for he was a most thoughtful man. When cigarette smokers were in the group, Dad remained at the table. Mom usually sat quietly listening to the babble of voices, occasionally beaming at the compliments for her culinary skill.

I remember one gathering on Halloween. It was a mild October evening, just right to be outside. Paper lanterns were strung about the yard. A galvanized tub sat filled with water for apple dunking.

The kitchen table was laden with the results of Mom's best efforts.

But this was a lighthouse and many of the planned events were pushed aside. Some of the guests strolled along the beaches, a few set about energetically digging clams. The pilot had invited another group along on a ride out to the ocean to meet an incoming steamer. Others sat around and chatted with Mom and Dad. However remarkable these events might have seemed to others, they were just a part of our everyday life and we were happy to have our friends enjoy the point as much as we did.

But soon the years of heavy physical work and the long hours shortened both my Dad's life and years of service. The two keepers at Ballast Point had charge of all the bay beacons and buoys, the ocean buoys, the station itself, two wharves, a launch, dwellings, and the lighthouse ground area. In addition they were standing a twenty-four hour watch, six on and six off. This meant that after doing a hard day's work, each keeper had to stand a six hour watch during the night. Finally, near the end of Dad's service the government began to realize that this was asking too much of two men and Mom was employed as a laborer for the specific purpose of standing watch. She was paid three hundred dollars a year for her efforts, less than a dollar a day.

The damage to Dad's health was now irreversible and in 1931 he applied for retirement on disability. On December 29, 1931, Dad made this entry in the lighthouse log. "Keeper arrived at station. Keeper moving off station." So few words to mark a man's many years of dedication to duty.

The next few years were even more difficult for my parents. My father's rapidly declining strength left him with little zest to enjoy his remaining time, and four years after leaving the Service he died.

But there remains with me, the wonderful memory that he lived exactly as he wanted to, near the sea. His sense of humor never dimmed, even in the worst of times.

The love my parents had for each other spilled over to cover us all and enrich our lives.

My life saw only "Two Beams of Light," Point Bonita and Ballast Point, and they were the happiest of times.

Suggestions for Further Reading

Beaver, Patrick. *A History of Lighthouses.* Secaucus, New Jersey: Citadel Press, 1973

Carse, Robert. *Keepers of the Lights:* Charles Scribner's Sons, New York, 1969
Stories of the coastal lighthouses of the United States, back to pre-Revoluntionary times.

Gibbs, James A. *West Coast Lighthouses.* Seattle, Washington: Superior Publishing Co., 1974
A pictorial history of the guiding lights of the sea.

Holland, Francis Ross. *America's Lighthouses.* Brattleboro, Vermont: The Stephen Greene Press, 1972
Their illustrated history since 1716

The Old Point Loma Lighthouse, symbol of the Pacific Coast's first lighthouse. San Diego, California: Cabrillo Historical Association, 1968

Majdalany, Fred. *The Eddystone Light.* Boston, Massachusetts: Houghton Mifflin Co., 1960

Moeser, June D. *Lighthouse Portraits.* San Diego, California. Brochure from her one-person show of oil paintings of lighthouses. 1973

Shanks, Ralph C. *Lighthouses and Lifeboats on the Redwood Coast.* San Anselmo, California: Costano Books

Lighthouses of San Francisco Bay. San Anselmo, California: Costano Books, 1976

Snow, Edward R. *Famous Lighthouses of America.* New York: Dodd-Mead, 1955

And just for those who might like fiction:
Verne, Jules. *Lighthouse at the End of the World*

Note: There are many children's books also available at the public libraries.

257

Appendix

Copy of a watercolor of Oakland Harbor Light Station painted by a construction worker on the back of a box and presented to Freda Engel, 1901.

Correspondence between Hermann Engel and the U.S. Lighthouse Service, 1901-1931.

404 Safe Deposit Building,

Office U. S. Light-House Inspector,

Twelfth District,

_____ Inclosures.

San Francisco, Cal., SEPLY ED

Sir:

Your application for examination under the civil service rules to enter the Light-House Service was considered by the Local Civil Service Board in San Francisco on *Sept. 7. 1900.*

The general average you obtained (*93.15*) places you on the list of eligibles as No. *1*, Class *1*.

Please call for your papers.

~~The papers filed with your application are returned herewith.~~

Respectfully,

U. SEBREE,

Commander, U. S. N.,

Chairman Local Civil Service Board for the Light-House Service (Inspector's Department).

Mr. *Herman Engel,* *City,*

 919 Florida St.

 S. F.

P. O. Box 2423.   *404 Safe Deposit Building.*   *Telephone Main—843.*

Light-House Establishment,

Office of the Light-House Inspector, Twelfth District,

_____ *Inclosures.*

San Francisco, Cal.,   30 October 1900.

Subject:

Mr. Herman Engel,

    919 Florida Street,

        San Francisco.

Sir:

    I inclose herewith your probationary appointment as Assistant Keeper Oakland Harbor Light-Station with pay at the rate of $500. per annum.

    You are directed to subscribe to the inclosed oath of office and fill out the accompanying blank form, which are to be returned to this office, and report to the Keeper Oakland Harbor Light-Station on November 1st for assignment to duty.

              Respectfully,

              Commander, U. S. N.,

                    Inspector.

DIVISION OF APPOINTMENTS.
Form 248.—Ed. 10 11 1900 1,000.

Treasury Department,

OFFICE OF THE SECRETARY,

Washington, D. C., August 13, 1901.

LIGHT HOUSE INSPECTOR
20 AUG-1901
SAN FRANCISCO, CAL.

Mr. Hermann Engel,

    Care of the Chairman

        of the Light-House Board.

Sir:

    Having served satisfactorily for the probationary period of

six months required by law, you are hereby *absolutely* appointed

THIRD   ASSISTANT   KEEPER of the———— Bonita Point ————

Light Station,——— California, ——with compensation at the rate

of————five hundred ——————————— dollars   ($500.)   per

annum from   May 4, 1901.

        Respectfully,

Secretary.

T

LIGHT HOUSE BOARD
AUG
14
1901
792
Received

DEPARTMENT OF COMMERCE AND LABOR
Lighthouse Service

WW-GMP

CIRCULAR NO. 10.   Office of Inspector, 18th District
                                                     Custom House
Furniture, bedding   San Francisco, Cal.
and cooking utensils   Oct. 26, 1912.
for stations.

TO KEEPERS AND ASSISTANT KEEPERS:

    1.   The following list is a standard schedule of furniture,
cooking utensils, etc., which may be furnished at government expense
to light and fog signal stations.   The schedule is the maximum of
what shall be supplied to any station, but the articles enumerated
will not be supplied unless considered necessary by the Inspector.

    2.   If the existing equipment is found satisfactory keepers
should **not** ask for articles just because they are listed in the
schedule.

SCHEDULE OF EQUIPMENT
For all Lightstations having quarters.

    1 Cooking stove, with pipe and damper, poker, shaker, lifter,
      coal hod, shovel, and zinc floor board, for each separate
      keeper's dwelling, each keeper's quarters with family, or
      for each lighthouse not having quarters for family.

    1 Heating stove, with pipe and damper, poker, shaker, lifter,
      coal hod, shovel, and zinc floor board, for each separate
      keeper's dwelling, each keeper's quarters with family, or
      for lighthouse not having quarters for family.

Notes:- Oil stoves, instead of coal or wood stoves, will be
     furnished where mineral oil is authorized as fuel.

     Heating stoves will not be furnished to stations
    where heating plants are provided.

For all Off-Shore and Isolated Land Stations where Families
    are not Permitted to Reside.

FURNITURE	BEDDING AND LINEN
For Station Use	For Each Keeper.
1 Desk, flat-top, 42 inches or smaller.	3 Colored mattress covers
1 Desk chair	3 Colored pillow cases
1 Kitchen table	6 Hand towels
	1 Mattress, hair.

CIRCULAR No. 10.   2.
Furniture, bedding, etc. (Continued)

For all Off-Shore and Isolated Land Stations where Families
   are Not Permitted to Reside,(continued)

FURNITURE   BEDDING AND LINEN
For Each Keeper.   For Each Keeper.

1 Chiffonier with mirror   1 Pair colored blankets
3 Hardwood chairs   1 Pillow, hair
1 Single iron bed with wire   1 Colored comforter (In 1,2,
   springs   3,4,5,10,11,12,16 & 17 Dists).

COOKING UTENSILS AND TABLEWARE
For Station Use.   For Station Use,(cont'd)

 1 Baking pan   1 Rolling pin
 1 Basting spoon   1 Salt shaker
 1 Bean pot   2 Soup bowls for spare
 2 Bread-baking pans   1 Soup ladle
 1 Bread board   1 Steamer for cooking pot
 1 Bread box   1 Sugar bowl
 2 Butcher knives   1 Tea kettle
 1 Butter dish   1 Teapot
 1 Chopping board   2 Vegetable dishes, open
 1 Chopping knife   1 Wash board
 2 Coffee mugs   1 Wash tub, cedar
 1 Coffee pot
 1 Clothes line   For Each Keeper.
50 Clothes pins
 1 Cook's fork   2 Coffee mugs
 2 Cooking pots with covers   2 Dinner plates
 1 Dish pan   2 Forks
 2 Frying pans   2 Knives
 1 Pepper shaker   1 Pail, galvanized
 3 Pie tins   1 Soup bowl
 2 Platters   2 Tablespoons
 1 Roasting pan   2 Teaspoons

     3.   All of the above articles must be asked for in annual
requisitions. As the annual requisitions for the coming fiscal
year have already been submitted to the Inspector, keepers are
authorized to submit supplementary requisitions on Form 95 for
such articles covered by the authorized schedule as are considered
absolutely necessary for use during the next fiscal year.

                         RHODES.

𝔇epartment of 𝔠ommerce and 𝔏abor

LIGHTHOUSE SERVICE

HWR-CHT

OFFICE OF INSPECTOR, 18TH DISTRICT
CUSTOMHOUSE
SAN FRANCISCO, CAL.

January 30, 1914.

Mr Hermann Engel,
    1st Asst, Bonita Point Lightstation,
        Through the Keeper,

1.   In accordance with the recommendation of this office you have been
                                   promoted
transferred ∧ and appointed Keeper of San Diego Bay Lights, California, with pay

at the rate of $720 per annum, effective on the date of your entrance on duty

at that station.   The transfer to be made at your own expense.   You are re-

quested to subscribe to the inclosed oath of office before a notary public and

return it to this office without delay.

2.   As soon as your arrangements can be perfected, you will apply to the

Keeper of Bonita Point to be relieved from duty and request him to promptly

notify this office whether you have made a satisfactory return of all the Gov-

ernment property in your possession at that station.

3.   Upon arrival at San Diego you will receipt to Keeper Newlin for all

the public property at that station (using columns 6 and 8 and certificate C on

Form 30 as per instructions thereon).   You are cautioned to carefully check up

all the property before signing to satisfy yourself that the articles are on

hand and in the condition stated, as thereafter you will be held responsible

for all contained therein.   One copy of the receipt is to be forwarded to this

office, one delivered to the retiring keeper, and the third retained on the

station.   *Rhodes.*
                                                Inspector

DEPARTMENT OF COMMERCE
OFFICE OF THE SECRETARY
WASHINGTON

January 13, 1917.

Sir:

The Department states that it has been brought to its attention that you voluntarily gave your time for one day each week during the past year for the purpose of polishing the lens and brass
work of the exhibit of the Lighthouse Service at the Panama-Cali-
fornia International Exposition at San Diego, California, in
addition to performing your duties as keeper of the Ballast Point
Light Station and of the San Diego Bay Lights, which are exacting,
inasmuch as they require long hours of service each day and a considerable amount of extra night work to maintain your lights in
good condition. Your performance of the extra work in connection
with the exhibit without additional compensation is most commend-
able, and the Department takes pleasure in expressing its appreciation of the fact.

The fact that you have been commended will be noted on the
records as part of your official history.

Respectfully,

E. F. Sweet

Acting Secretary.

Mr. Hermann Engel, Keeper,
   Ballast Point Light Station, etc., Cal.
(Through Commissioner of Lighthouses)

ADDRESS ALL COMMUNICATIONS TO
SUPERINTENDENT OF LIGHTHOUSES
SAN FRANCISCO. CALIF.

DEPARTMENT OF COMMERCE

LIGHTHOUSE SERVICE

HWR:AMC

LIGHTHOUSE
SUPERINTENDENT
NOV 30 1921
SAN FRANCISCO

OFFICE OF SUPERINTENDENT, 18TH DISTRICT

CUSTOMHOUSE

SAN FRANCISCO, CALIF.

Andrew,
Supr. Con:
Mar. Engr
Personnel
Accounts.
Contracts
Chf. Clk.
Sup. Comm
Comm.

Nov. 18,1921.

Commissioner of Lighthouses:

Saving of life

1. Reports covering the following cases of the saving of life and
property have been made to this office:

(a) On October 14th, Hermann Engel, Keeper of the Ballast
Point Light Station, jumped overboard and rescued from drowning
a little girl who had fallen off the station wharf.

(b) On October 31st, Herman Engel, Keeper of the Ballast
Point Light Station, received a telephone call from Roseville,
a small town on San Diego Bay, requesting him to make search
for two women who had drifted out to sea in a small skiff on
a strong ebb tide.   The Keeper went out in the station launch
and rescued the women, bringing them safely into the station and
later towed the skiff to Roseville.

(c) On October 24th, Hermann Engel, Keeper of the Ballast
Point Light Station, observed a fishing launch broken down and in
a sinking condition with two men on board.   Assistant Keeper,
Harry H. Hoddinott, of the Ballast Point Station, and one of the
Harbor Pilots, who has an anchorage near the light station, went out
in the pilot boat and rescued the men, towing the launch into San
Diego.   The station launch could not be used in this case on
account of the extremely strong ebb tide which was running.

H. W. RHODES

Copy for to Keeper, Ballast Point Light Station, for his information

and files.

H. W. RHODES

July 10, 1922.

Sir:

Referring to report of assistance rendered by you on June 8, 1922, in rescuing two men from a sinking U. S. Army airplane, which had fallen in the channel near your station, and in keeping the plane afloat until the arrival of a Naval tug, the Department takes pleasure in commending you for the services rendered, which will be noted on the records as part of your official history.

Respectfully,

Herbert Hoover

Secretary of Commerce.

Herman Engel, Keeper,
    Ballast Point Light Station, Calif.
(Through Commissioner of Lighthouses).

DEPARTMENT OF COMMERCE
OFFICE OF THE SECRETARY
WASHINGTON

December 10, 1923.

My dear Mr. Engel:

    I have read with interest your report of November 16, 1923 forwarded from the Superintendent at San Francisco, with reference to the assistance rendered by the assistant keeper and yourself to the Navy Plane HS 2 of the Battle Fleet Air Squadron, which was badly damaged when it hit the rocks on the jetty. I am sincerely pleased to commend you for the assistance rendered in getting the plane off the jetty and towing it to safety, which commendation will be noted on official records.

                              Cordially yours,

                                    Acting Secretary of Commerce.

Mr. Hermann Engel, Keeper,
    Ballast Point Light Station, California.
(Through Commissioner of Lighthouses).

ADDRESS ALL COMMUNICATIONS TO
SUPERINTENDENT OF LIGHTHOUSES
SAN FRANCISCO, CALIF.

DEPARTMENT OF COMMERCE
LIGHTHOUSE SERVICE

EIGHTEENTH DISTRICT

Ballast Point
(Station, Depot, or Vessel.)

Sept. 14-1928 , 19

Superintendent of Lighthouses:

San Francisco, Calif.

Sir:

Respectfully request reconsideration of increase in salary
scale for the personnel of Ballast Point Light House Station,
San Diego, California. for the following reasons:

The Keepers are receiving less salary, but have
more responsibilities and increased duties than ~~the~~ a
number
~~majority~~ of other stations in this district. (18th.)

Major duties and responsibilities at this Station
are:

    10 lights,(9 beacons and Station light.)
    2 Fog Signals.
    4 Gas Buoys. (at station & 1 at Quarantine)

Dwellings, workhouses, ~~wharves~~, launch and
garages and road. The above duties are
handled entirely by two keepers. The laborer
provided only for standing watch.

These numerous and widespread duties make it
impossible for the keepers to complete all duties
within the alloted time, thereby extending the

ADDRESS ALL COMMUNICATIONS TO
SUPERINTENDENT OF LIGHTHOUSES
SAN FRANCISCO, CALIF.

DEPARTMENT OF COMMERCE

LIGHTHOUSE SERVICE

EIGHTEENTH DISTRICT

Ballast Point
(Station, Depot, or Vessel.)

Sept. 14, 1928, 19

work day beyond the regular hours.

For these reasons I respectfully request the Superintendent
recommend an increase in the salary scale for all employes
at this Station.

Respectfully

H. Engel.

Keeper.

ADDRESS ALL COMMUNICATIONS TO
SUPERINTENDENT OF LIGHTHOUSES
SAN FRANCISCO, CALIF.

DEPARTMENT OF COMMERCE

LIGHTHOUSE SERVICE

HWR:SM
ENCL.

OFFICE OF SUPERINTENDENT, 18TH DISTRICT
CUSTOMHOUSE
SAN FRANCISCO, CALIF.

December 30th, 1931.

Mr. Herman Engel,
Keeper,
Ballast Point Light Station.

Dear Mr. Engel:

    1. There is enclosed herewith a letter from the Secretary of Commerce expressing his appreciation of your long service with the Department.

    2. Upon the eve of your retirement, after more than thirty-seven years of Government service, I desire to convey to you my appreciation of your long and faithful service, and to commend you for your efficiency and zeal in the discharge of your duties.

    3. I trust that you may regain your health when relieved of the duties of your present position, and that you may enjoy for many years the rest which you have so well earned.

                 Very sincerely yours,

                     H. W. Rhodes

Inspected Dec. 14 1931 HWR

JOURNAL OF LIGHT STATION AT Ballast Point and San Diego Bay Beacons December 1931

1931 MONTH	DAY.	STATE WORK PERFORMED BY KEEPERS REGARDING UPKEEP OF STATION, AND RECORD OF IMPORTANT EVENTS, WEATHER CONDITIONS, ETC.	
Tuesday	22	Trimmed light	Light N.W.
Wednesday	23		
Thursday	24		
Friday	25		1100 " S.W. 8.7 Clouds
Saturday	26	Trimmed lights	" 28. clear
Sunday	27		1.01/00 " W
Monday	28	Working on beacon	9=6 - Built S.W. to 9 W clouds
Tuesday	29	Return morning off station	light & W clear
Wednesday	30	To city with turning motor	" " "
Thursday	31	Working up the log on beacons	Vermont

3.85/00